Disney

THE MUPPETS

THE FOUR SEASONS

WRITTEN AND ILLUSTRATED BY **Roger Langridge**

COLORS **Kawaii Creative Studio**

LETTERS **Litomilano S.r.l.**

COVER ART **Elisabetta Melaranci**

COVER COLORS **Silvano Scolari, Gianluca Barone & Mirka Andolfo**

DISNEY PUBLISHING WORLDWIDE – GLOBAL MAGAZINES

Creative Director
Gianfranco Cordara

Project Supervision
Guido Frazzini (*Director, Comics & Digital Development*)

Editorial Team
Enrico Soave (*Senior Designer*), Antonella Donola (*Comics Editor*), Virpi Korhonen (*Editorial Coordinator*)

Creative Operations
Silvia Figini (*Director, Marketing, Franchise and Creative Management Publishing EMEA – Associate Publisher Global Magazines DPW*), Camilla Vedove (*Senior Project Manager*), Mariantonietta Galla (*Franchise Manager*), Cristina Fusetti (*Associate Marketing Manager Digital*)

Contributors Creative Operations
Chiara Zanetti (*Digital Localization Coordinator*)

MARVEL ENTERTAINMENT

Collection Editor
Cory Levine

Assistant Editors
Alex Starbuck & Nelson Ribeiro

Editors, Special Projects
Jennifer Grünwald & Mark D. Beazley

Senior Editor, Special Projects
Jeff Youngquist

Senior Vice President of Sales
David Gabriel

SVP of Brand Planning & Communications
Michael Pasciullo

Editor In Chief
Axel Alonso

Chief Creative Officer
Joe Quesada

Publisher
Dan Buckley

MUPPETS: THE FOUR SEASONS. Contains material originally published in magazine form as MUPPETS #1-4. First printing 2012. ISBN# 978-0-7851-6538-5. Published by MARVEL WORLDWIDE, INC., a subsidiary of MARVEL ENTERTAINMENT, LLC. OFFICE OF PUBLICATION: 135 West 50th Street, New York, NY 10020. Copyright © 2012 Disney. All rights reserved. $14.99 per copy in the U.S. and $16.99 in Canada (GST #R127032852); Canadian Agreement #40668537. No similarity between any of the names, characters, persons, and/or institutions in this magazine with those of any living or dead person or institution is intended, and any such similarity which may exist is purely coincidental. Marvel and its logos are TM & © Marvel Characters, Inc. Printed in the U.S.A. ALAN FINE, EVP - Office of the President, Marvel Worldwide, Inc. and EVP & CMO Marvel Characters B.V.; DAN BUCKLEY, Publisher & President - Print, Animation & Digital Divisions; JOE QUESADA, Chief Creative Officer; TOM BREVOORT, SVP of Publishing; DAVID BOGART, SVP of Operations & Procurement, Publishing; RUWAN JAYATILLEKE, SVP & Associate Publisher, Publishing; C.B. CEBULSKI, Creator & Content Development; DAVID GABRIEL, SVP of Publishing Sales & Circulation; MICHAEL PASCIULLO, SVP of Brand Planning & Communications; JIM O'KEEFE, VP of Operations & Logistics; DAN CARR, Executive Director of Technology; SUSAN CRESPI, Editorial Operations Manager; ALEX MORALES, Publishing Operations Manager; STAN LEE, Chairman Emeritus. For information regarding advertising in Marvel Comics or on Marvel.com, please contact Director of Marvel Partnerships, at ndisla@marvel.com. For Marvel subscription inquiries, please call 800-217-9158. Manufactured between 10/18/2012 and 11/20/2012 by QUAD/GRAPHICS, DUBUQUE, IA, USA.

10 9 8 7 6 5 4 3 2 1

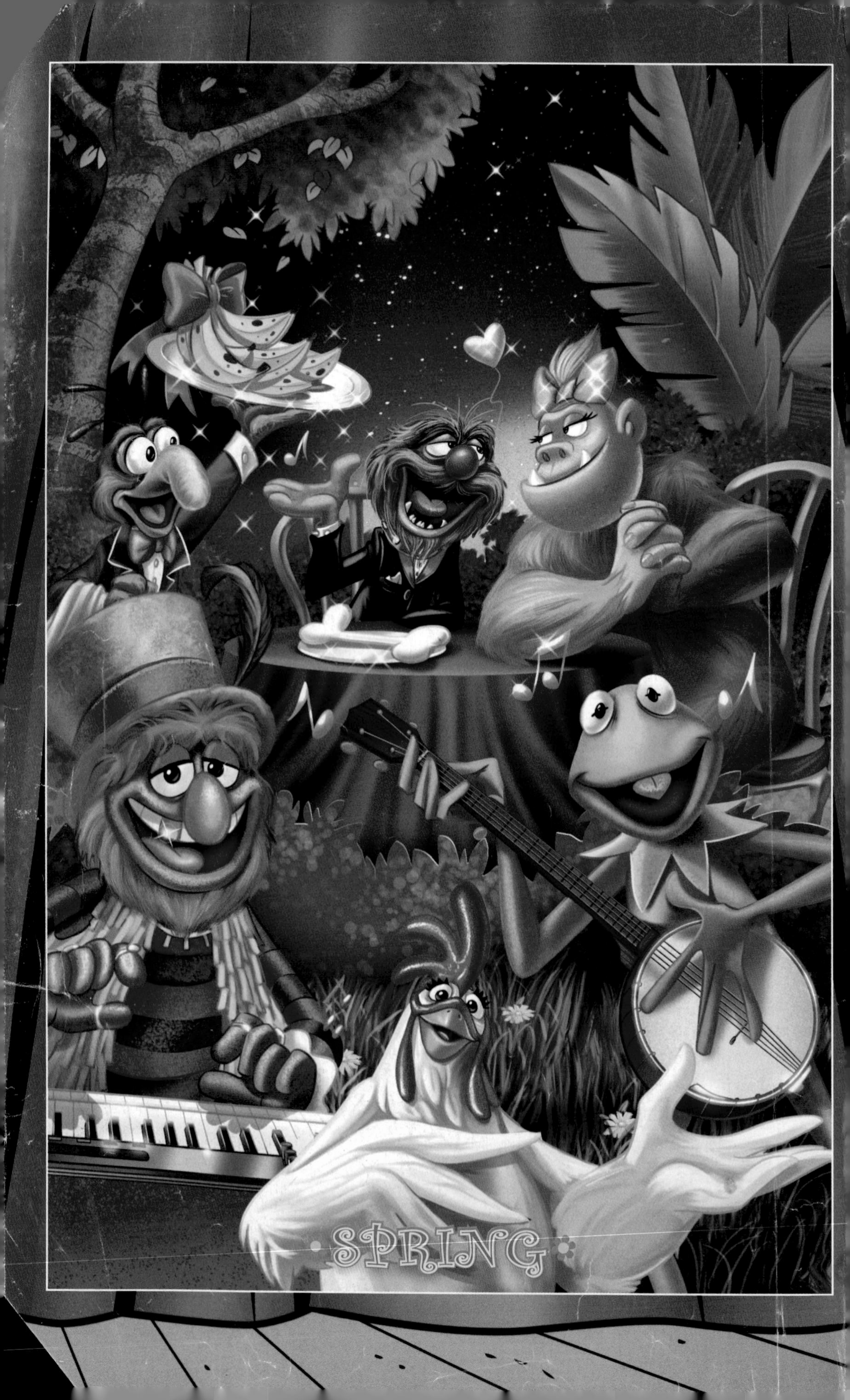
SPRING

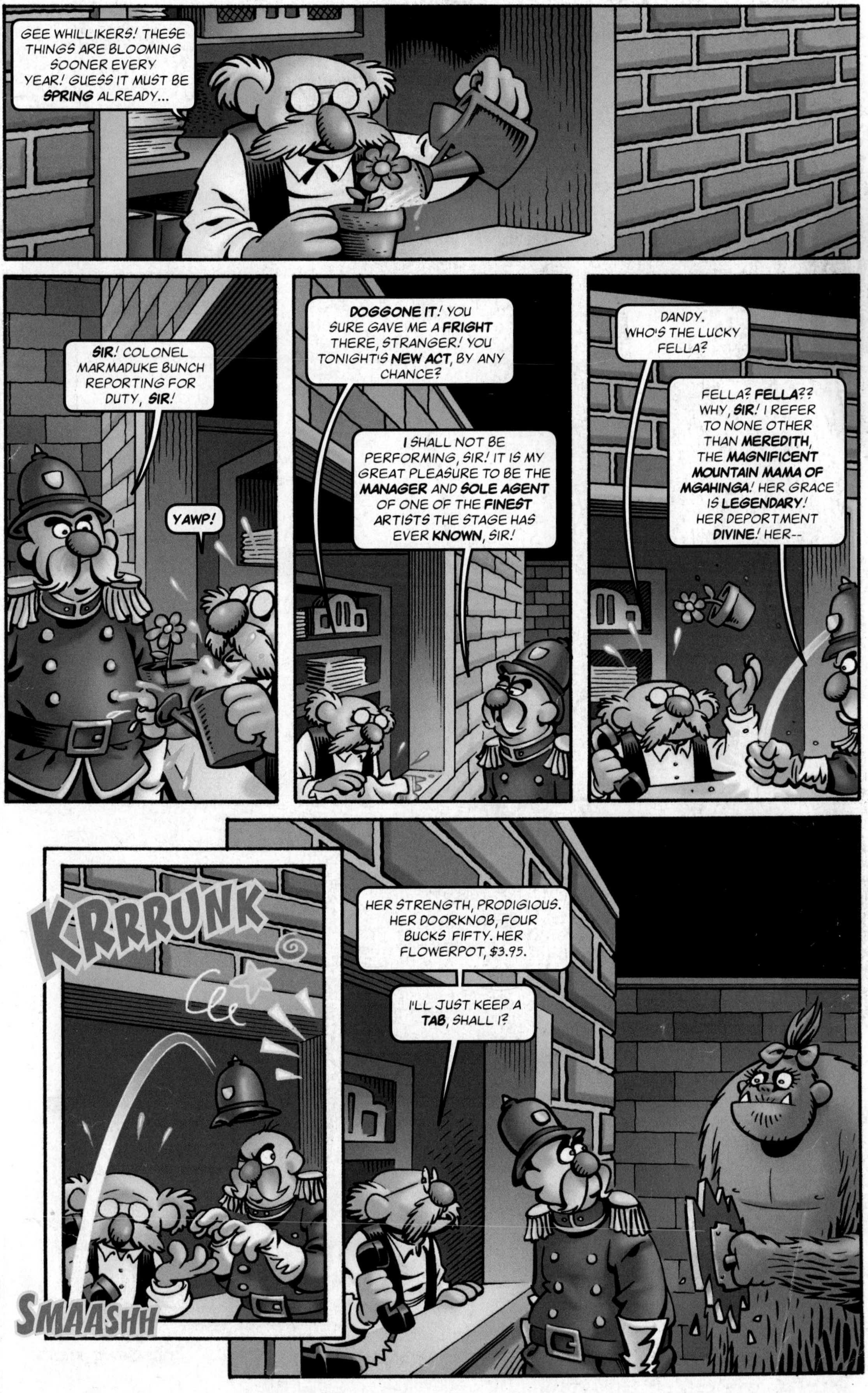
GEE WHILLIKERS! THESE THINGS ARE BLOOMING SOONER EVERY YEAR! GUESS IT MUST BE SPRING ALREADY...
SIR! COLONEL MARMADUKE BUNCH REPORTING FOR DUTY, SIR!
YAWP!
DOGGONE IT! YOU SURE GAVE ME A FRIGHT THERE, STRANGER! YOU TONIGHT'S NEW ACT, BY ANY CHANCE?
I SHALL NOT BE PERFORMING, SIR! IT IS MY GREAT PLEASURE TO BE THE MANAGER AND SOLE AGENT OF ONE OF THE FINEST ARTISTS THE STAGE HAS EVER KNOWN, SIR!
DANDY. WHO'S THE LUCKY FELLA?
FELLA? FELLA?? WHY, SIR! I REFER TO NONE OTHER THAN MEREDITH, THE MAGNIFICENT MOUNTAIN MAMA OF MGAHINGA! HER GRACE IS LEGENDARY! HER DEPORTMENT DIVINE! HER--
KRRRUNK
SMAASHH
HER STRENGTH, PRODIGIOUS. HER DOORKNOB, FOUR BUCKS FIFTY. HER FLOWERPOT, $3.95.
I'LL JUST KEEP A TAB, SHALL I?

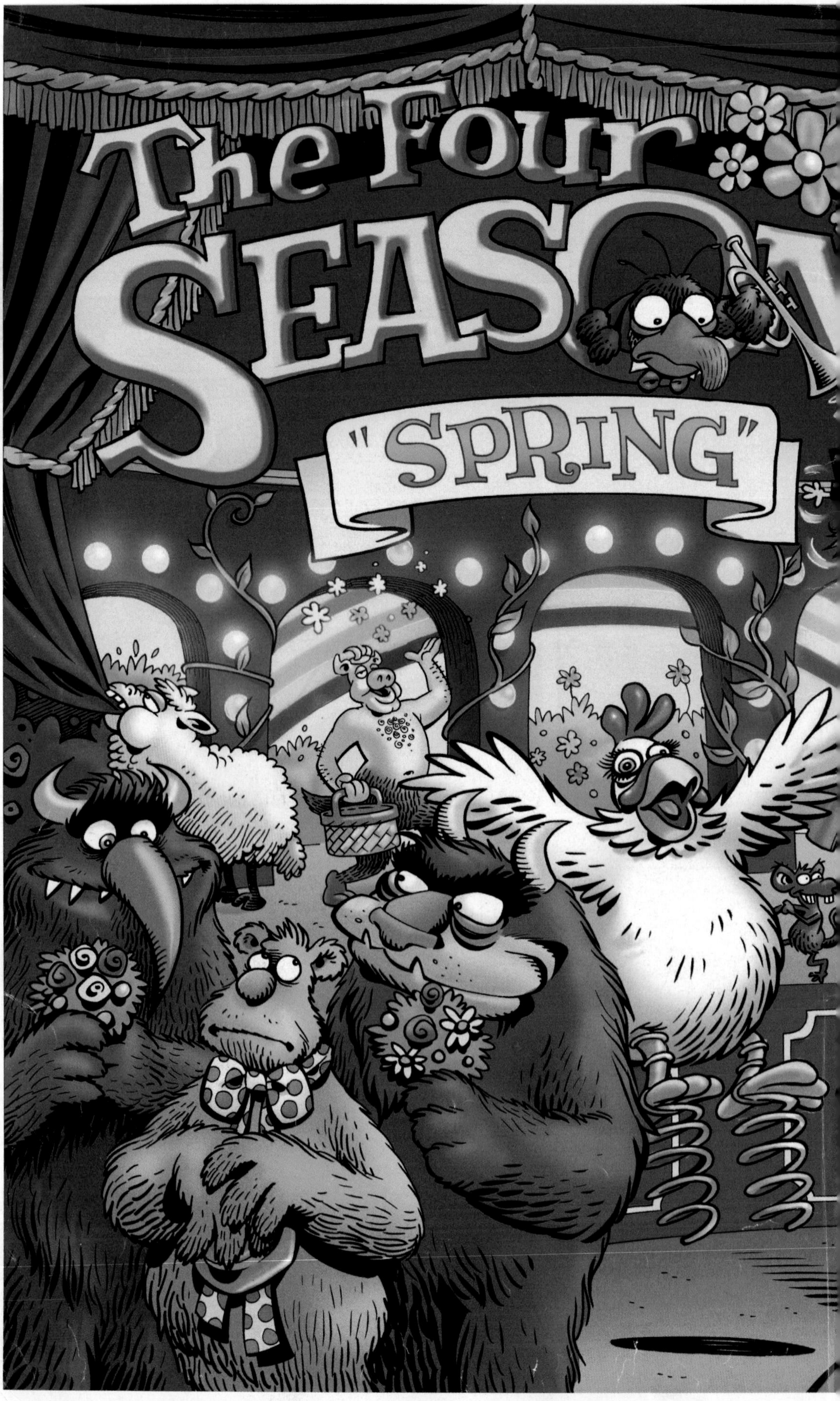
The Four
SEASO
"SPRING"

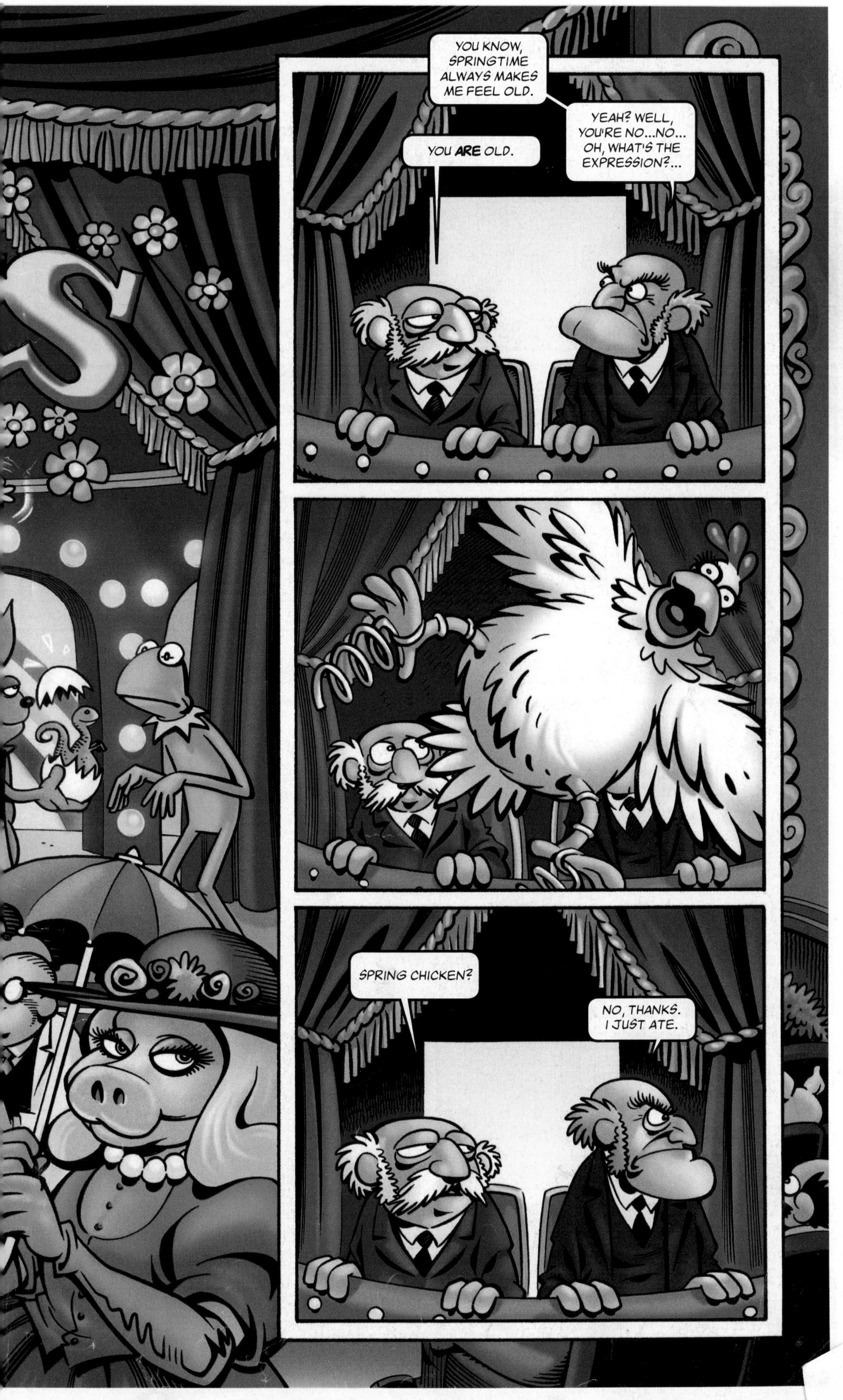
YOU KNOW, SPRINGTIME ALWAYS MAKES ME FEEL OLD.
YOU **ARE** OLD.
YEAH? WELL, YOU'RE NO...NO... OH, WHAT'S THE EXPRESSION?...
SPRING CHICKEN?
NO, THANKS. I JUST ATE.

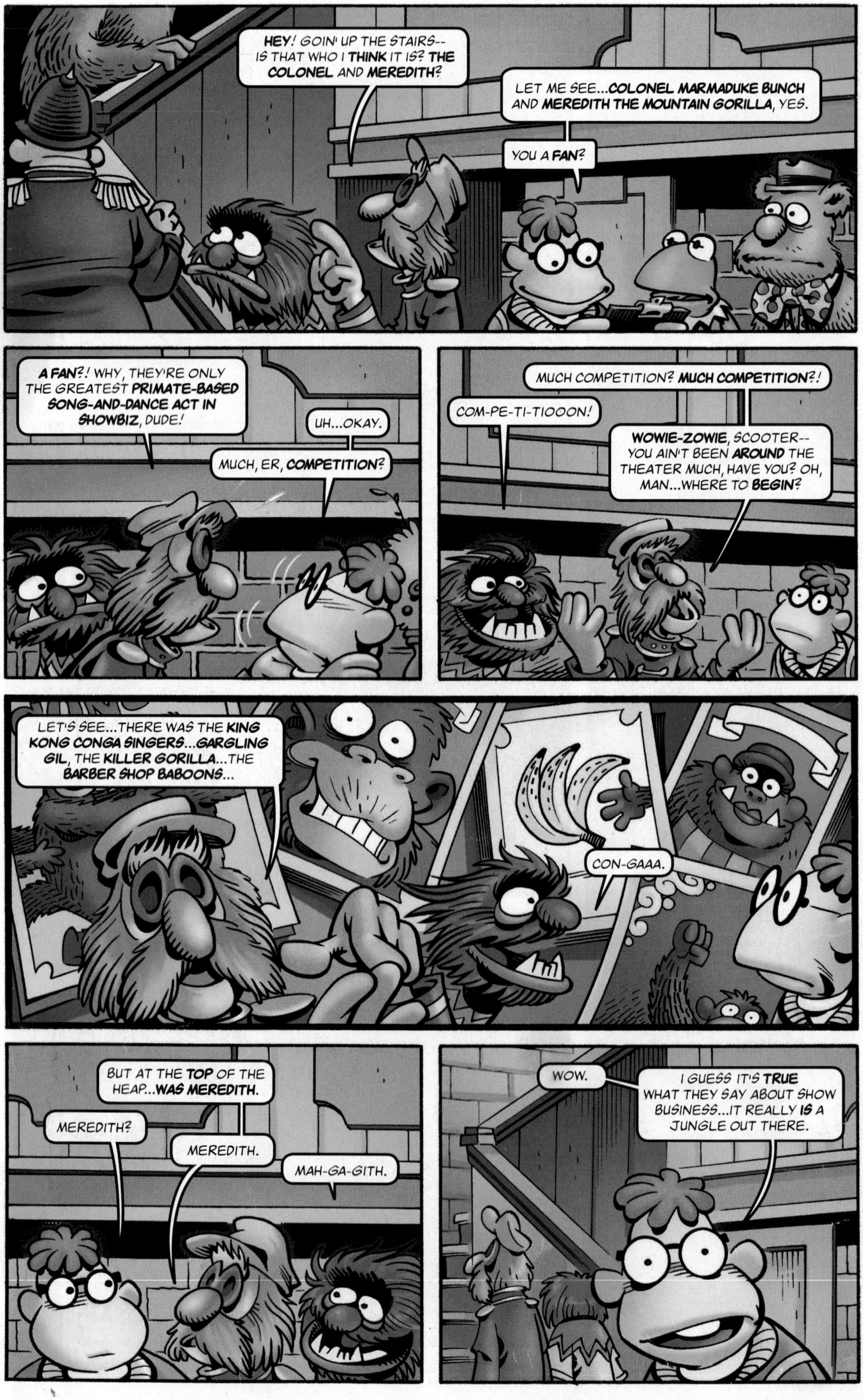
HEY! GOIN' UP THE STAIRS-- IS THAT WHO I THINK IT IS? THE COLONEL AND MEREDITH?
LET ME SEE...COLONEL MARMADUKE BUNCH AND MEREDITH THE MOUNTAIN GORILLA, YES.
YOU A FAN?
A FAN?! WHY, THEY'RE ONLY THE GREATEST PRIMATE-BASED SONG-AND-DANCE ACT IN SHOWBIZ, DUDE!
UH...OKAY.
MUCH, ER, COMPETITION?
MUCH COMPETITION? MUCH COMPETITION?!
COM-PE-TI-TIOOON!
WOWIE-ZOWIE, SCOOTER-- YOU AIN'T BEEN AROUND THE THEATER MUCH, HAVE YOU? OH, MAN...WHERE TO BEGIN?
LET'S SEE...THERE WAS THE KING KONG CONGA SINGERS...GARGLING GIL, THE KILLER GORILLA...THE BARBER SHOP BABOONS...
CON-GAAA.
BUT AT THE TOP OF THE HEAP...WAS MEREDITH.
MEREDITH?
MEREDITH.
MAH-GA-GITH.
WOW.
I GUESS IT'S TRUE WHAT THEY SAY ABOUT SHOW BUSINESS...IT REALLY IS A JUNGLE OUT THERE.

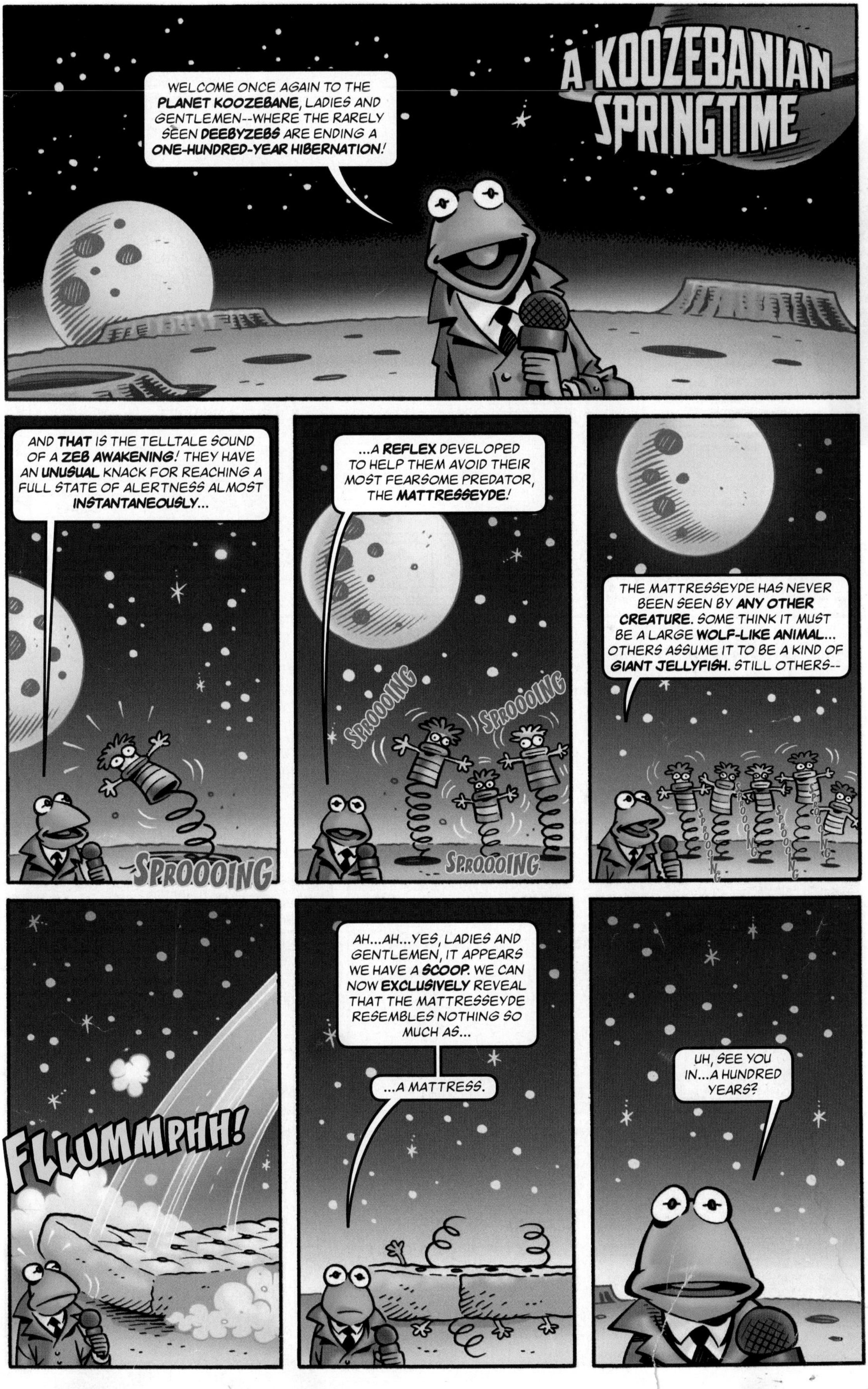
A KOOZEBANIAN SPRINGTIME
WELCOME ONCE AGAIN TO THE PLANET KOOZEBANE, LADIES AND GENTLEMEN--WHERE THE RARELY SEEN DEEBYZEBS ARE ENDING A ONE-HUNDRED-YEAR HIBERNATION!
AND THAT IS THE TELLTALE SOUND OF A ZEB AWAKENING! THEY HAVE AN UNUSUAL KNACK FOR REACHING A FULL STATE OF ALERTNESS ALMOST INSTANTANEOUSLY...
SPROOOOING
...A REFLEX DEVELOPED TO HELP THEM AVOID THEIR MOST FEARSOME PREDATOR, THE MATTRESSEYDE!
SPROOOING
SPROOOING
SPROOOING
THE MATTRESSEYDE HAS NEVER BEEN SEEN BY ANY OTHER CREATURE. SOME THINK IT MUST BE A LARGE WOLF-LIKE ANIMAL... OTHERS ASSUME IT TO BE A KIND OF GIANT JELLYFISH. STILL OTHERS--
FLLUMMPHH!
AH...AH...YES, LADIES AND GENTLEMEN, IT APPEARS WE HAVE A SCOOP. WE CAN NOW EXCLUSIVELY REVEAL THAT THE MATTRESSEYDE RESEMBLES NOTHING SO MUCH AS...
...A MATTRESS.
UH, SEE YOU IN...A HUNDRED YEARS?

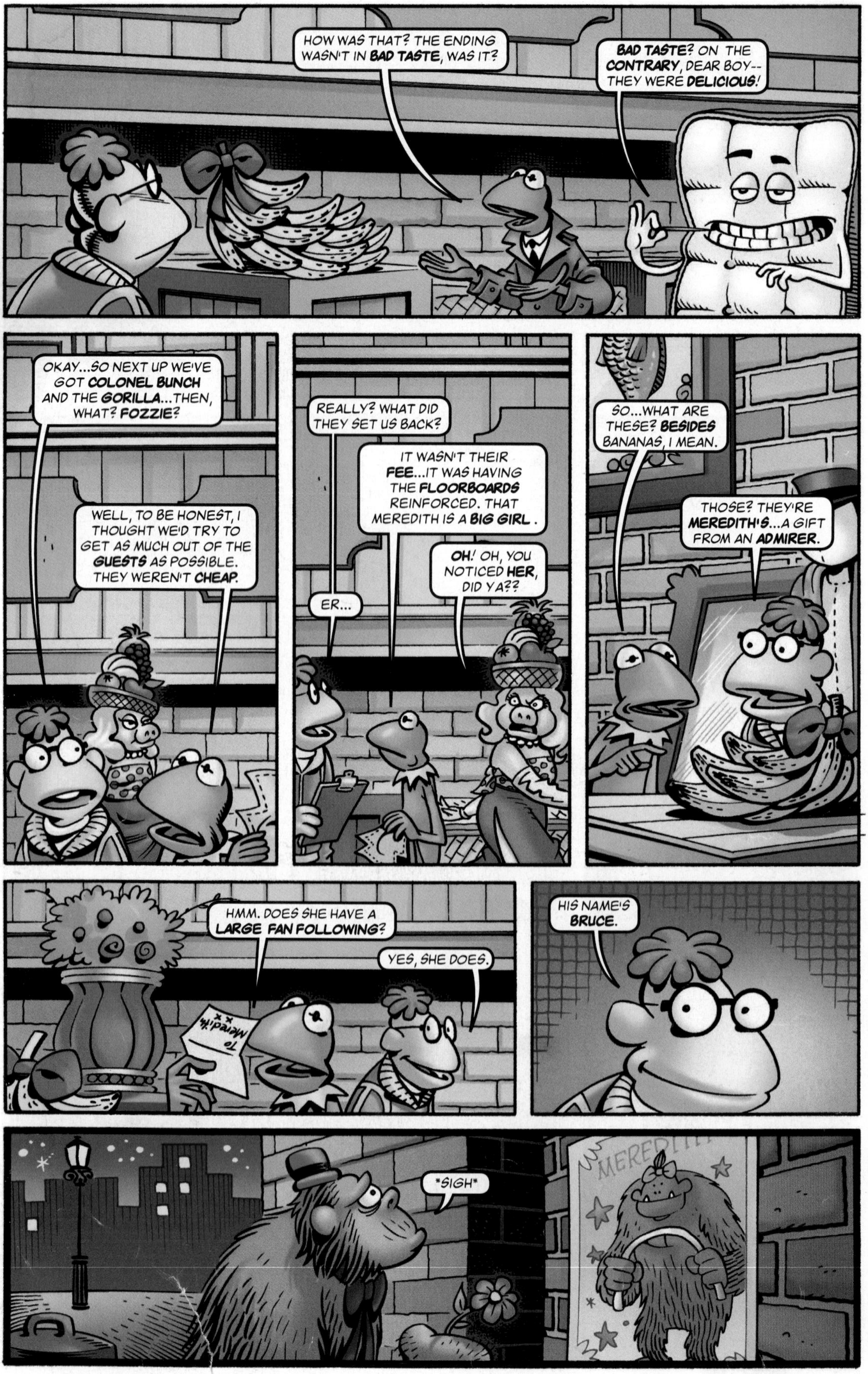
HOW WAS THAT? THE ENDING WASN'T IN BAD TASTE, WAS IT?
BAD TASTE? ON THE CONTRARY, DEAR BOY-- THEY WERE DELICIOUS!
OKAY...SO NEXT UP WE'VE GOT COLONEL BUNCH AND THE GORILLA...THEN, WHAT? FOZZIE?
WELL, TO BE HONEST, I THOUGHT WE'D TRY TO GET AS MUCH OUT OF THE GUESTS AS POSSIBLE. THEY WEREN'T CHEAP.
REALLY? WHAT DID THEY SET US BACK?
IT WASN'T THEIR FEE...IT WAS HAVING THE FLOORBOARDS REINFORCED. THAT MEREDITH IS A BIG GIRL.
ER...
OH! OH, YOU NOTICED HER, DID YA??
SO...WHAT ARE THESE? BESIDES BANANAS, I MEAN.
THOSE? THEY'RE MEREDITH'S...A GIFT FROM AN ADMIRER.
HMM. DOES SHE HAVE A LARGE FAN FOLLOWING?
YES, SHE DOES.
HIS NAME'S BRUCE.
SIGH

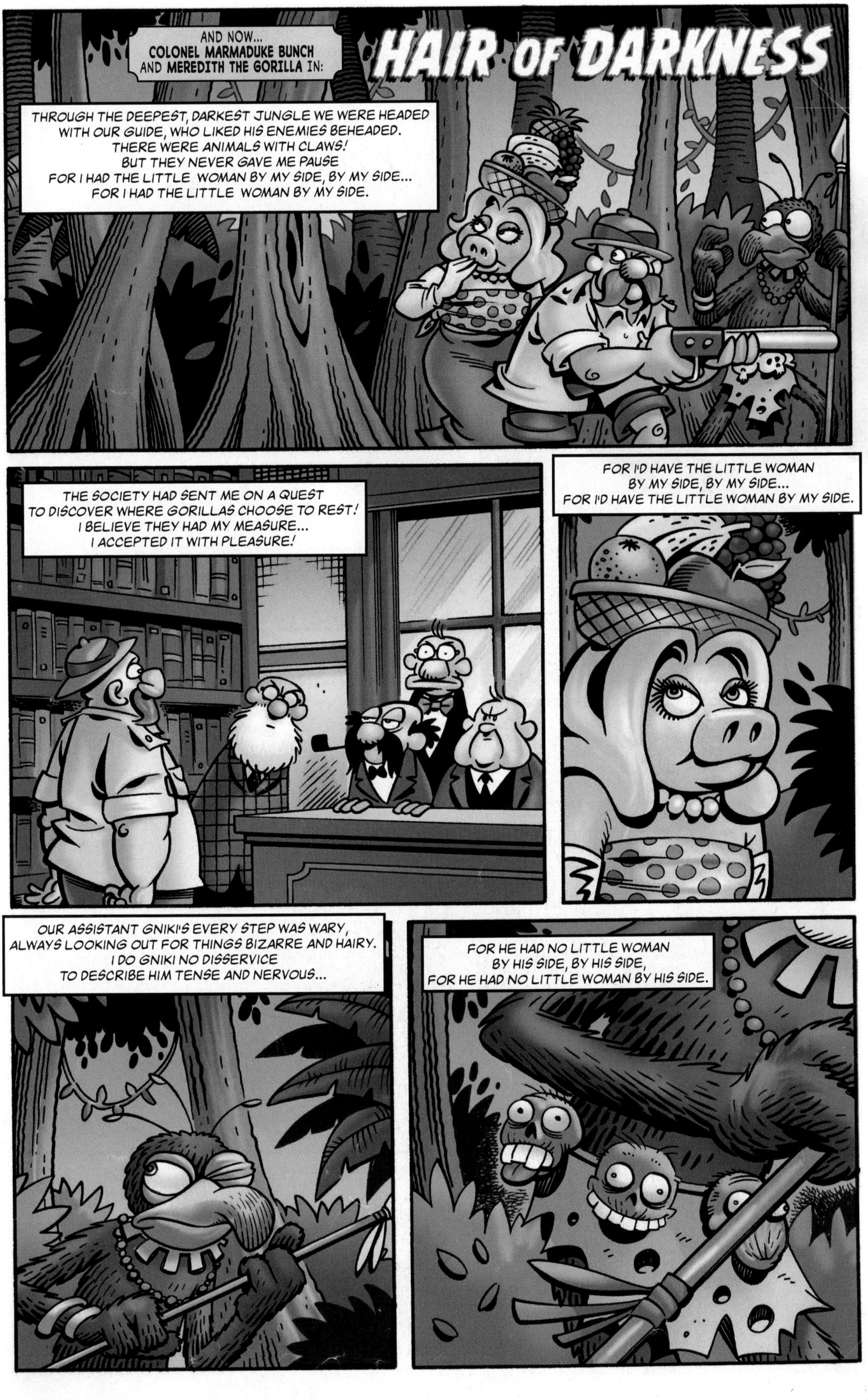
AND NOW... COLONEL MARMADUKE BUNCH AND MEREDITH THE GORILLA IN:
HAIR OF DARKNESS
THROUGH THE DEEPEST, DARKEST JUNGLE WE WERE HEADED WITH OUR GUIDE, WHO LIKED HIS ENEMIES BEHEADED. THERE WERE ANIMALS WITH CLAWS! BUT THEY NEVER GAVE ME PAUSE FOR I HAD THE LITTLE WOMAN BY MY SIDE, BY MY SIDE... FOR I HAD THE LITTLE WOMAN BY MY SIDE.
THE SOCIETY HAD SENT ME ON A QUEST TO DISCOVER WHERE GORILLAS CHOOSE TO REST! I BELIEVE THEY HAD MY MEASURE... I ACCEPTED IT WITH PLEASURE!
FOR I'D HAVE THE LITTLE WOMAN BY MY SIDE, BY MY SIDE... FOR I'D HAVE THE LITTLE WOMAN BY MY SIDE.
OUR ASSISTANT GNIKI'S EVERY STEP WAS WARY, ALWAYS LOOKING OUT FOR THINGS BIZARRE AND HAIRY. I DO GNIKI NO DISSERVICE TO DESCRIBE HIM TENSE AND NERVOUS...
FOR HE HAD NO LITTLE WOMAN BY HIS SIDE, BY HIS SIDE, FOR HE HAD NO LITTLE WOMAN BY HIS SIDE.

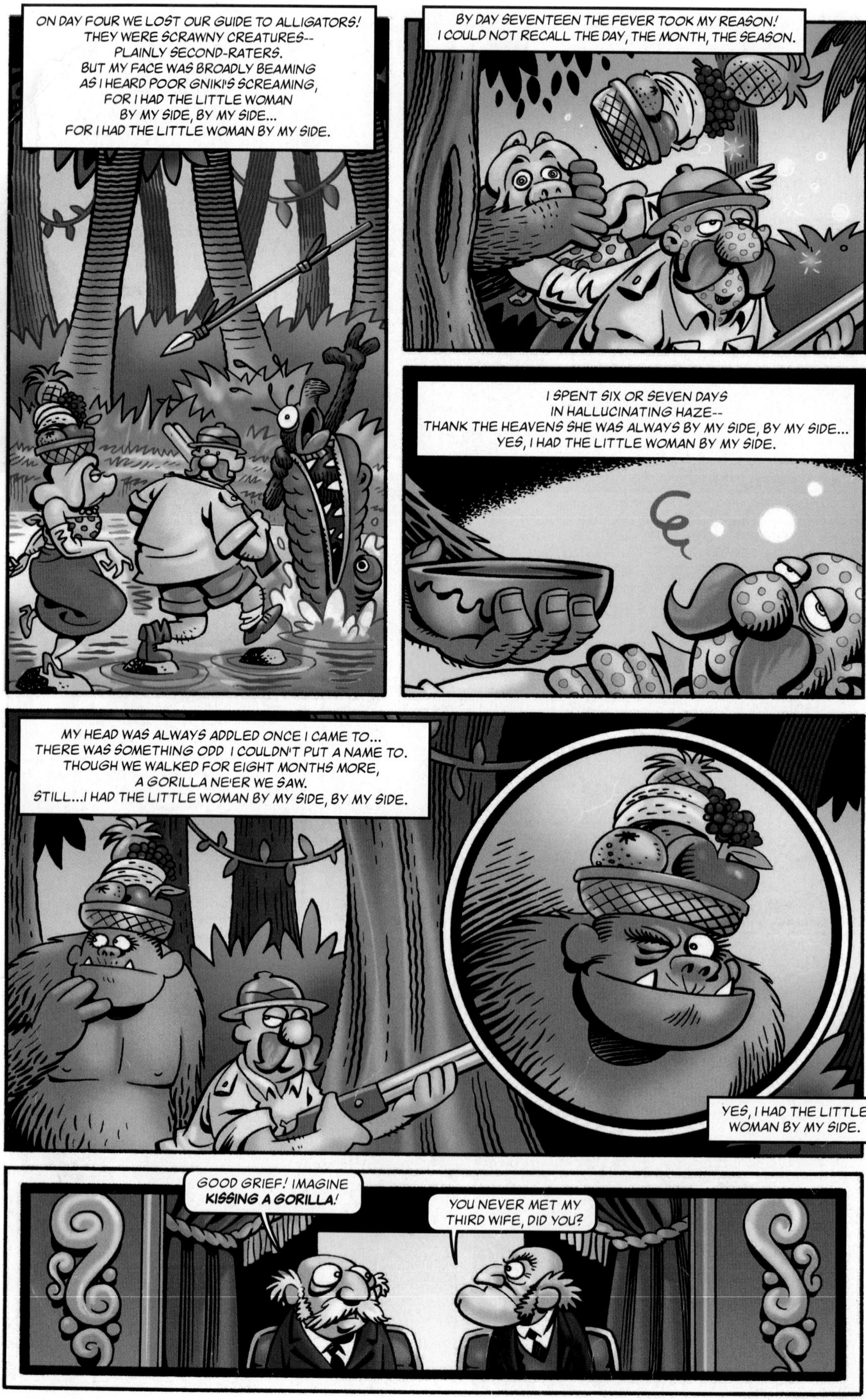
ON DAY FOUR WE LOST OUR GUIDE TO ALLIGATORS! THEY WERE SCRAWNY CREATURES-- PLAINLY SECOND-RATERS. BUT MY FACE WAS BROADLY BEAMING AS I HEARD POOR GNIKI'S SCREAMING, FOR I HAD THE LITTLE WOMAN BY MY SIDE, BY MY SIDE... FOR I HAD THE LITTLE WOMAN BY MY SIDE.
BY DAY SEVENTEEN THE FEVER TOOK MY REASON! I COULD NOT RECALL THE DAY, THE MONTH, THE SEASON.
I SPENT SIX OR SEVEN DAYS IN HALLUCINATING HAZE-- THANK THE HEAVENS SHE WAS ALWAYS BY MY SIDE, BY MY SIDE... YES, I HAD THE LITTLE WOMAN BY MY SIDE.
MY HEAD WAS ALWAYS ADDLED ONCE I CAME TO... THERE WAS SOMETHING ODD I COULDN'T PUT A NAME TO. THOUGH WE WALKED FOR EIGHT MONTHS MORE, A GORILLA NE'ER WE SAW. STILL...I HAD THE LITTLE WOMAN BY MY SIDE, BY MY SIDE.
YES, I HAD THE LITTLE WOMAN BY MY SIDE.
GOOD GRIEF! IMAGINE **KISSING A GORILLA**!
YOU NEVER MET MY THIRD WIFE, DID YOU?

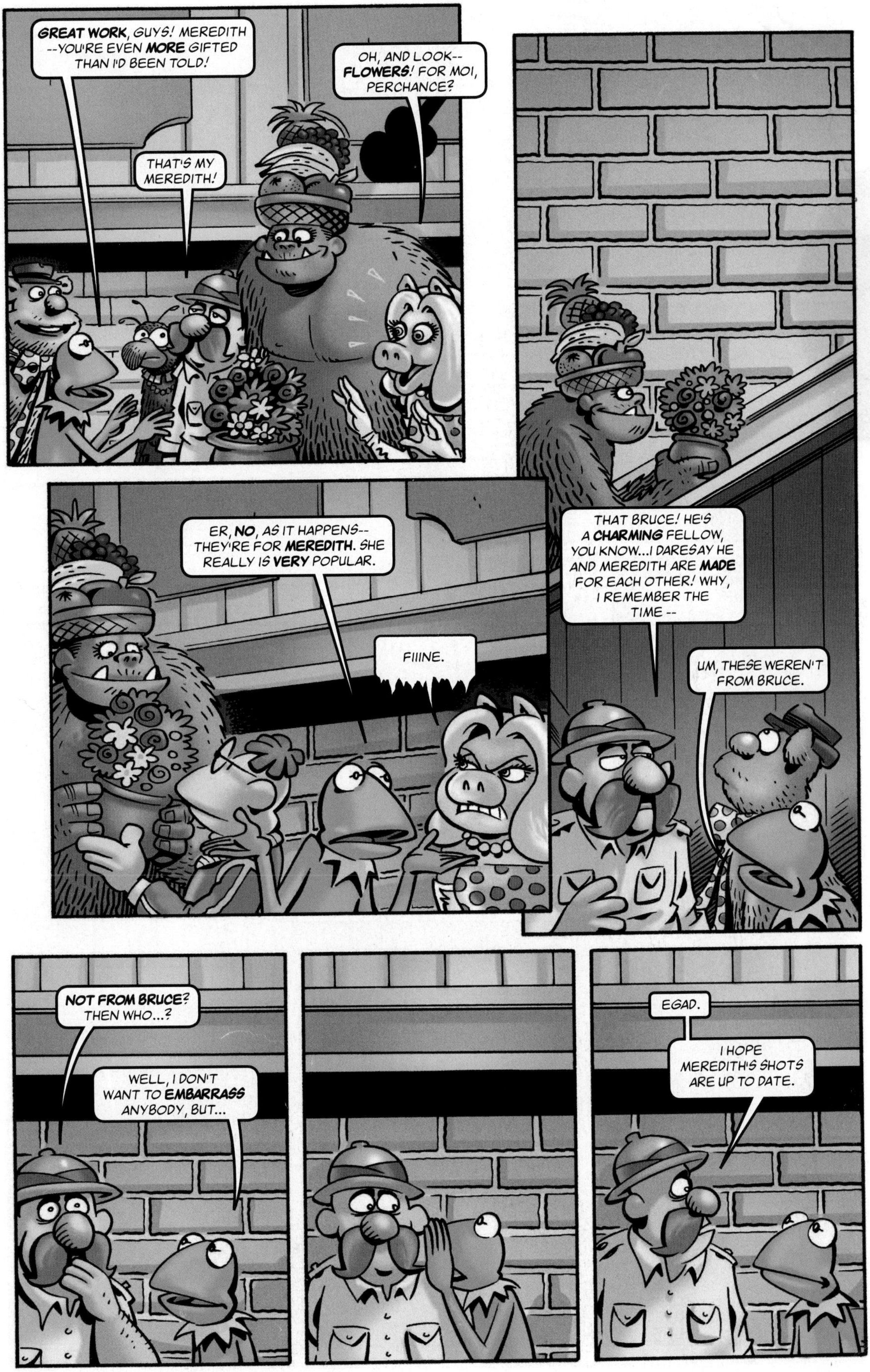
GREAT WORK, GUYS! MEREDITH --YOU'RE EVEN MORE GIFTED THAN I'D BEEN TOLD!
THAT'S MY MEREDITH!
OH, AND LOOK-- FLOWERS! FOR MOI, PERCHANCE?
ER, NO, AS IT HAPPENS-- THEY'RE FOR MEREDITH. SHE REALLY IS VERY POPULAR.
FIIINE.
THAT BRUCE! HE'S A CHARMING FELLOW, YOU KNOW...I DARESAY HE AND MEREDITH ARE MADE FOR EACH OTHER! WHY, I REMEMBER THE TIME --
UM, THESE WEREN'T FROM BRUCE.
NOT FROM BRUCE? THEN WHO...?
WELL, I DON'T WANT TO EMBARRASS ANYBODY, BUT...
EGAD.
I HOPE MEREDITH'S SHOTS ARE UP TO DATE.

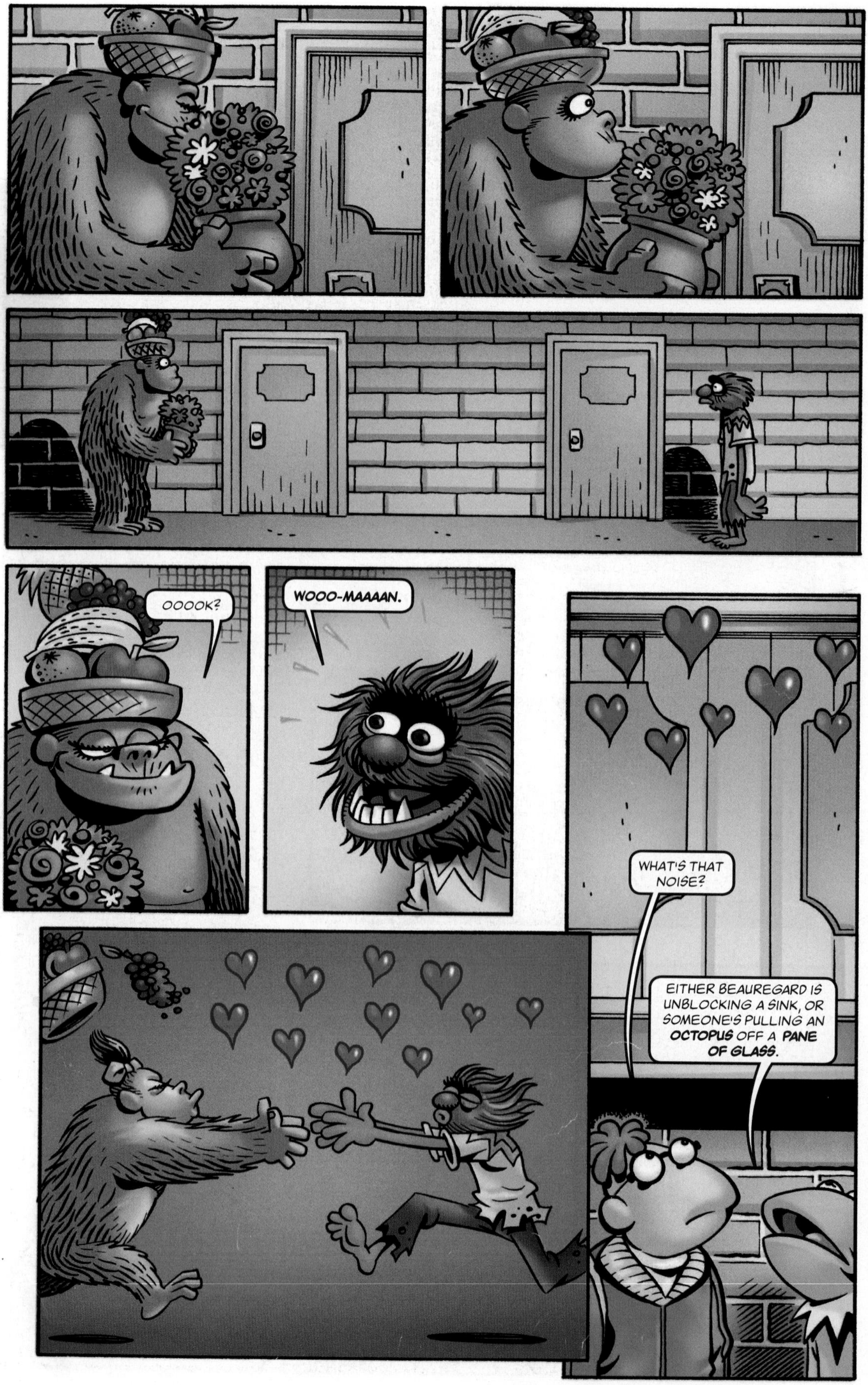
OOOOK?
WOOO-MAAAAN.
WHAT'S THAT NOISE?
EITHER BEAUREGARD IS UNBLOCKING A SINK, OR SOMEONE'S PULLING AN **OCTOPUS** OFF A **PANE OF GLASS**.

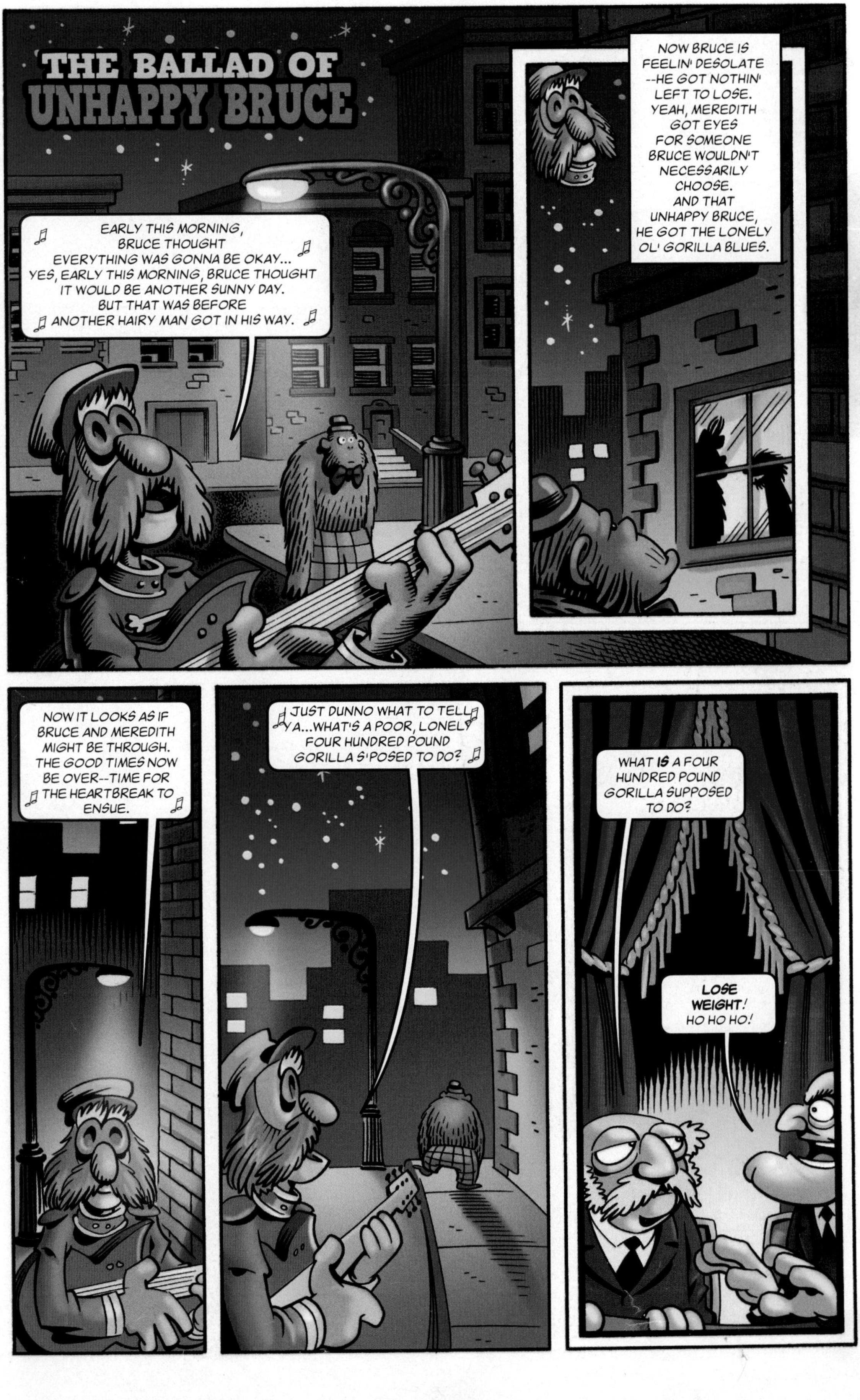
THE BALLAD OF UNHAPPY BRUCE
EARLY THIS MORNING, BRUCE THOUGHT EVERYTHING WAS GONNA BE OKAY... YES, EARLY THIS MORNING, BRUCE THOUGHT IT WOULD BE ANOTHER SUNNY DAY. BUT THAT WAS BEFORE ANOTHER HAIRY MAN GOT IN HIS WAY.
NOW BRUCE IS FEELIN' DESOLATE --HE GOT NOTHIN' LEFT TO LOSE. YEAH, MEREDITH GOT EYES FOR SOMEONE BRUCE WOULDN'T NECESSARILY CHOOSE. AND THAT UNHAPPY BRUCE, HE GOT THE LONELY OL' GORILLA BLUES.
NOW IT LOOKS AS IF BRUCE AND MEREDITH MIGHT BE THROUGH. THE GOOD TIMES NOW BE OVER--TIME FOR THE HEARTBREAK TO ENSUE.
JUST DUNNO WHAT TO TELL YA...WHAT'S A POOR, LONELY FOUR HUNDRED POUND GORILLA S'POSED TO DO?
WHAT IS A FOUR HUNDRED POUND GORILLA SUPPOSED TO DO?
LOSE WEIGHT! HO HO HO!

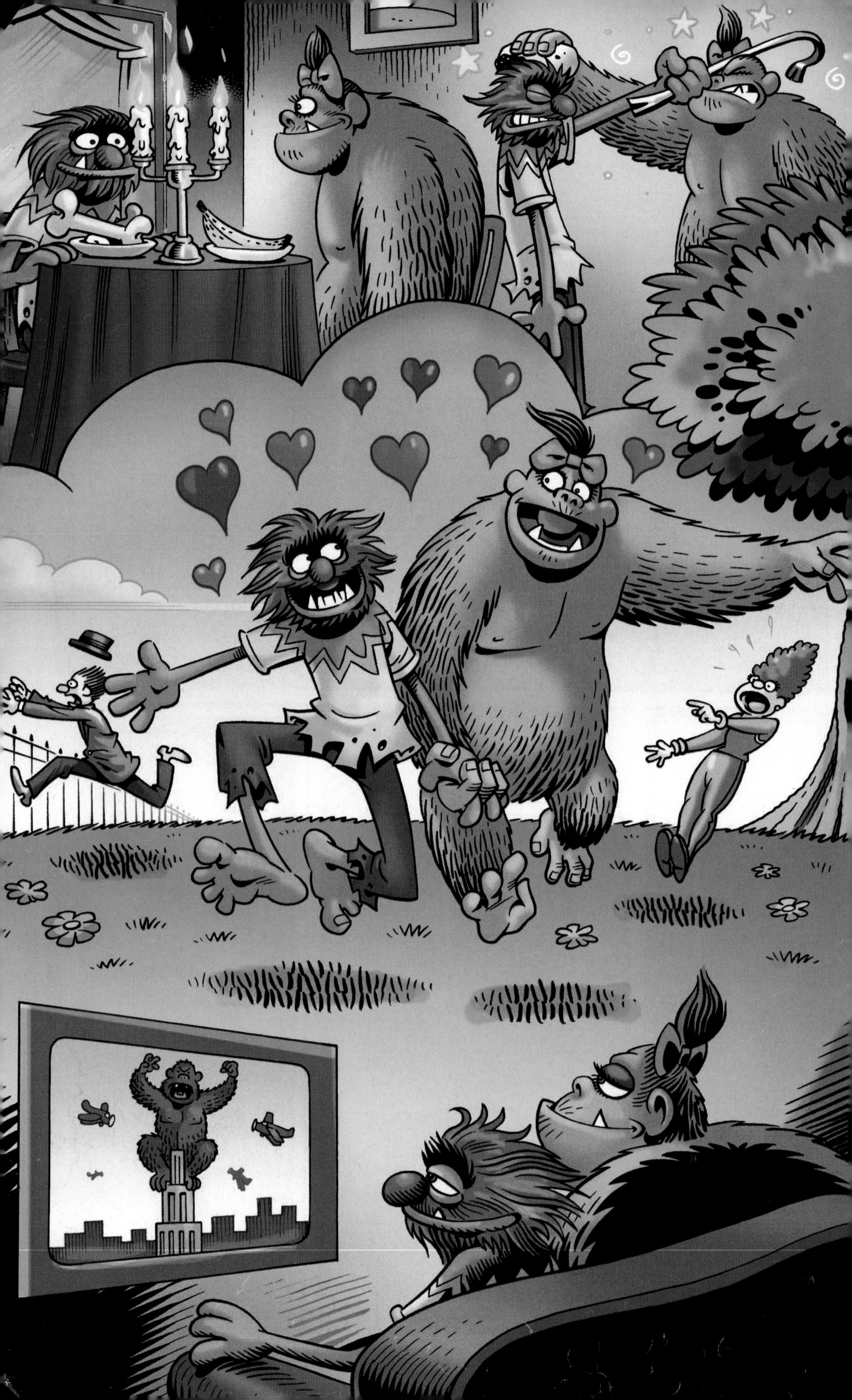

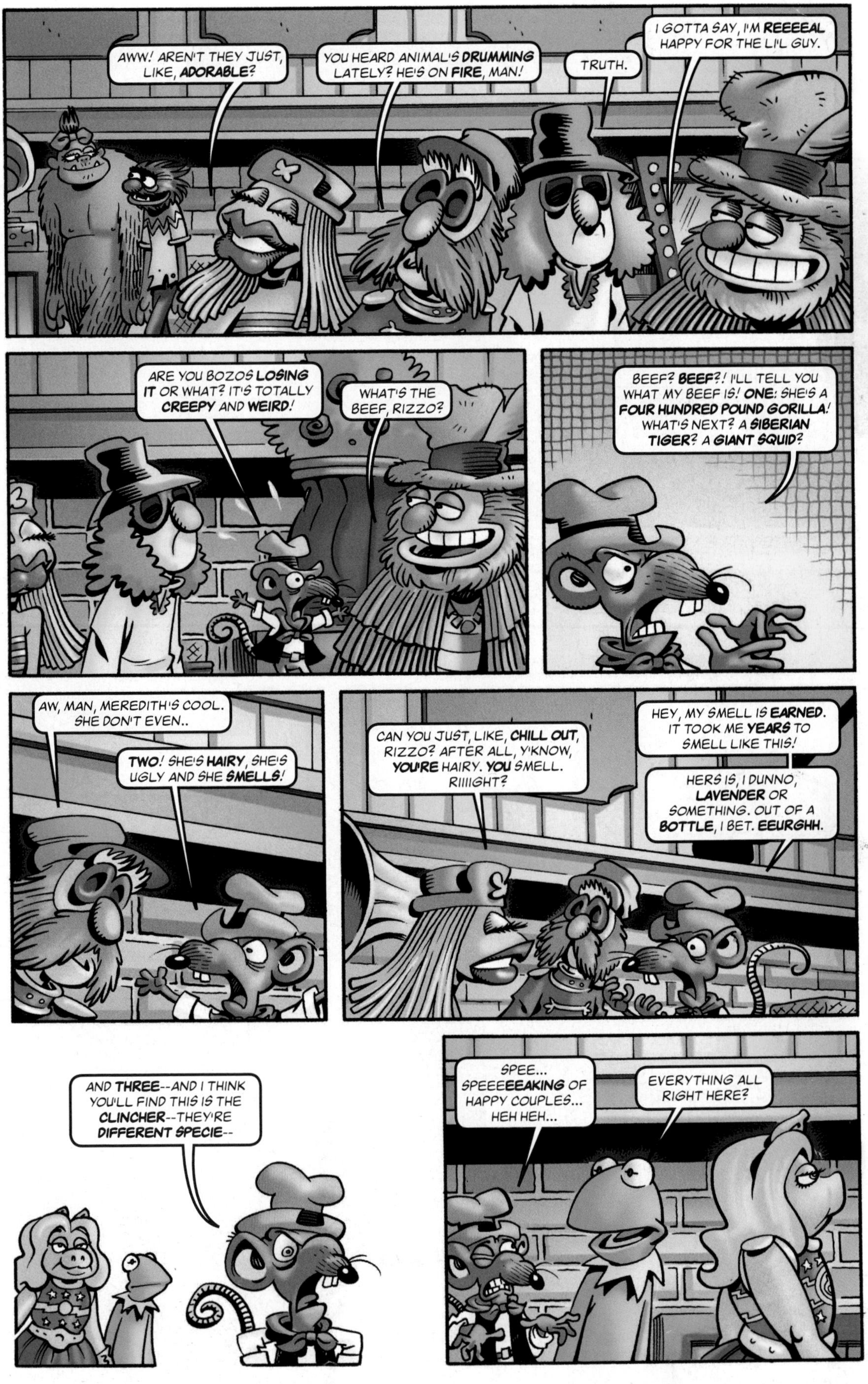

AWW! AREN'T THEY JUST, LIKE, ADORABLE?
YOU HEARD ANIMAL'S DRUMMING LATELY? HE'S ON FIRE, MAN!
TRUTH.
I GOTTA SAY, I'M REEEEAL HAPPY FOR THE LI'L GUY.
ARE YOU BOZOS LOSING IT OR WHAT? IT'S TOTALLY CREEPY AND WEIRD!
WHAT'S THE BEEF, RIZZO?
BEEF? BEEF?! I'LL TELL YOU WHAT MY BEEF IS! ONE: SHE'S A FOUR HUNDRED POUND GORILLA! WHAT'S NEXT? A SIBERIAN TIGER? A GIANT SQUID?
AW, MAN, MEREDITH'S COOL. SHE DON'T EVEN..
TWO! SHE'S HAIRY, SHE'S UGLY AND SHE SMELLS!
CAN YOU JUST, LIKE, CHILL OUT, RIZZO? AFTER ALL, Y'KNOW, YOU'RE HAIRY. YOU SMELL. RIIIIGHT?
HEY, MY SMELL IS EARNED. IT TOOK ME YEARS TO SMELL LIKE THIS!
HERS IS, I DUNNO, LAVENDER OR SOMETHING. OUT OF A BOTTLE, I BET. EEURGHH.
AND THREE--AND I THINK YOU'LL FIND THIS IS THE CLINCHER--THEY'RE DIFFERENT SPECIE--
SPEE... SPEEEEEAKING OF HAPPY COUPLES... HEH HEH...
EVERYTHING ALL RIGHT HERE?

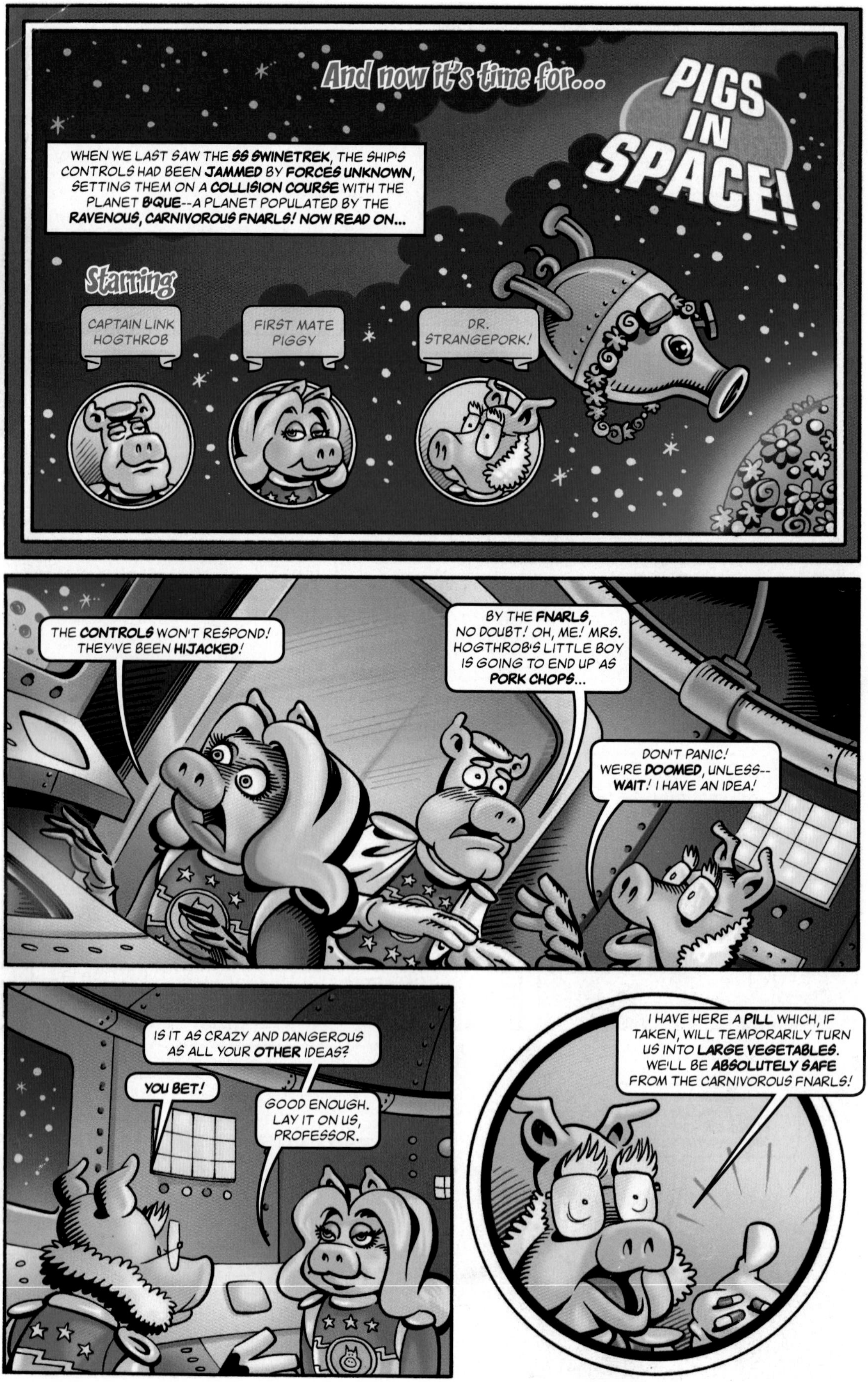
And now it's time for...
PIGS IN SPACE!
WHEN WE LAST SAW THE SS SWINETREK, THE SHIP'S CONTROLS HAD BEEN JAMMED BY FORCES UNKNOWN, SETTING THEM ON A COLLISION COURSE WITH THE PLANET B'QUE--A PLANET POPULATED BY THE RAVENOUS, CARNIVOROUS FNARLS! NOW READ ON...
Starring
CAPTAIN LINK HOGTHROB
FIRST MATE PIGGY
DR. STRANGEPORK!
THE CONTROLS WON'T RESPOND! THEY'VE BEEN HIJACKED!
BY THE FNARLS, NO DOUBT! OH, ME! MRS. HOGTHROB'S LITTLE BOY IS GOING TO END UP AS PORK CHOPS...
DON'T PANIC! WE'RE DOOMED, UNLESS-- WAIT! I HAVE AN IDEA!
IS IT AS CRAZY AND DANGEROUS AS ALL YOUR OTHER IDEAS?
YOU BET!
GOOD ENOUGH. LAY IT ON US, PROFESSOR.
I HAVE HERE A PILL WHICH, IF TAKEN, WILL TEMPORARILY TURN US INTO LARGE VEGETABLES. WE'LL BE ABSOLUTELY SAFE FROM THE CARNIVOROUS FNARLS!

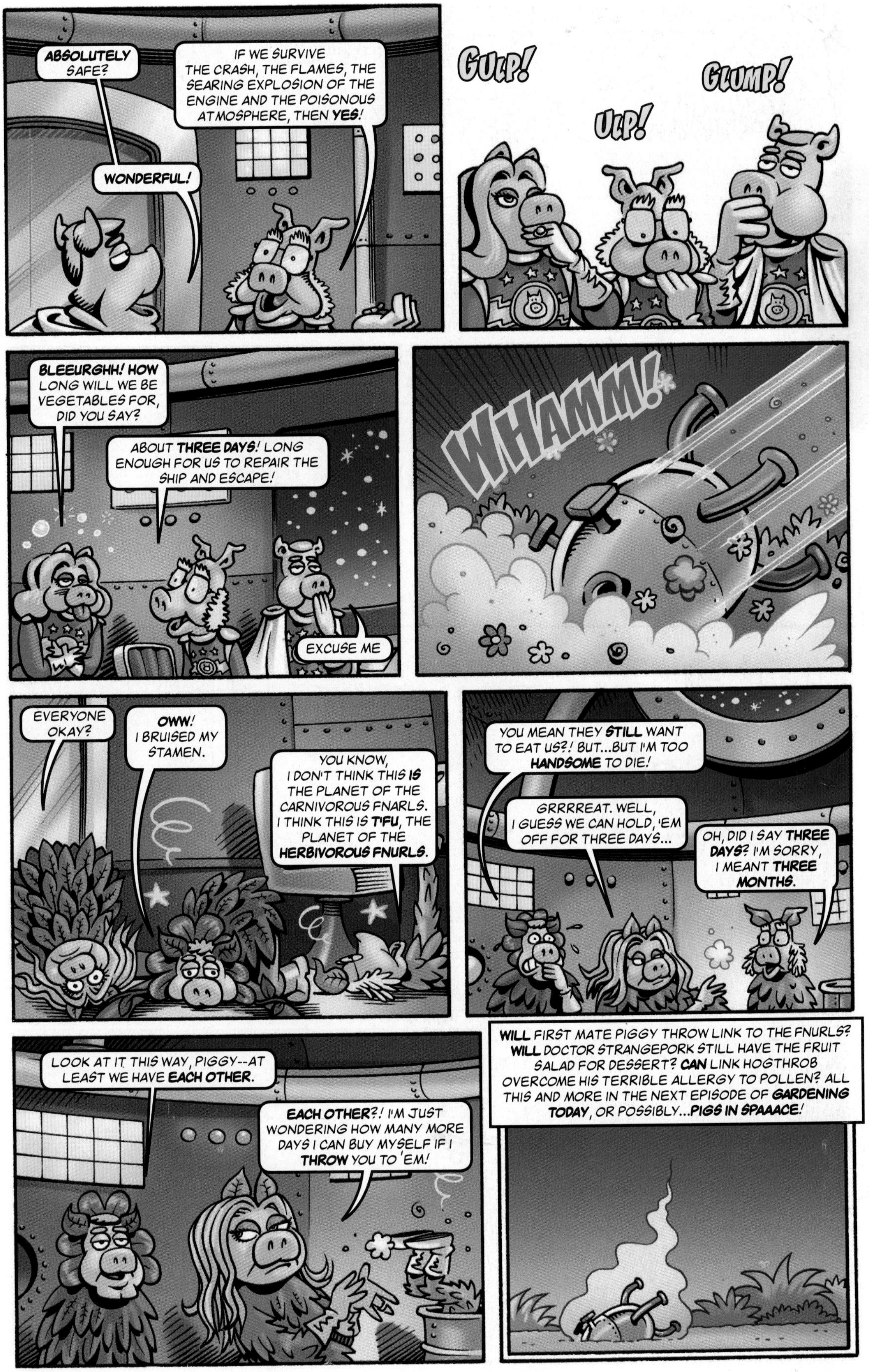
ABSOLUTELY SAFE?
IF WE SURVIVE THE CRASH, THE FLAMES, THE SEARING EXPLOSION OF THE ENGINE AND THE POISONOUS ATMOSPHERE, THEN YES!
WONDERFUL!
GULP!
ULP!
GLUMP!
BLEEURGHH! HOW LONG WILL WE BE VEGETABLES FOR, DID YOU SAY?
ABOUT THREE DAYS! LONG ENOUGH FOR US TO REPAIR THE SHIP AND ESCAPE!
EXCUSE ME
WHAMM!
EVERYONE OKAY?
OWW! I BRUISED MY STAMEN.
YOU KNOW, I DON'T THINK THIS IS THE PLANET OF THE CARNIVOROUS FNARLS. I THINK THIS IS T'FU, THE PLANET OF THE HERBIVOROUS FNURLS.
YOU MEAN THEY STILL WANT TO EAT US?! BUT...BUT I'M TOO HANDSOME TO DIE!
GRRRREAT. WELL, I GUESS WE CAN HOLD 'EM OFF FOR THREE DAYS...
OH, DID I SAY THREE DAYS? I'M SORRY, I MEANT THREE MONTHS.
LOOK AT IT THIS WAY, PIGGY--AT LEAST WE HAVE EACH OTHER.
EACH OTHER?! I'M JUST WONDERING HOW MANY MORE DAYS I CAN BUY MYSELF IF I THROW YOU TO 'EM!
WILL FIRST MATE PIGGY THROW LINK TO THE FNURLS? WILL DOCTOR STRANGEPORK STILL HAVE THE FRUIT SALAD FOR DESSERT? CAN LINK HOGTHROB OVERCOME HIS TERRIBLE ALLERGY TO POLLEN? ALL THIS AND MORE IN THE NEXT EPISODE OF GARDENING TODAY, OR POSSIBLY...PIGS IN SPAAACE!

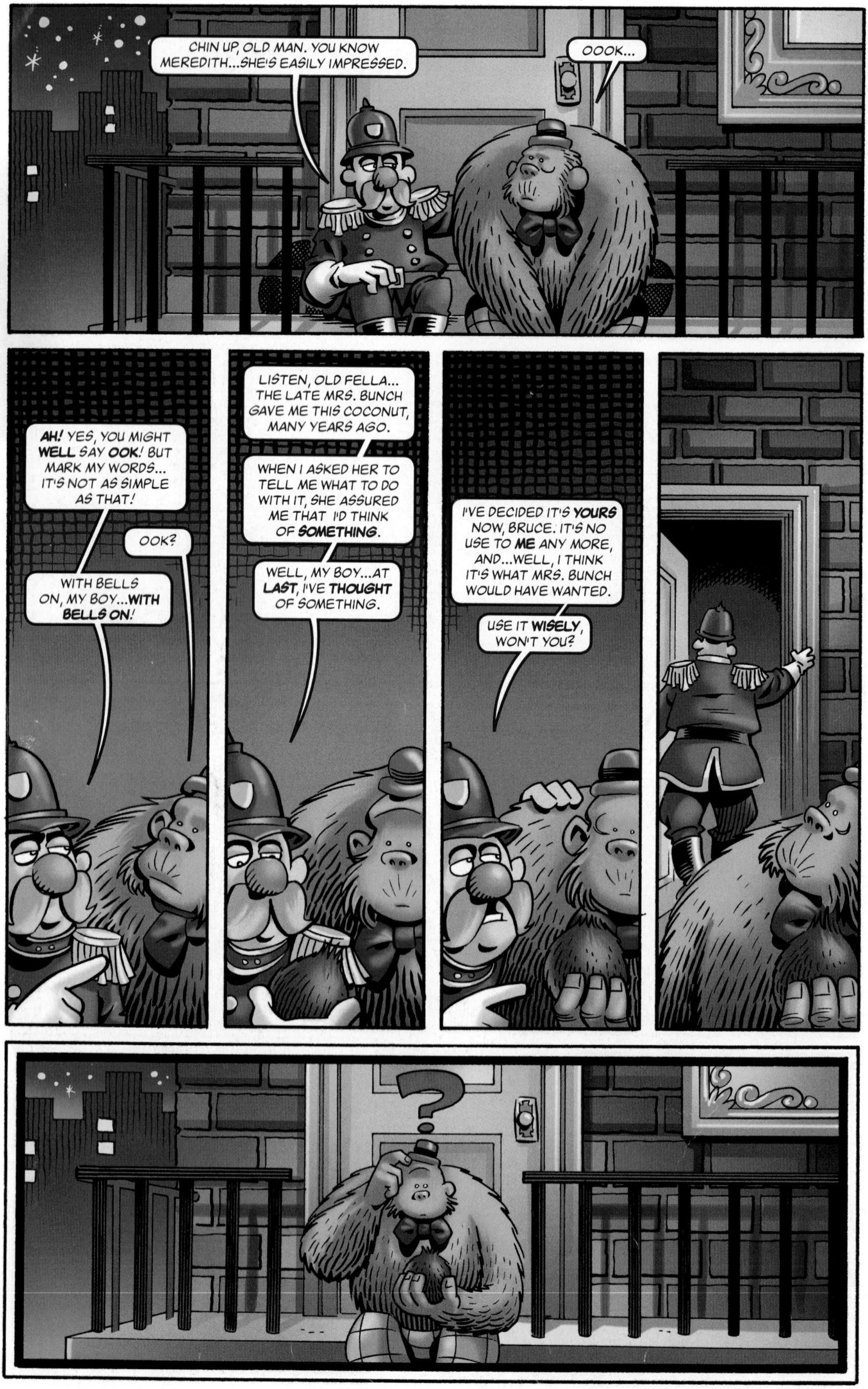
CHIN UP, OLD MAN. YOU KNOW MEREDITH...SHE'S EASILY IMPRESSED.
OOOK...
AH! YES, YOU MIGHT WELL SAY OOK! BUT MARK MY WORDS... IT'S NOT AS SIMPLE AS THAT!
OOK?
WITH BELLS ON, MY BOY...WITH BELLS ON!
LISTEN, OLD FELLA... THE LATE MRS. BUNCH GAVE ME THIS COCONUT, MANY YEARS AGO.
WHEN I ASKED HER TO TELL ME WHAT TO DO WITH IT, SHE ASSURED ME THAT I'D THINK OF SOMETHING.
WELL, MY BOY...AT LAST, I'VE THOUGHT OF SOMETHING.
I'VE DECIDED IT'S YOURS NOW, BRUCE. IT'S NO USE TO ME ANY MORE, AND...WELL, I THINK IT'S WHAT MRS. BUNCH WOULD HAVE WANTED.
USE IT WISELY, WON'T YOU?
?

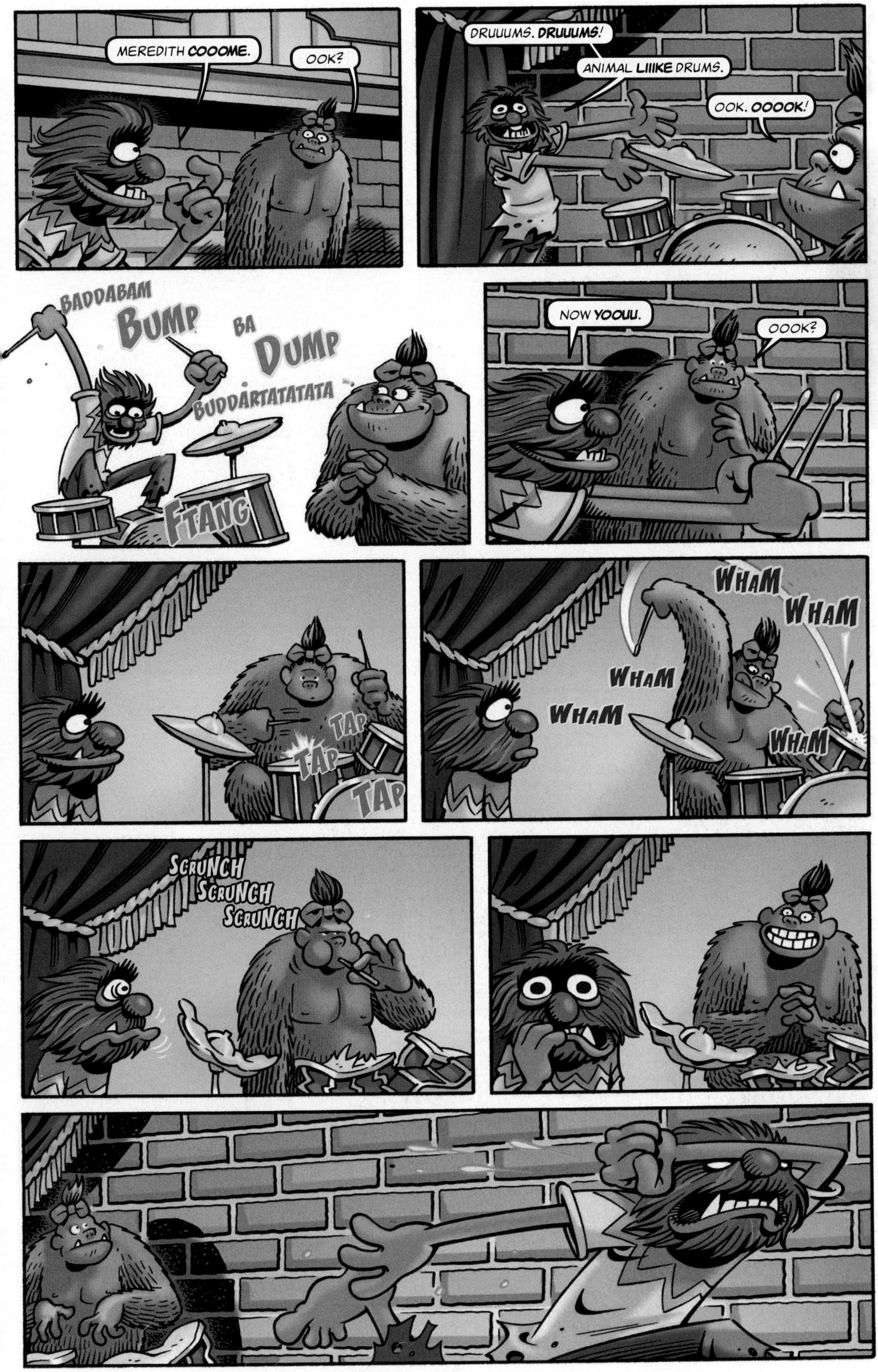

MEREDITH COOOME.
OOK?
DRUUUMS. DRUUUMS!
ANIMAL LIIIKE DRUMS.
OOK. OOOOK!
BADDABAM
BUMP
BA
DUMP
BUDDARTATATATA
FTANG
NOW YOOUU.
OOOK?
TAP
TAP
TAP
WHAM
WHAM
WHAM
WHAM
WHAM
SCRUNCH
SCRUNCH
SCRUNCH

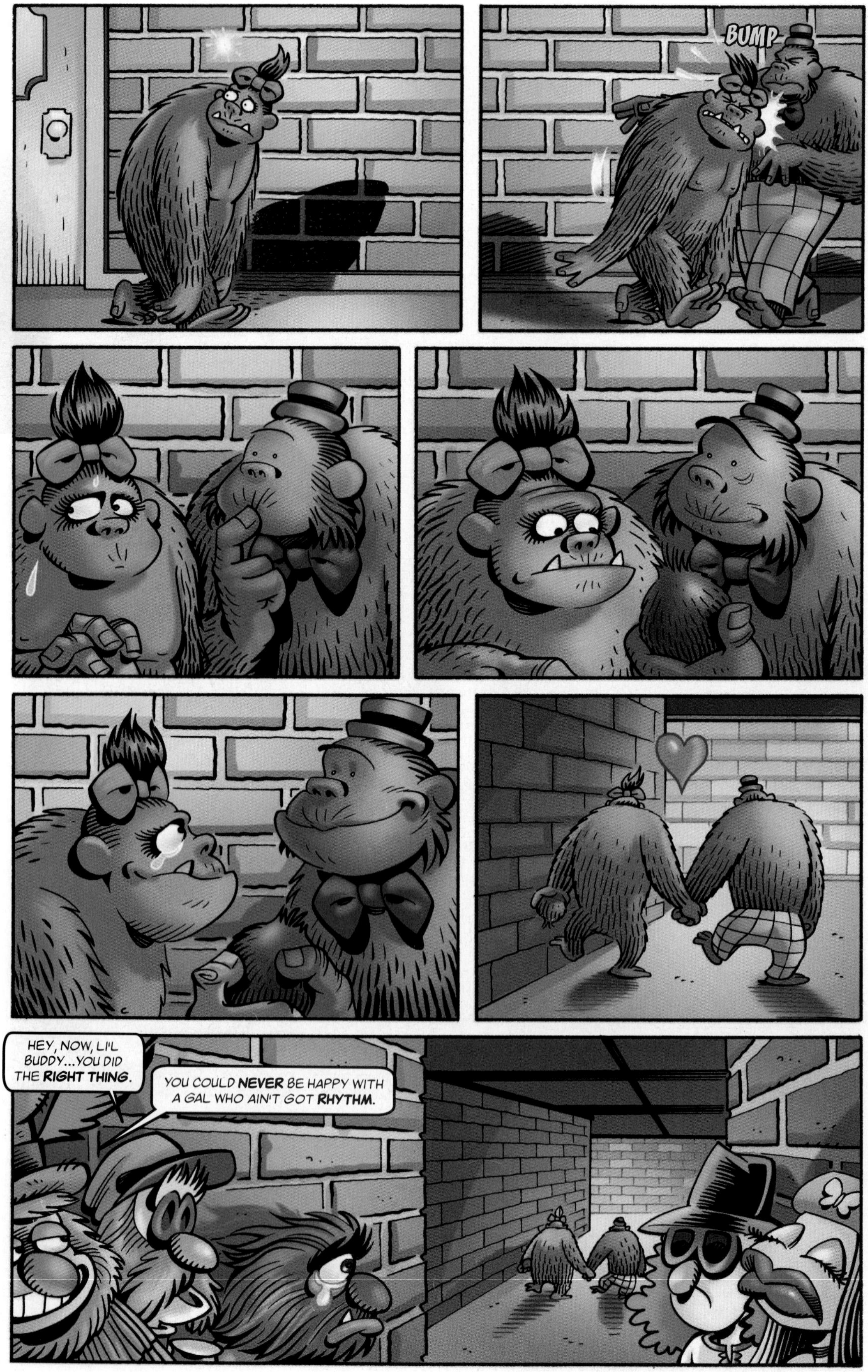
BUMP
HEY, NOW, LI'L BUDDY...YOU DID THE RIGHT THING.
YOU COULD NEVER BE HAPPY WITH A GAL WHO AIN'T GOT RHYTHM.

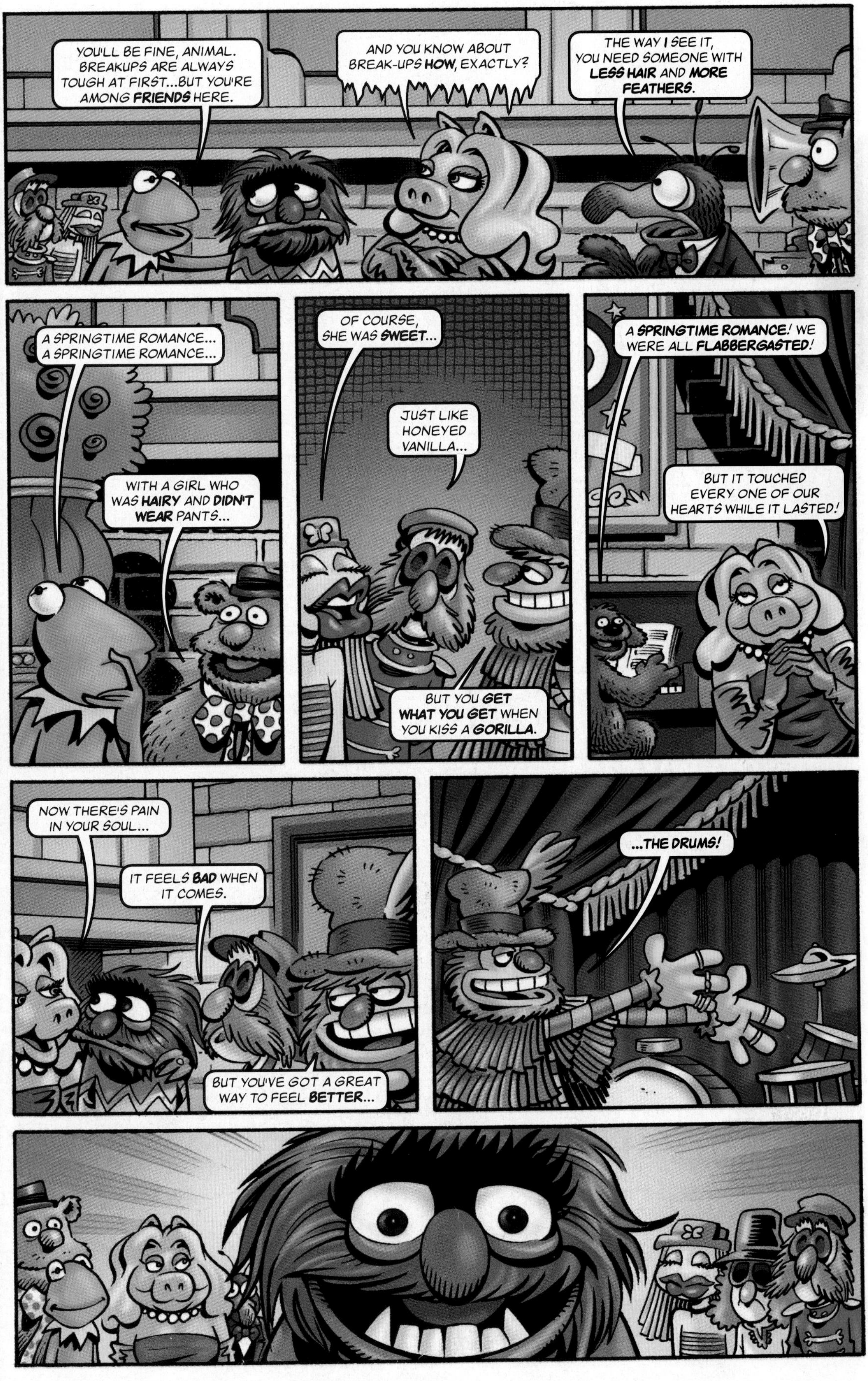

YOU'LL BE FINE, ANIMAL. BREAKUPS ARE ALWAYS TOUGH AT FIRST...BUT YOU'RE AMONG FRIENDS HERE.
AND YOU KNOW ABOUT BREAK-UPS HOW, EXACTLY?
THE WAY I SEE IT, YOU NEED SOMEONE WITH LESS HAIR AND MORE FEATHERS.
A SPRINGTIME ROMANCE... A SPRINGTIME ROMANCE...
WITH A GIRL WHO WAS HAIRY AND DIDN'T WEAR PANTS...
OF COURSE, SHE WAS SWEET...
JUST LIKE HONEYED VANILLA...
BUT YOU GET WHAT YOU GET WHEN YOU KISS A GORILLA.
A SPRINGTIME ROMANCE! WE WERE ALL FLABBERGASTED!
BUT IT TOUCHED EVERY ONE OF OUR HEARTS WHILE IT LASTED!
NOW THERE'S PAIN IN YOUR SOUL...
IT FEELS BAD WHEN IT COMES.
BUT YOU'VE GOT A GREAT WAY TO FEEL BETTER...
...THE DRUMS!

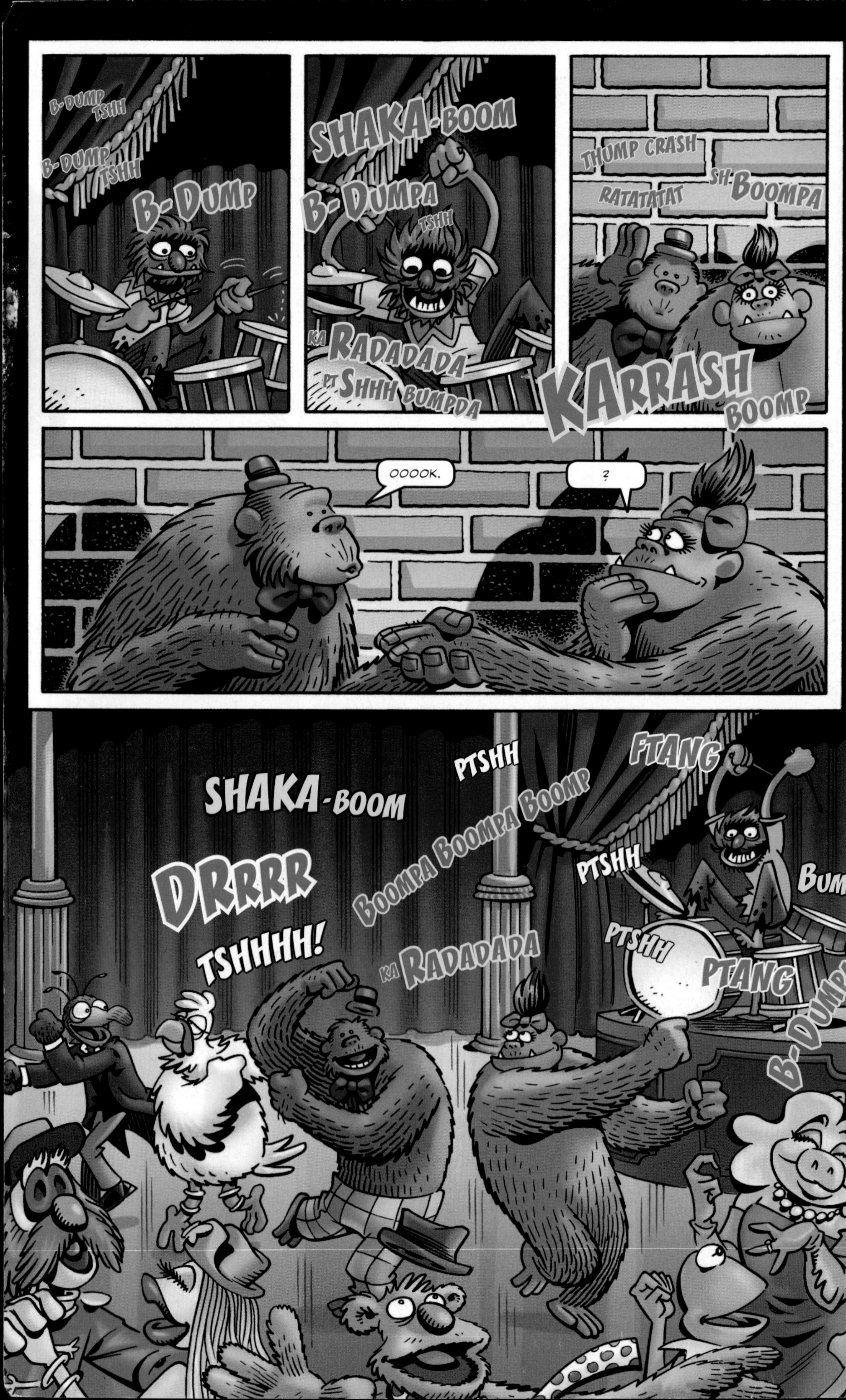
B-DUMP TSHH
B-DUMP TSHH
B-DUMP
SHAKA-BOOM
B-DUMPA
TSHH
KA RADADADA
PT SHHH BUMPDA
THUMP CRASH
RATATATAT
SH-BOOMPA
KARRASH
BOOMP
OOOOK.
?
SHAKA-BOOM
PTSHH
FTANG
BOOMPA BOOMPA BOOMP
DRRRR
PTSHH
TSHHHH!
KA RADADADA
PTSHH
PTANG

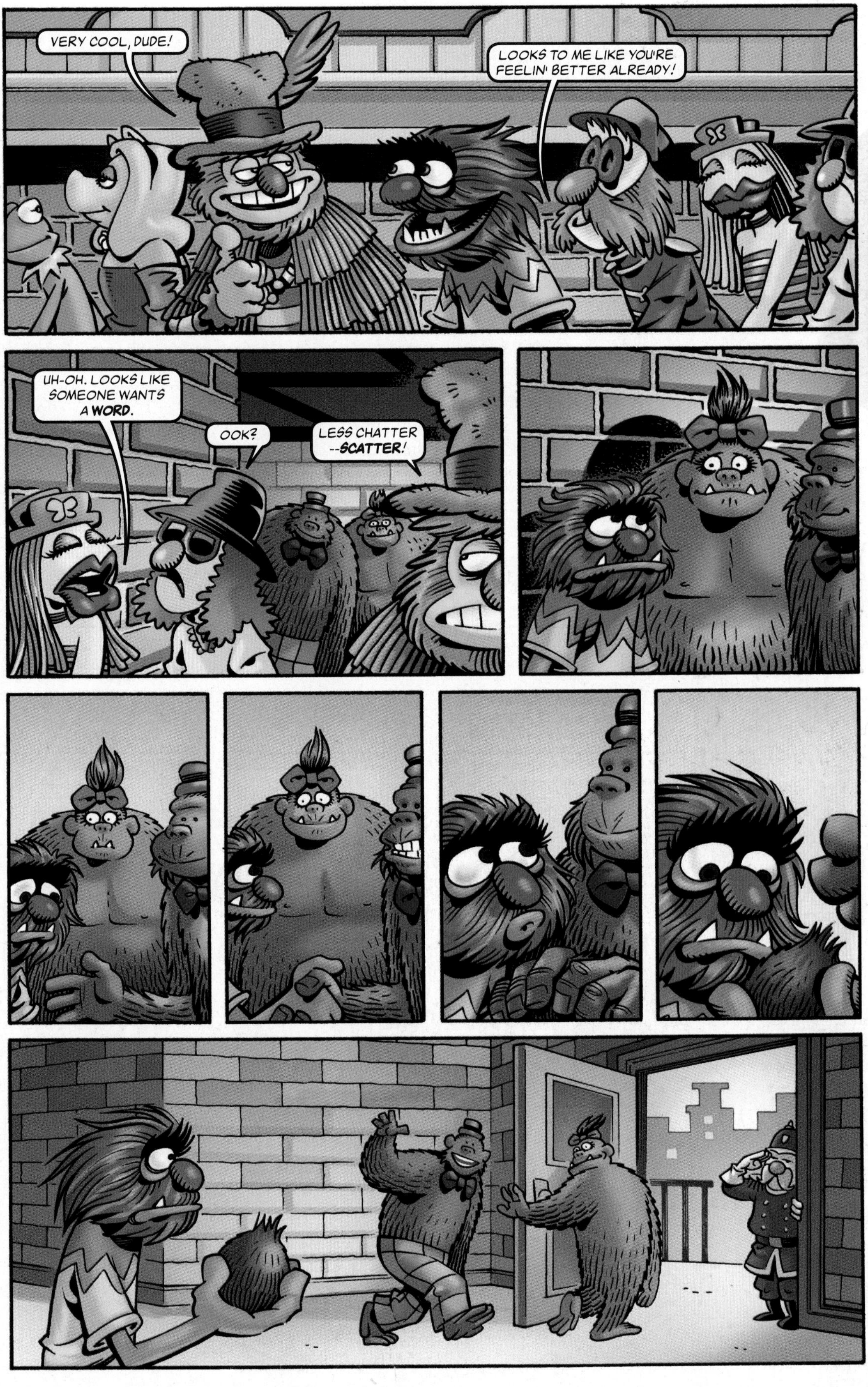
VERY COOL, DUDE!
LOOKS TO ME LIKE YOU'RE FEELIN' BETTER ALREADY!
UH-OH. LOOKS LIKE SOMEONE WANTS A **WORD**.
OOK?
LESS CHATTER --**SCATTER**!

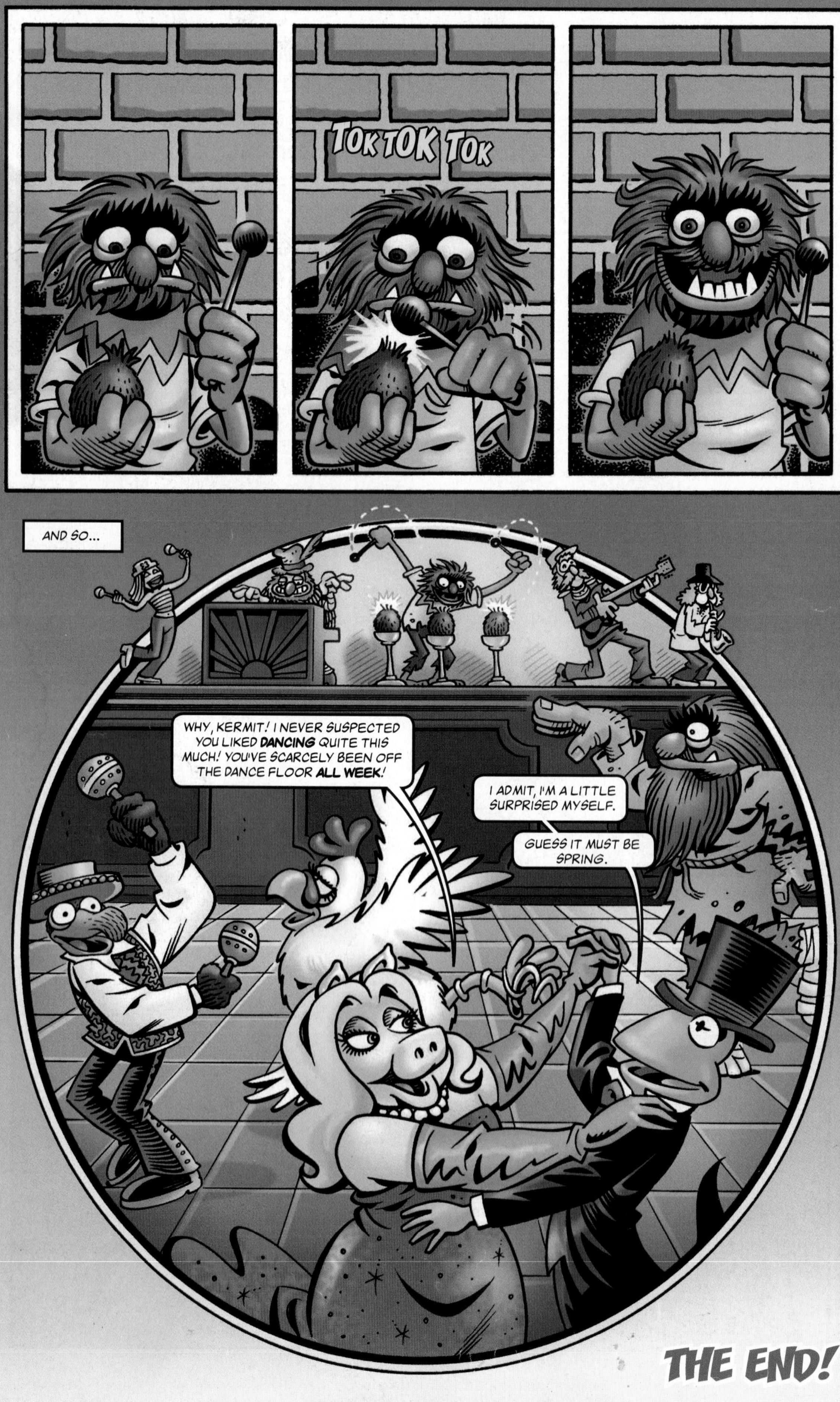
TOK TOK TOK
AND SO...
WHY, KERMIT! I NEVER SUSPECTED YOU LIKED DANCING QUITE THIS MUCH! YOU'VE SCARCELY BEEN OFF THE DANCE FLOOR ALL WEEK!
I ADMIT, I'M A LITTLE SURPRISED MYSELF.
GUESS IT MUST BE SPRING.
THE END!

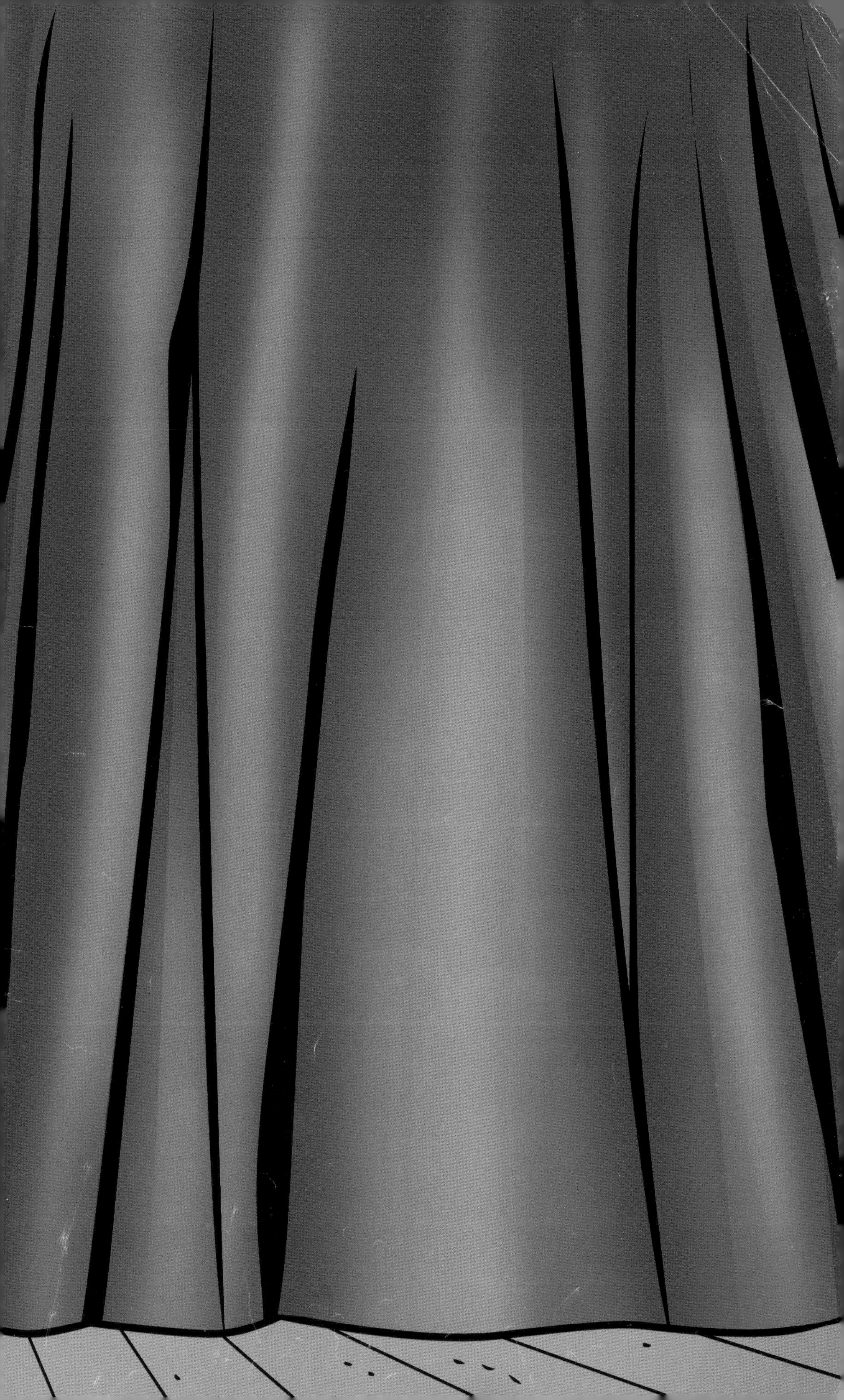

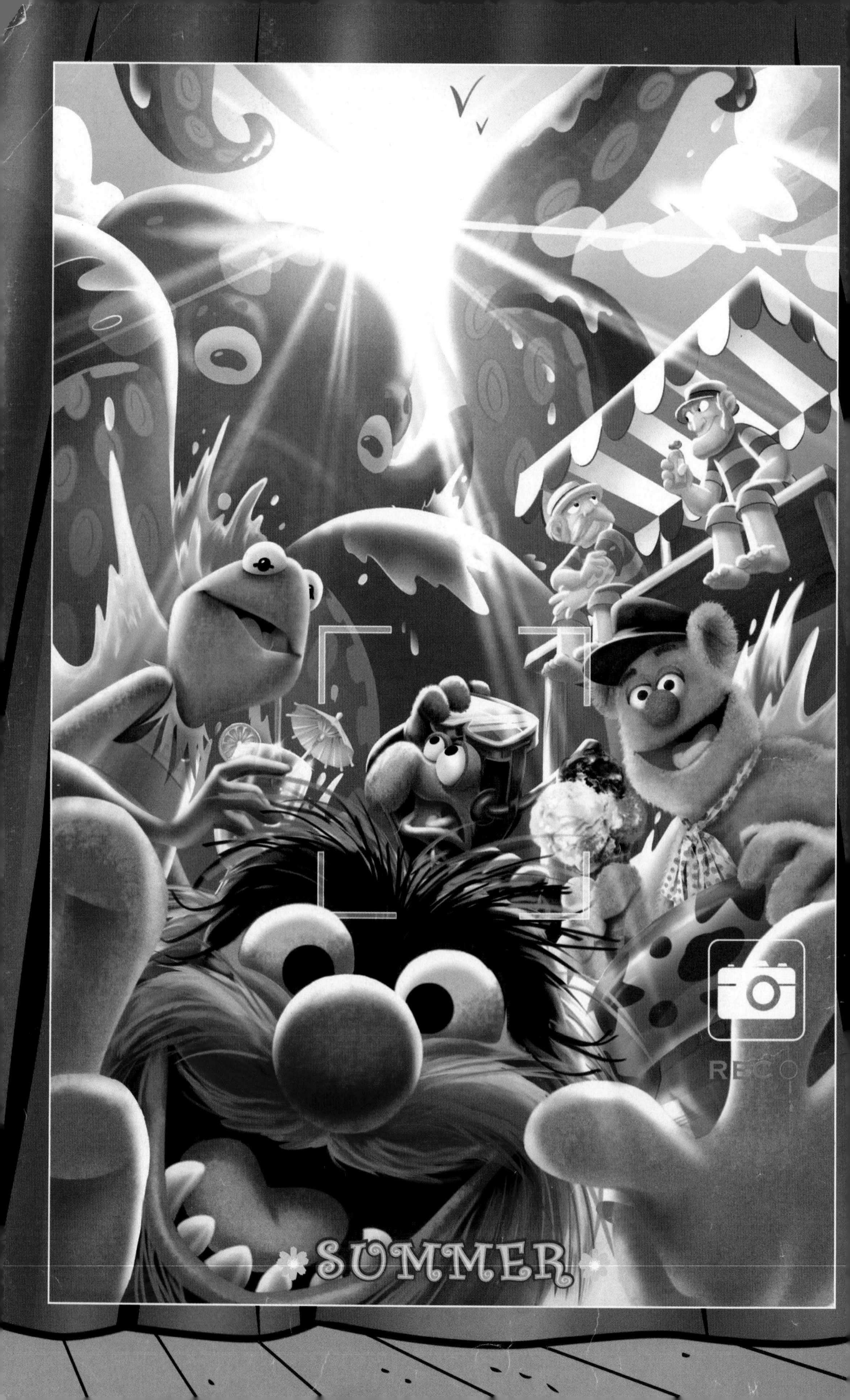
REC
SUMMER

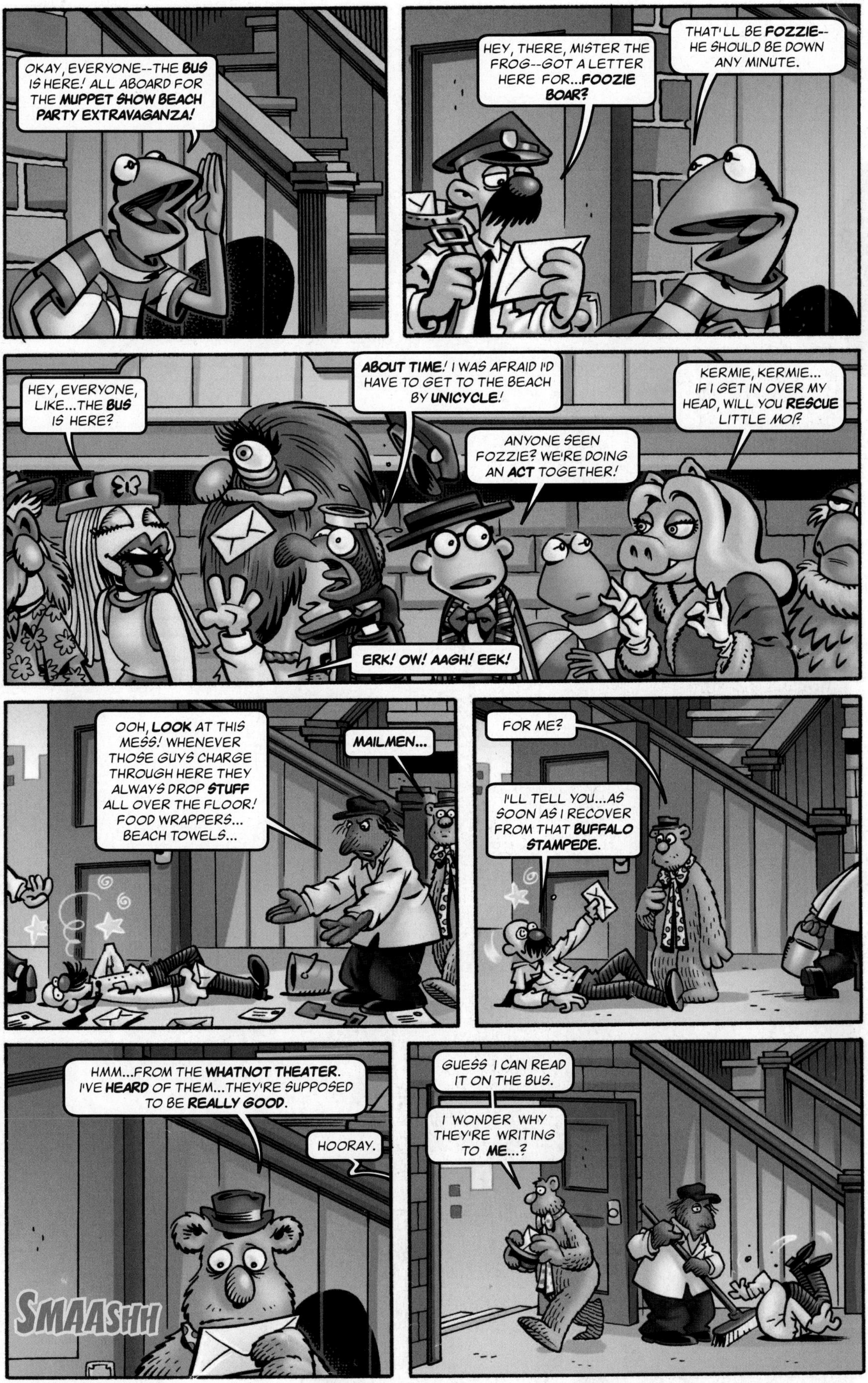

OKAY, EVERYONE--THE BUS IS HERE! ALL ABOARD FOR THE MUPPET SHOW BEACH PARTY EXTRAVAGANZA!
HEY, THERE, MISTER THE FROG--GOT A LETTER HERE FOR...FOOZIE BOAR?
THAT'LL BE FOZZIE--HE SHOULD BE DOWN ANY MINUTE.
HEY, EVERYONE, LIKE...THE BUS IS HERE?
ABOUT TIME! I WAS AFRAID I'D HAVE TO GET TO THE BEACH BY UNICYCLE!
ANYONE SEEN FOZZIE? WE'RE DOING AN ACT TOGETHER!
KERMIE, KERMIE... IF I GET IN OVER MY HEAD, WILL YOU RESCUE LITTLE MOI?
ERK! OW! AAGH! EEK!
OOH, LOOK AT THIS MESS! WHENEVER THOSE GUYS CHARGE THROUGH HERE THEY ALWAYS DROP STUFF ALL OVER THE FLOOR! FOOD WRAPPERS... BEACH TOWELS...
MAILMEN...
FOR ME?
I'LL TELL YOU...AS SOON AS I RECOVER FROM THAT BUFFALO STAMPEDE.
HMM...FROM THE WHATNOT THEATER. I'VE HEARD OF THEM...THEY'RE SUPPOSED TO BE REALLY GOOD.
HOORAY.
SMAASHH
GUESS I CAN READ IT ON THE BUS.
I WONDER WHY THEY'RE WRITING TO ME...?

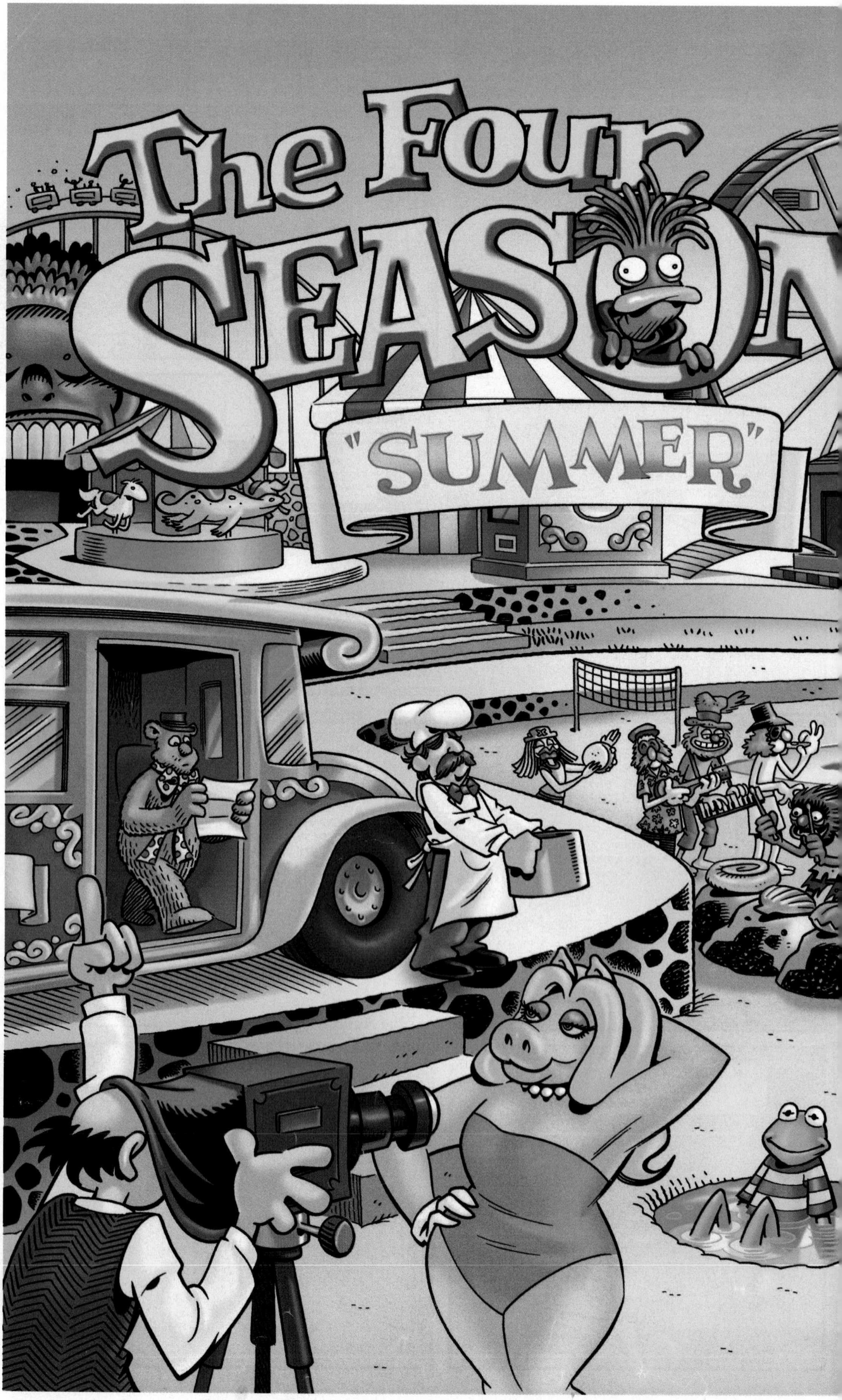
The Four
SEAS
"SUMMER"

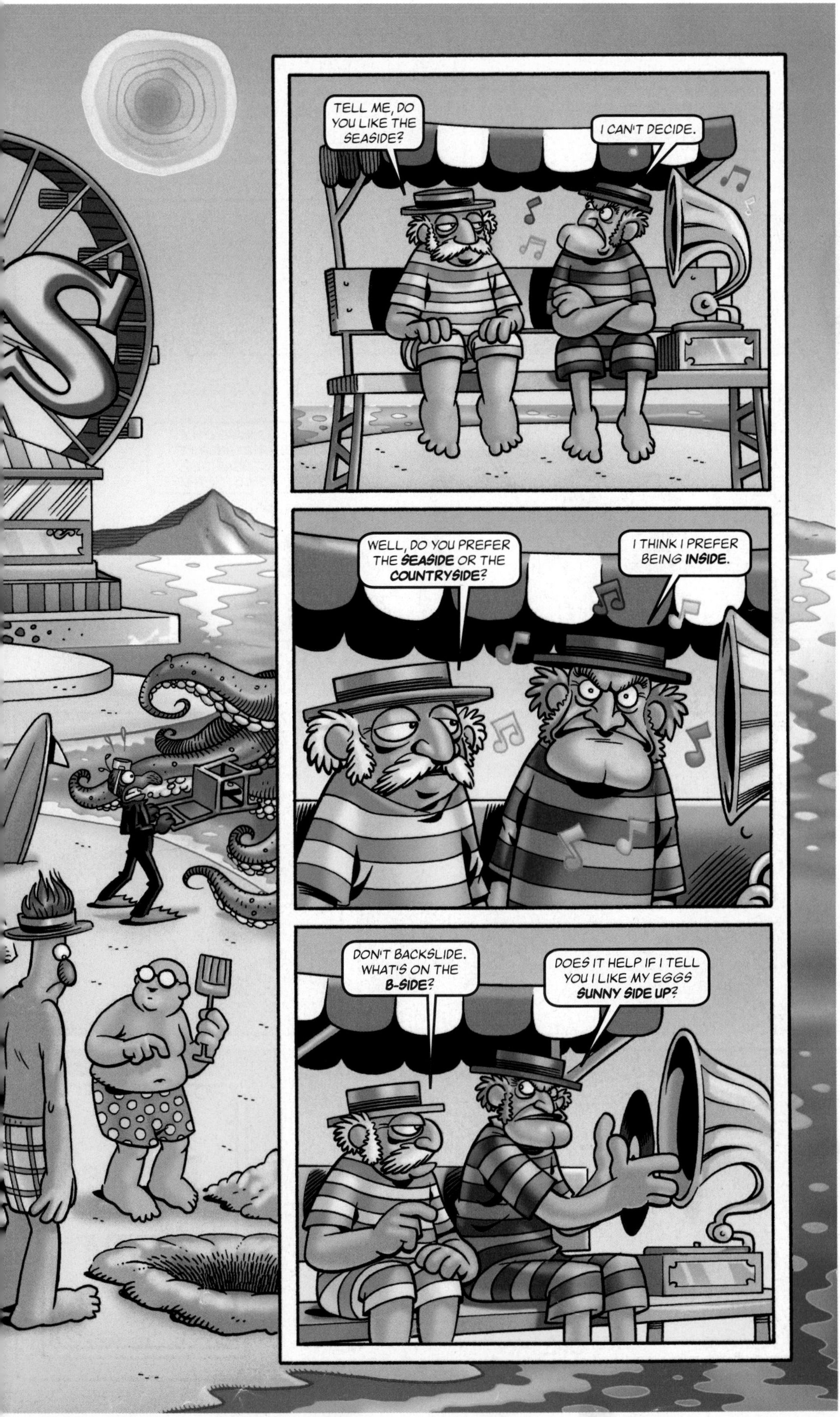

TELL ME, DO YOU LIKE THE SEASIDE?
I CAN'T DECIDE.
WELL, DO YOU PREFER THE **SEASIDE** OR THE **COUNTRYSIDE**?
I THINK I PREFER BEING **INSIDE**.
DON'T BACKSLIDE. WHAT'S ON THE **B-SIDE**?
DOES IT HELP IF I TELL YOU I LIKE MY EGGS **SUNNY SIDE UP**?

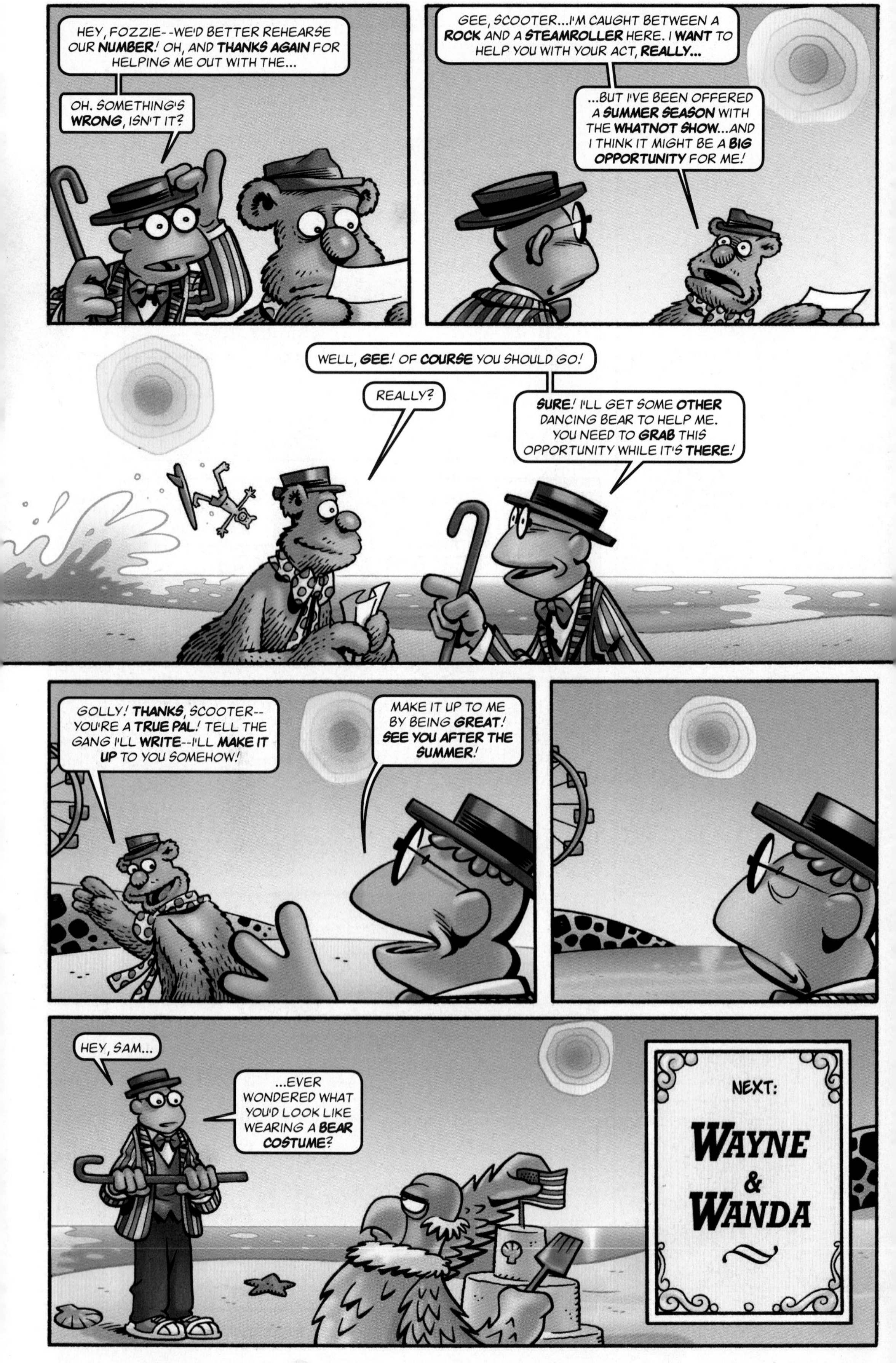

HEY, FOZZIE--WE'D BETTER REHEARSE OUR NUMBER! OH, AND THANKS AGAIN FOR HELPING ME OUT WITH THE...
OH. SOMETHING'S WRONG, ISN'T IT?
GEE, SCOOTER...I'M CAUGHT BETWEEN A ROCK AND A STEAMROLLER HERE. I WANT TO HELP YOU WITH YOUR ACT, REALLY...
...BUT I'VE BEEN OFFERED A SUMMER SEASON WITH THE WHATNOT SHOW...AND I THINK IT MIGHT BE A BIG OPPORTUNITY FOR ME!
WELL, GEE! OF COURSE YOU SHOULD GO!
REALLY?
SURE! I'LL GET SOME OTHER DANCING BEAR TO HELP ME. YOU NEED TO GRAB THIS OPPORTUNITY WHILE IT'S THERE!
GOLLY! THANKS, SCOOTER--YOU'RE A TRUE PAL! TELL THE GANG I'LL WRITE--I'LL MAKE IT UP TO YOU SOMEHOW!
MAKE IT UP TO ME BY BEING GREAT! SEE YOU AFTER THE SUMMER!
HEY, SAM...
...EVER WONDERED WHAT YOU'D LOOK LIKE WEARING A BEAR COSTUME?
NEXT:
WAYNE & WANDA

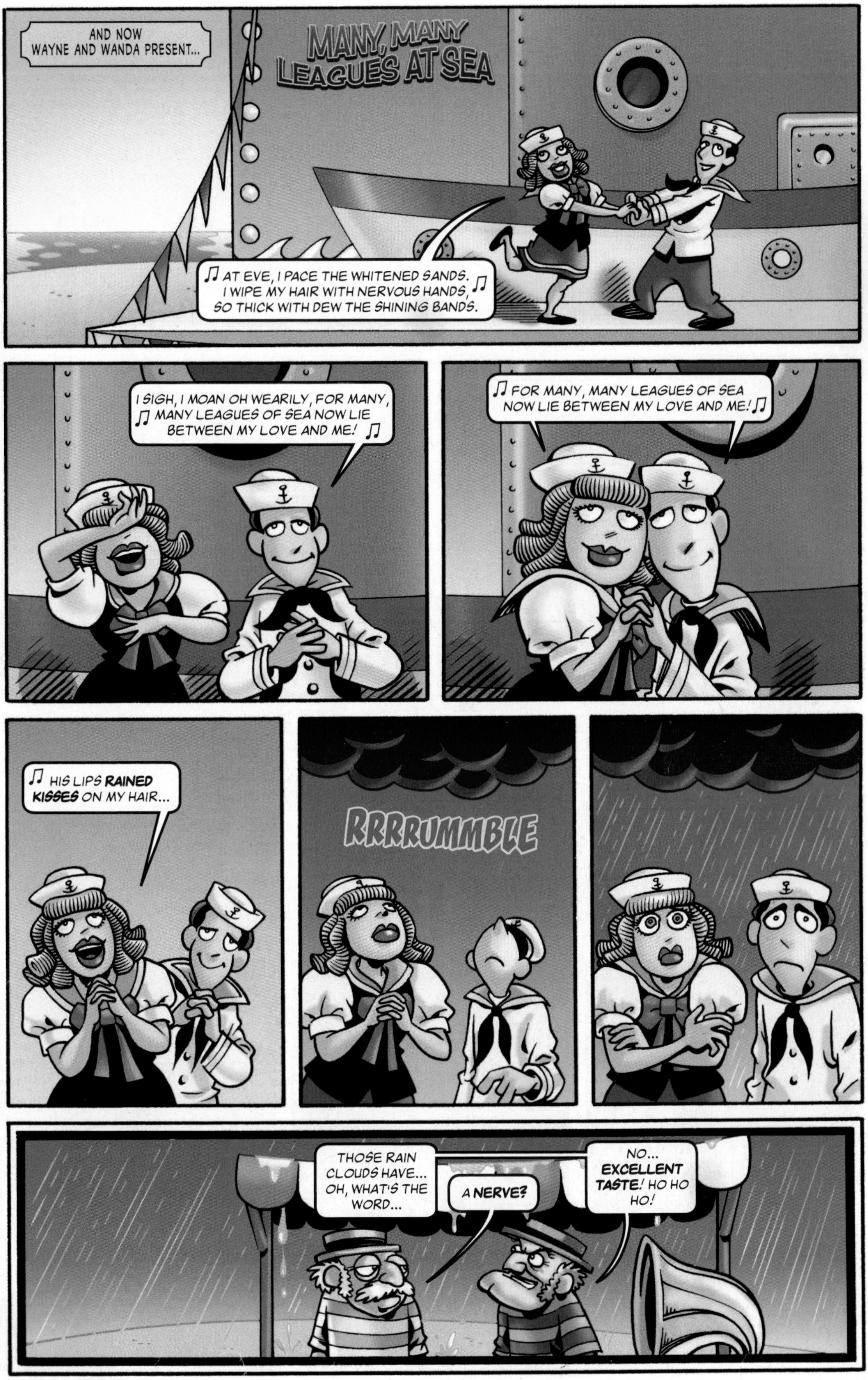
AND NOW WAYNE AND WANDA PRESENT...
MANY, MANY LEAGUES AT SEA
♫ AT EVE, I PACE THE WHITENED SANDS. I WIPE MY HAIR WITH NERVOUS HANDS, ♫ SO THICK WITH DEW THE SHINING BANDS.
I SIGH, I MOAN OH WEARILY, FOR MANY, ♫ MANY LEAGUES OF SEA NOW LIE BETWEEN MY LOVE AND ME! ♫
♫ FOR MANY, MANY LEAGUES OF SEA NOW LIE BETWEEN MY LOVE AND ME! ♫
♫ HIS LIPS **RAINED KISSES** ON MY HAIR...
RRRRUMMBLE
THOSE RAIN CLOUDS HAVE... OH, WHAT'S THE WORD...
A **NERVE**?
NO... **EXCELLENT TASTE**! HO HO HO!

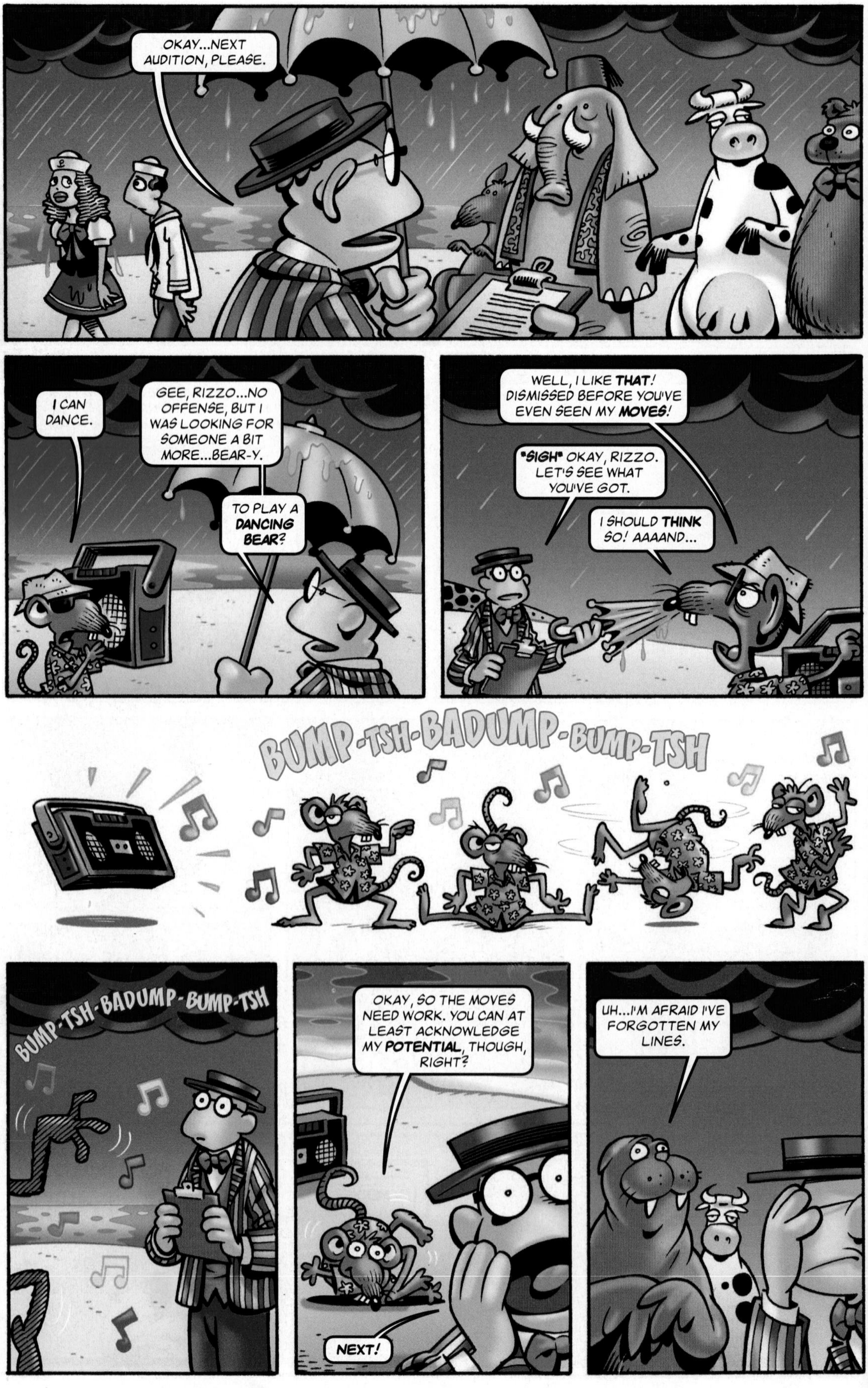
OKAY...NEXT AUDITION, PLEASE.
I CAN DANCE.
GEE, RIZZO...NO OFFENSE, BUT I WAS LOOKING FOR SOMEONE A BIT MORE...BEAR-Y.
TO PLAY A DANCING BEAR?
WELL, I LIKE THAT! DISMISSED BEFORE YOU'VE EVEN SEEN MY MOVES!
SIGH OKAY, RIZZO. LET'S SEE WHAT YOU'VE GOT.
I SHOULD THINK SO! AAAAND...
BUMP-TSH-BADUMP-BUMP-TSH
BUMP-TSH-BADUMP-BUMP-TSH
OKAY, SO THE MOVES NEED WORK. YOU CAN AT LEAST ACKNOWLEDGE MY POTENTIAL, THOUGH, RIGHT?
NEXT!
UH...I'M AFRAID I'VE FORGOTTEN MY LINES.

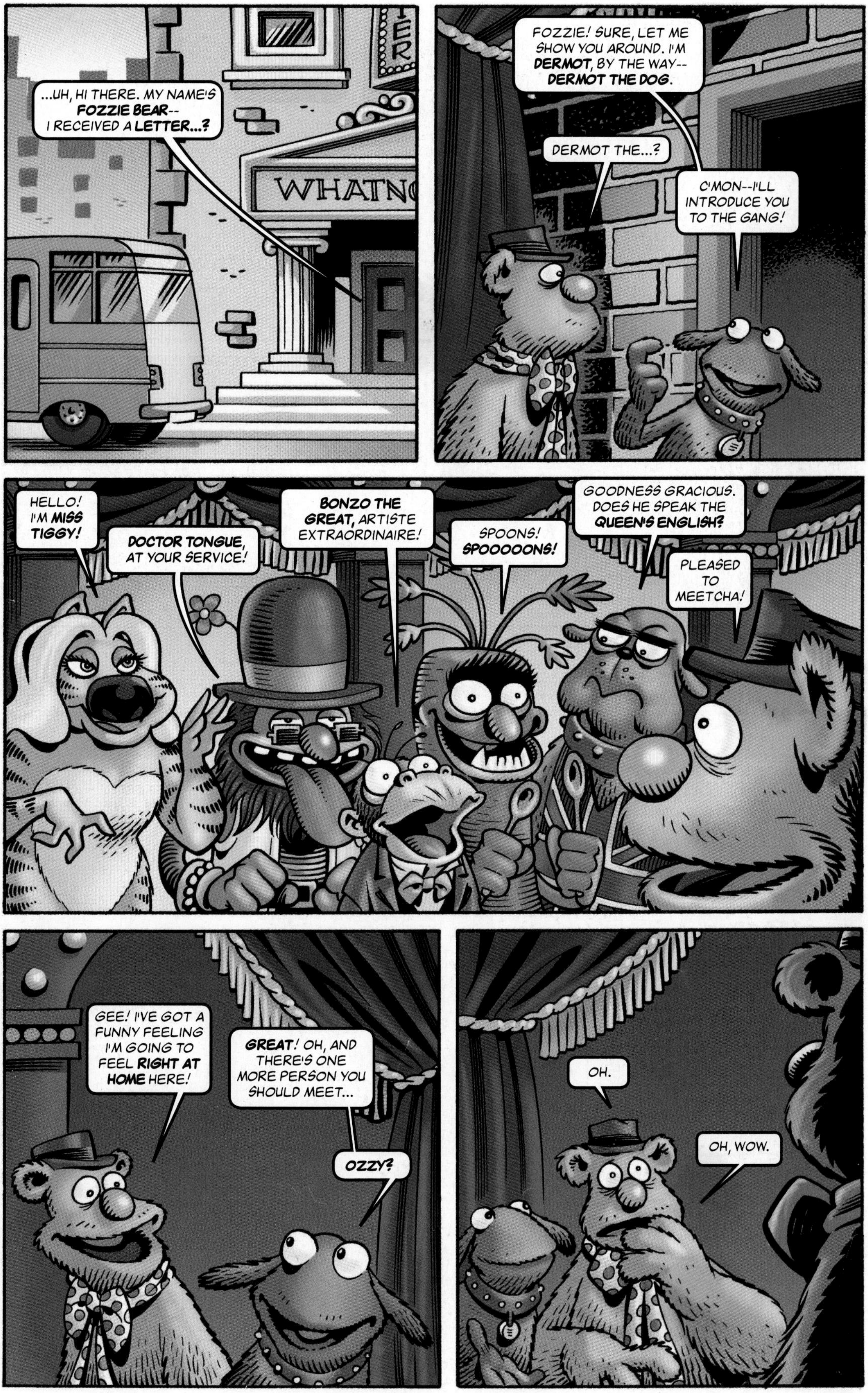
...UH, HI THERE. MY NAME'S FOZZIE BEAR-- I RECEIVED A LETTER...?
WHATN
FOZZIE! SURE, LET ME SHOW YOU AROUND. I'M DERMOT, BY THE WAY-- DERMOT THE DOG.
DERMOT THE...?
C'MON--I'LL INTRODUCE YOU TO THE GANG!
HELLO! I'M MISS TIGGY!
DOCTOR TONGUE, AT YOUR SERVICE!
BONZO THE GREAT, ARTISTE EXTRAORDINAIRE!
SPOONS! SPOOOOONS!
GOODNESS GRACIOUS. DOES HE SPEAK THE QUEEN'S ENGLISH?
PLEASED TO MEETCHA!
GEE! I'VE GOT A FUNNY FEELING I'M GOING TO FEEL RIGHT AT HOME HERE!
GREAT! OH, AND THERE'S ONE MORE PERSON YOU SHOULD MEET...
OZZY?
OH.
OH, WOW.

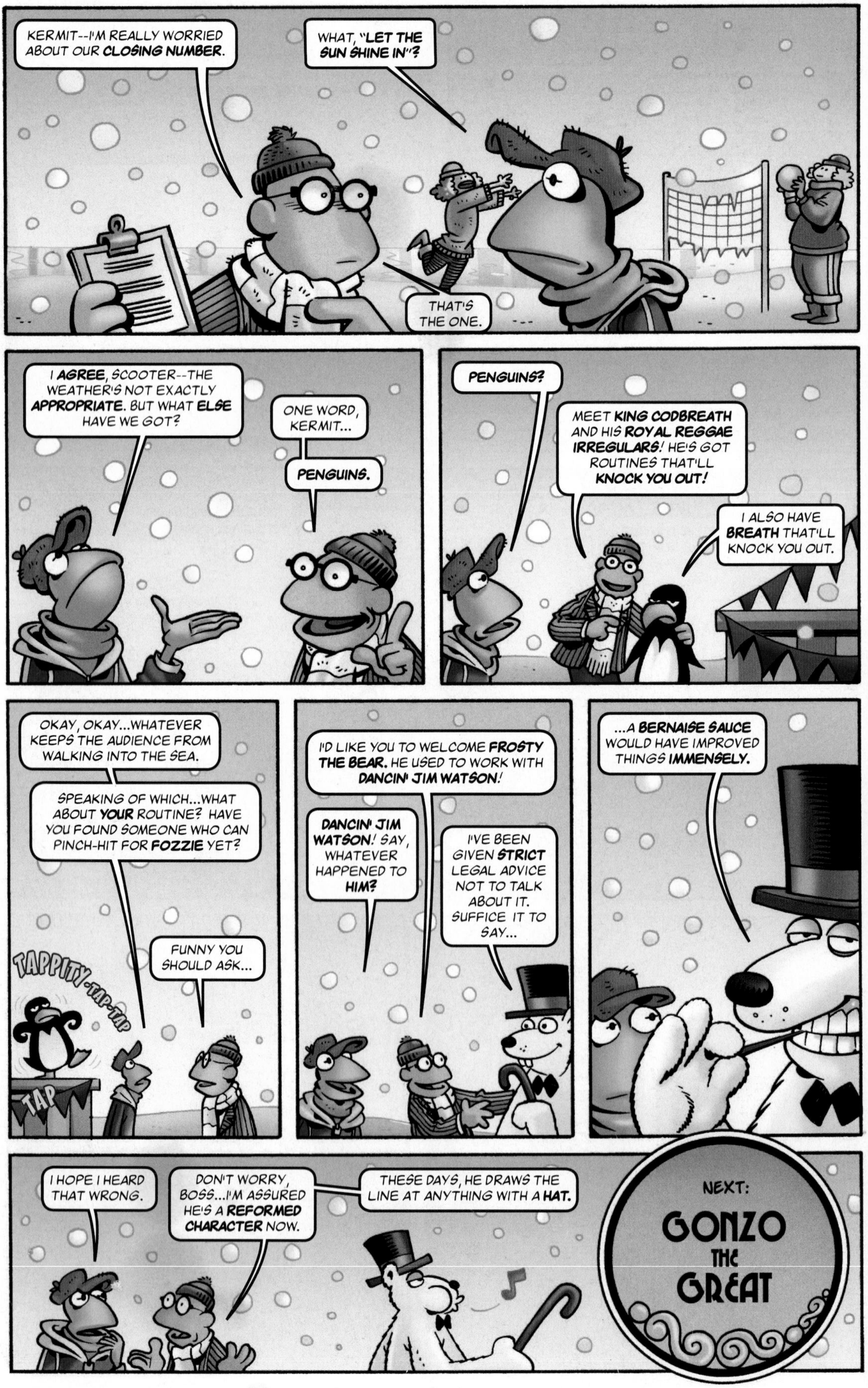
KERMIT--I'M REALLY WORRIED ABOUT OUR CLOSING NUMBER.
WHAT, "LET THE SUN SHINE IN"?
THAT'S THE ONE.
I AGREE, SCOOTER--THE WEATHER'S NOT EXACTLY APPROPRIATE. BUT WHAT ELSE HAVE WE GOT?
ONE WORD, KERMIT...
PENGUINS.
PENGUINS?
MEET KING CODBREATH AND HIS ROYAL REGGAE IRREGULARS! HE'S GOT ROUTINES THAT'LL KNOCK YOU OUT!
I ALSO HAVE BREATH THAT'LL KNOCK YOU OUT.
OKAY, OKAY...WHATEVER KEEPS THE AUDIENCE FROM WALKING INTO THE SEA.
SPEAKING OF WHICH...WHAT ABOUT YOUR ROUTINE? HAVE YOU FOUND SOMEONE WHO CAN PINCH-HIT FOR FOZZIE YET?
FUNNY YOU SHOULD ASK...
TAPPITY-TAP-TAP
TAP
I'D LIKE YOU TO WELCOME FROSTY THE BEAR. HE USED TO WORK WITH DANCIN' JIM WATSON!
DANCIN' JIM WATSON! SAY, WHATEVER HAPPENED TO HIM?
I'VE BEEN GIVEN STRICT LEGAL ADVICE NOT TO TALK ABOUT IT. SUFFICE IT TO SAY...
...A BERNAISE SAUCE WOULD HAVE IMPROVED THINGS IMMENSELY.
I HOPE I HEARD THAT WRONG.
DON'T WORRY, BOSS...I'M ASSURED HE'S A REFORMED CHARACTER NOW.
THESE DAYS, HE DRAWS THE LINE AT ANYTHING WITH A HAT.
NEXT:
GONZO THE GREAT

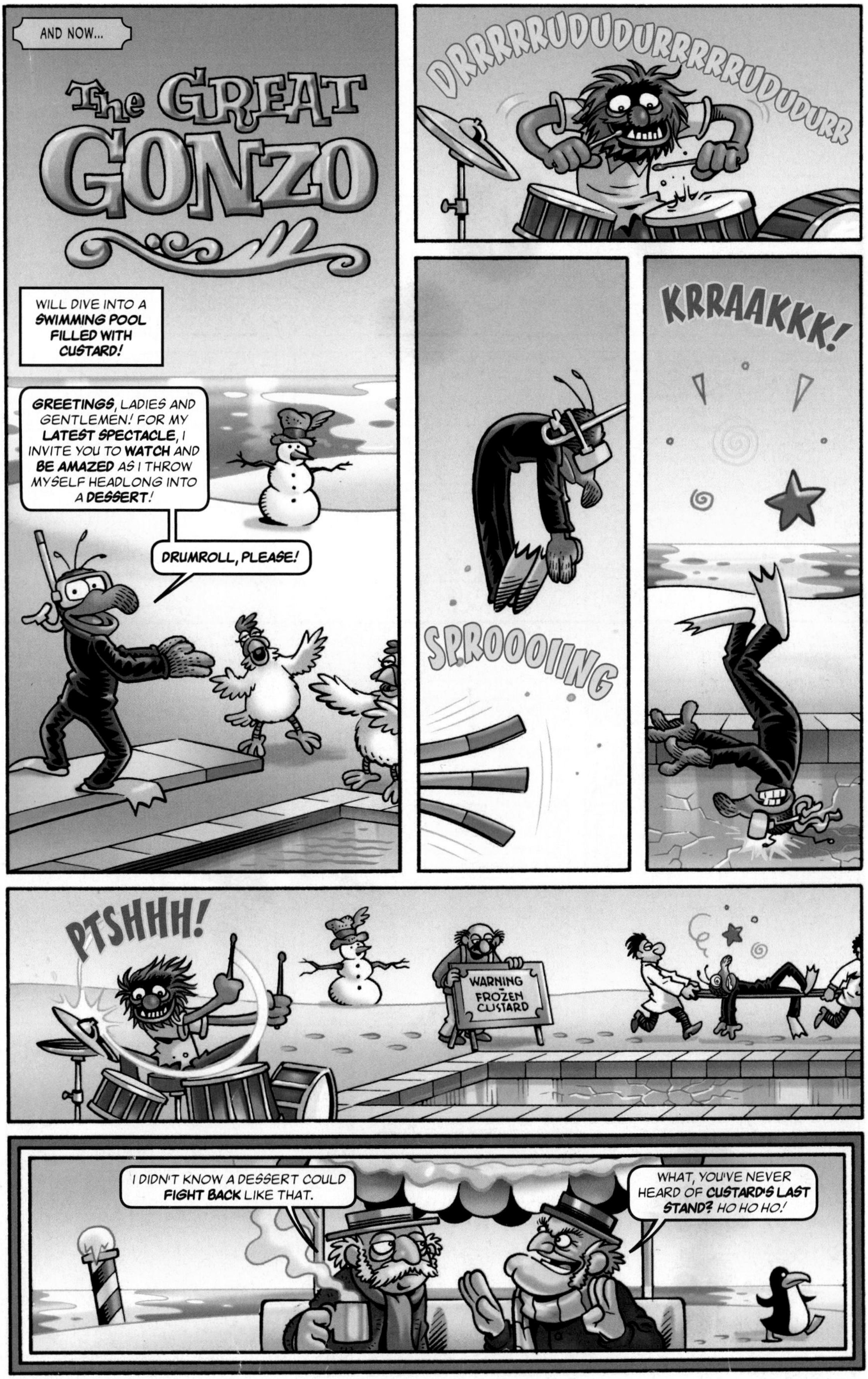
AND NOW...
The GREAT GONZO
WILL DIVE INTO A SWIMMING POOL FILLED WITH CUSTARD!
GREETINGS, LADIES AND GENTLEMEN! FOR MY LATEST SPECTACLE, I INVITE YOU TO WATCH AND BE AMAZED AS I THROW MYSELF HEADLONG INTO A DESSERT!
DRUMROLL, PLEASE!
DRRRRRUDUDURRRRRRRUDUDURR
SPROOOIING
KRRAAKKK!
PTSHHH!
WARNING FROZEN CUSTARD
I DIDN'T KNOW A DESSERT COULD FIGHT BACK LIKE THAT.
WHAT, YOU'VE NEVER HEARD OF CUSTARD'S LAST STAND? HO HO HO!

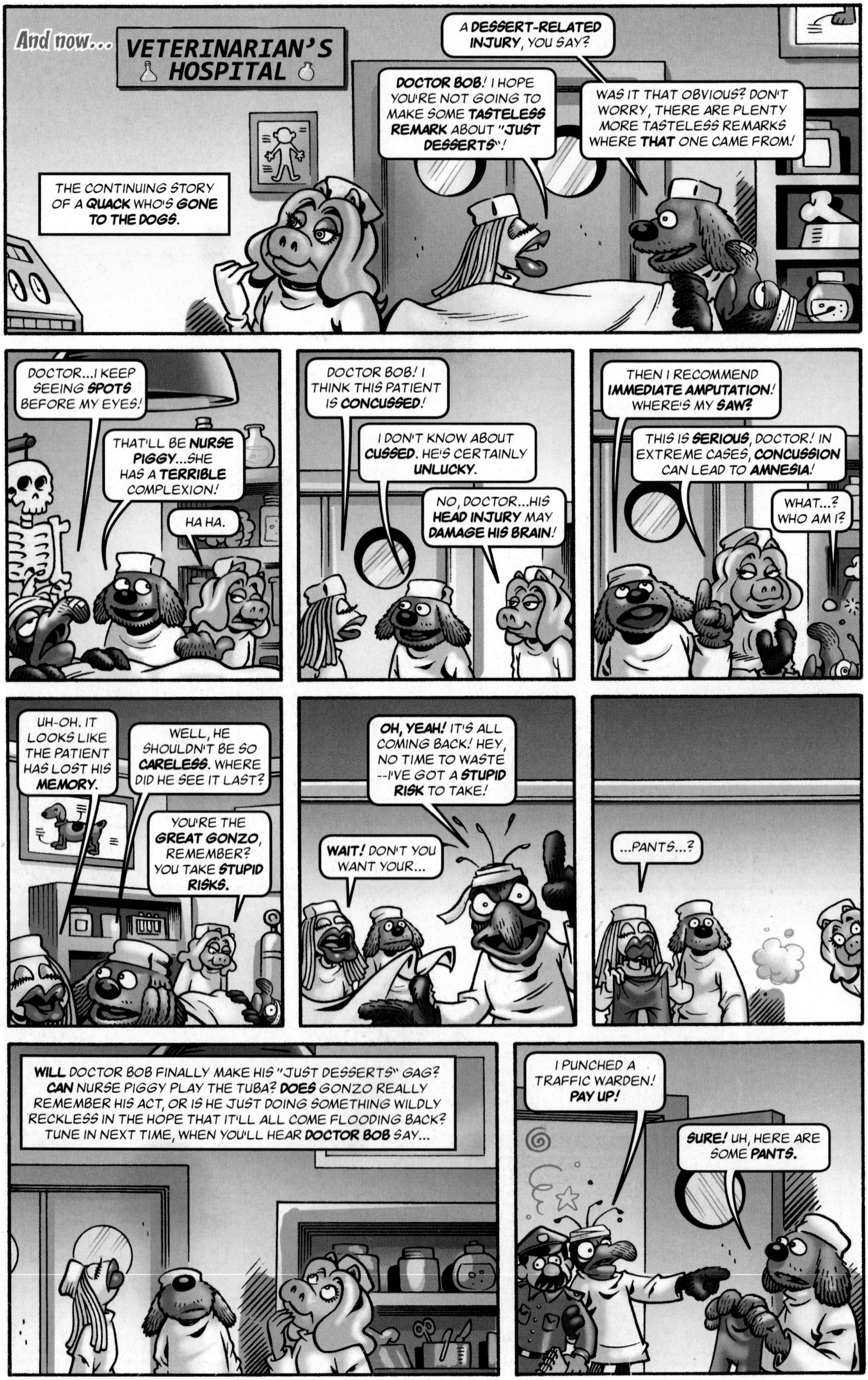
And now...
VETERINARIAN'S HOSPITAL
THE CONTINUING STORY OF A QUACK WHO'S GONE TO THE DOGS.
DOCTOR BOB! I HOPE YOU'RE NOT GOING TO MAKE SOME TASTELESS REMARK ABOUT "JUST DESSERTS"!
A DESSERT-RELATED INJURY, YOU SAY?
WAS IT THAT OBVIOUS? DON'T WORRY, THERE ARE PLENTY MORE TASTELESS REMARKS WHERE THAT ONE CAME FROM!
DOCTOR...I KEEP SEEING SPOTS BEFORE MY EYES!
THAT'LL BE NURSE PIGGY...SHE HAS A TERRIBLE COMPLEXION!
HA HA.
DOCTOR BOB! I THINK THIS PATIENT IS CONCUSSED!
I DON'T KNOW ABOUT CUSSED. HE'S CERTAINLY UNLUCKY.
NO, DOCTOR...HIS HEAD INJURY MAY DAMAGE HIS BRAIN!
THEN I RECOMMEND IMMEDIATE AMPUTATION! WHERE'S MY SAW?
THIS IS SERIOUS, DOCTOR! IN EXTREME CASES, CONCUSSION CAN LEAD TO AMNESIA!
WHAT...? WHO AM I?
UH-OH. IT LOOKS LIKE THE PATIENT HAS LOST HIS MEMORY.
WELL, HE SHOULDN'T BE SO CARELESS. WHERE DID HE SEE IT LAST?
YOU'RE THE GREAT GONZO, REMEMBER? YOU TAKE STUPID RISKS.
OH, YEAH! IT'S ALL COMING BACK! HEY, NO TIME TO WASTE --I'VE GOT A STUPID RISK TO TAKE!
WAIT! DON'T YOU WANT YOUR...
...PANTS...?
WILL DOCTOR BOB FINALLY MAKE HIS "JUST DESSERTS" GAG? CAN NURSE PIGGY PLAY THE TUBA? DOES GONZO REALLY REMEMBER HIS ACT, OR IS HE JUST DOING SOMETHING WILDLY RECKLESS IN THE HOPE THAT IT'LL ALL COME FLOODING BACK? TUNE IN NEXT TIME, WHEN YOU'LL HEAR DOCTOR BOB SAY...
I PUNCHED A TRAFFIC WARDEN! PAY UP!
SURE! UH, HERE ARE SOME PANTS.

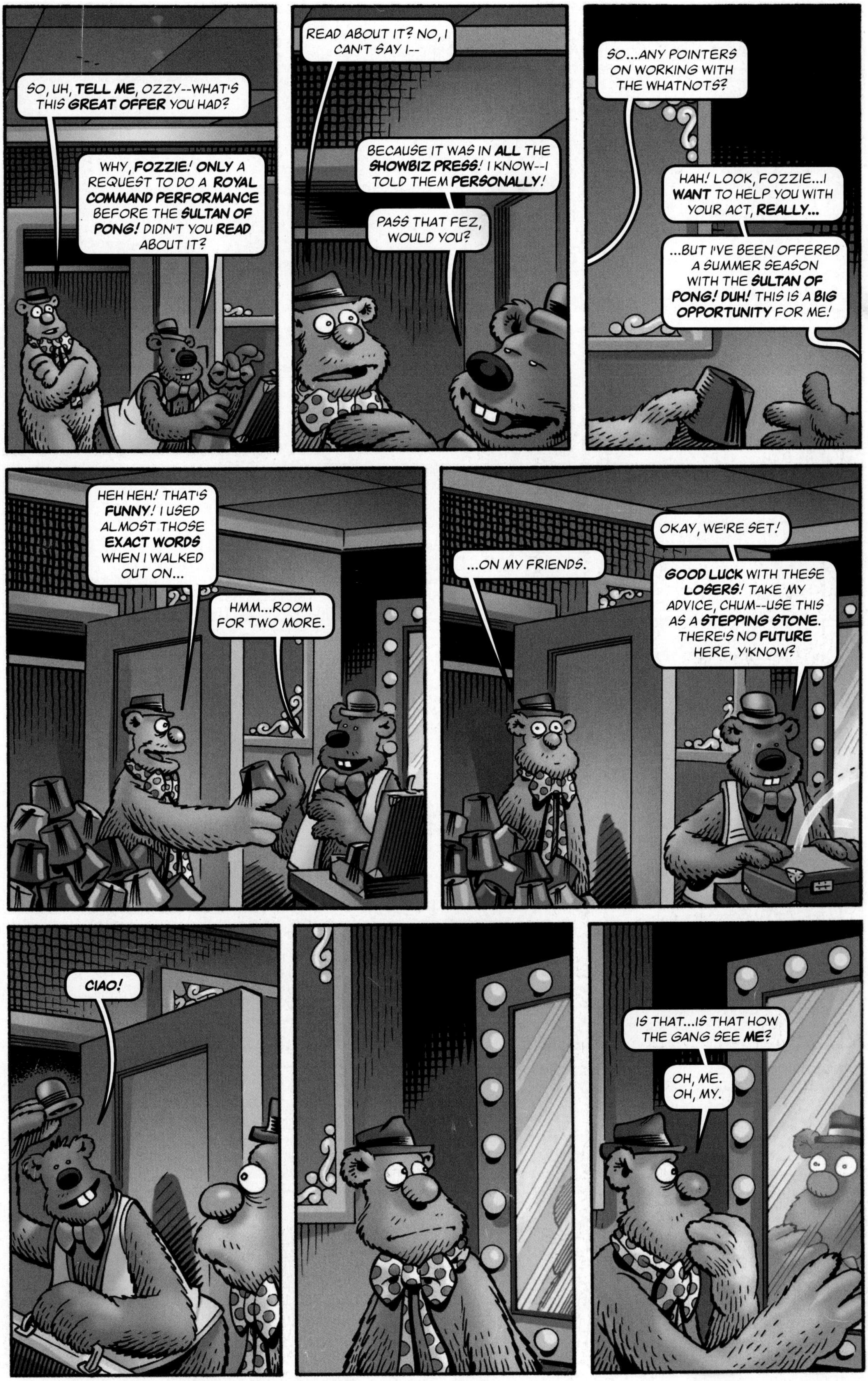
SO, UH, TELL ME, OZZY--WHAT'S THIS GREAT OFFER YOU HAD?
WHY, FOZZIE! ONLY A REQUEST TO DO A ROYAL COMMAND PERFORMANCE BEFORE THE SULTAN OF PONG! DIDN'T YOU READ ABOUT IT?
READ ABOUT IT? NO, I CAN'T SAY I--
BECAUSE IT WAS IN ALL THE SHOWBIZ PRESS! I KNOW--I TOLD THEM PERSONALLY!
PASS THAT FEZ, WOULD YOU?
SO...ANY POINTERS ON WORKING WITH THE WHATNOTS?
HAH! LOOK, FOZZIE...I WANT TO HELP YOU WITH YOUR ACT, REALLY...
...BUT I'VE BEEN OFFERED A SUMMER SEASON WITH THE SULTAN OF PONG! DUH! THIS IS A BIG OPPORTUNITY FOR ME!
HEH HEH! THAT'S FUNNY! I USED ALMOST THOSE EXACT WORDS WHEN I WALKED OUT ON...
HMM...ROOM FOR TWO MORE.
...ON MY FRIENDS.
OKAY, WE'RE SET!
GOOD LUCK WITH THESE LOSERS! TAKE MY ADVICE, CHUM--USE THIS AS A STEPPING STONE. THERE'S NO FUTURE HERE, Y'KNOW?
CIAO!
IS THAT...IS THAT HOW THE GANG SEE ME?
OH, ME. OH, MY.

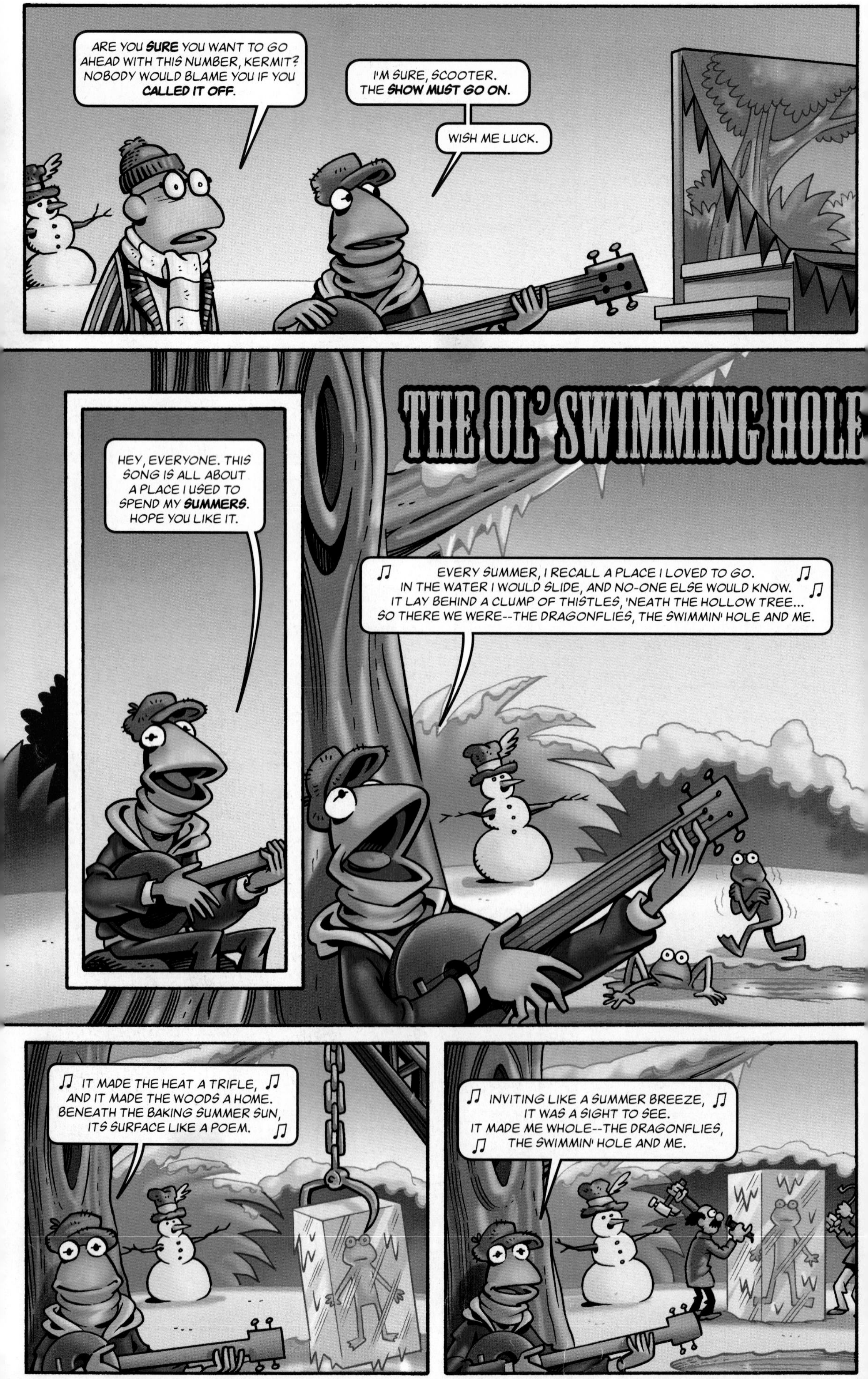
ARE YOU SURE YOU WANT TO GO AHEAD WITH THIS NUMBER, KERMIT? NOBODY WOULD BLAME YOU IF YOU CALLED IT OFF.
I'M SURE, SCOOTER. THE SHOW MUST GO ON.
WISH ME LUCK.
THE OL' SWIMMING HOLE
HEY, EVERYONE. THIS SONG IS ALL ABOUT A PLACE I USED TO SPEND MY SUMMERS. HOPE YOU LIKE IT.
♫ EVERY SUMMER, I RECALL A PLACE I LOVED TO GO. ♫ IN THE WATER I WOULD SLIDE, AND NO-ONE ELSE WOULD KNOW. ♫ IT LAY BEHIND A CLUMP OF THISTLES, 'NEATH THE HOLLOW TREE... SO THERE WE WERE--THE DRAGONFLIES, THE SWIMMIN' HOLE AND ME.
♫ IT MADE THE HEAT A TRIFLE, ♫ AND IT MADE THE WOODS A HOME. BENEATH THE BAKING SUMMER SUN, ITS SURFACE LIKE A POEM. ♫
♫ INVITING LIKE A SUMMER BREEZE, ♫ IT WAS A SIGHT TO SEE. IT MADE ME WHOLE--THE DRAGONFLIES, ♫ THE SWIMMIN' HOLE AND ME.

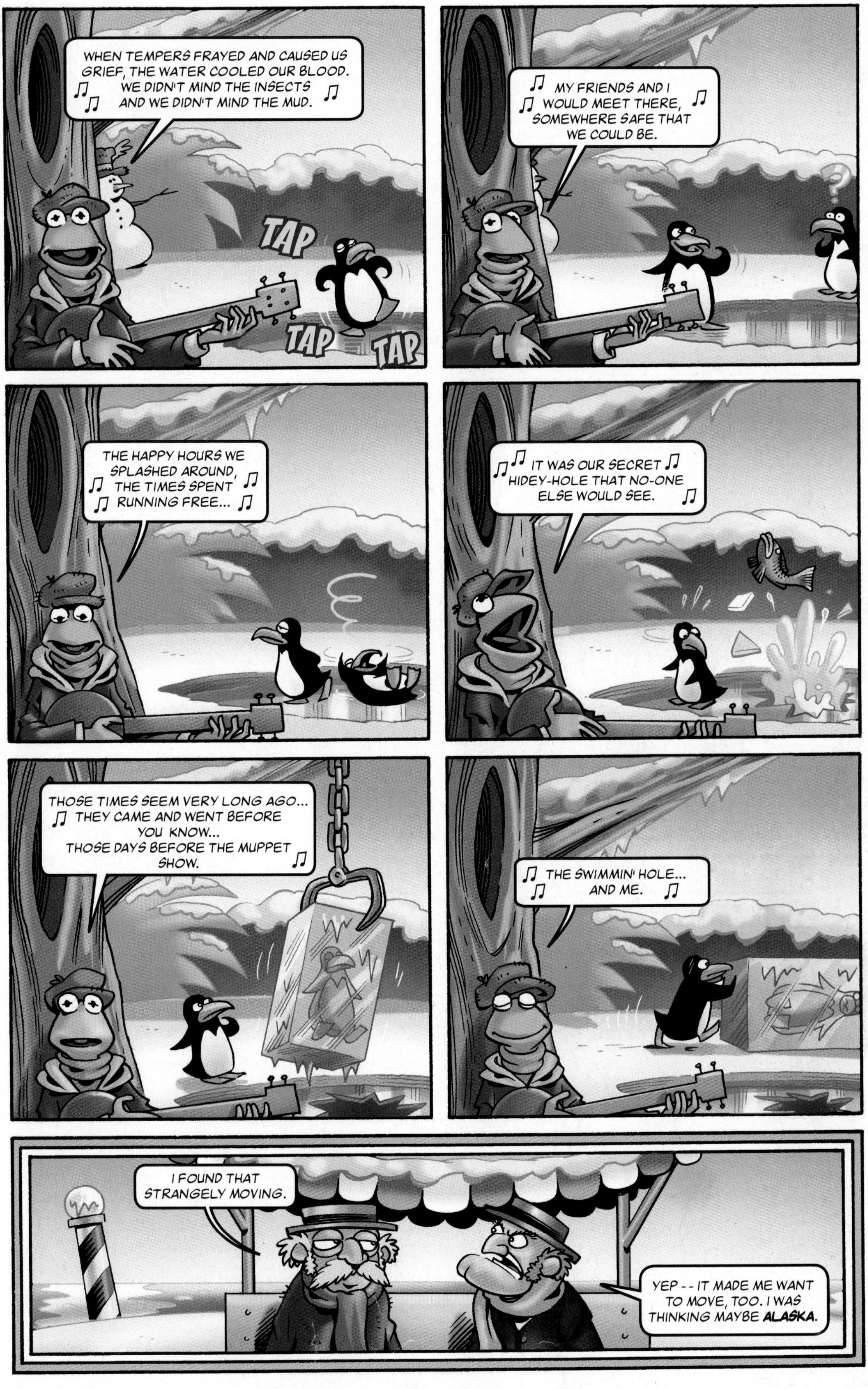
WHEN TEMPERS FRAYED AND CAUSED US GRIEF, THE WATER COOLED OUR BLOOD. ♫ ♫ WE DIDN'T MIND THE INSECTS AND WE DIDN'T MIND THE MUD. ♫
TAP TAP TAP
♫ MY FRIENDS AND I ♫ WOULD MEET THERE, ♫ SOMEWHERE SAFE THAT WE COULD BE.
THE HAPPY HOURS WE SPLASHED AROUND, ♫ THE TIMES SPENT ♫ ♫ RUNNING FREE... ♫
♫♫ IT WAS OUR SECRET ♫ HIDEY-HOLE THAT NO-ONE ELSE WOULD SEE. ♫
THOSE TIMES SEEM VERY LONG AGO... ♫ THEY CAME AND WENT BEFORE YOU KNOW... THOSE DAYS BEFORE THE MUPPET SHOW. ♫
♫ THE SWIMMIN' HOLE... ♫ AND ME. ♫
I FOUND THAT STRANGELY MOVING.
YEP -- IT MADE ME WANT TO MOVE, TOO. I WAS THINKING MAYBE **ALASKA**.

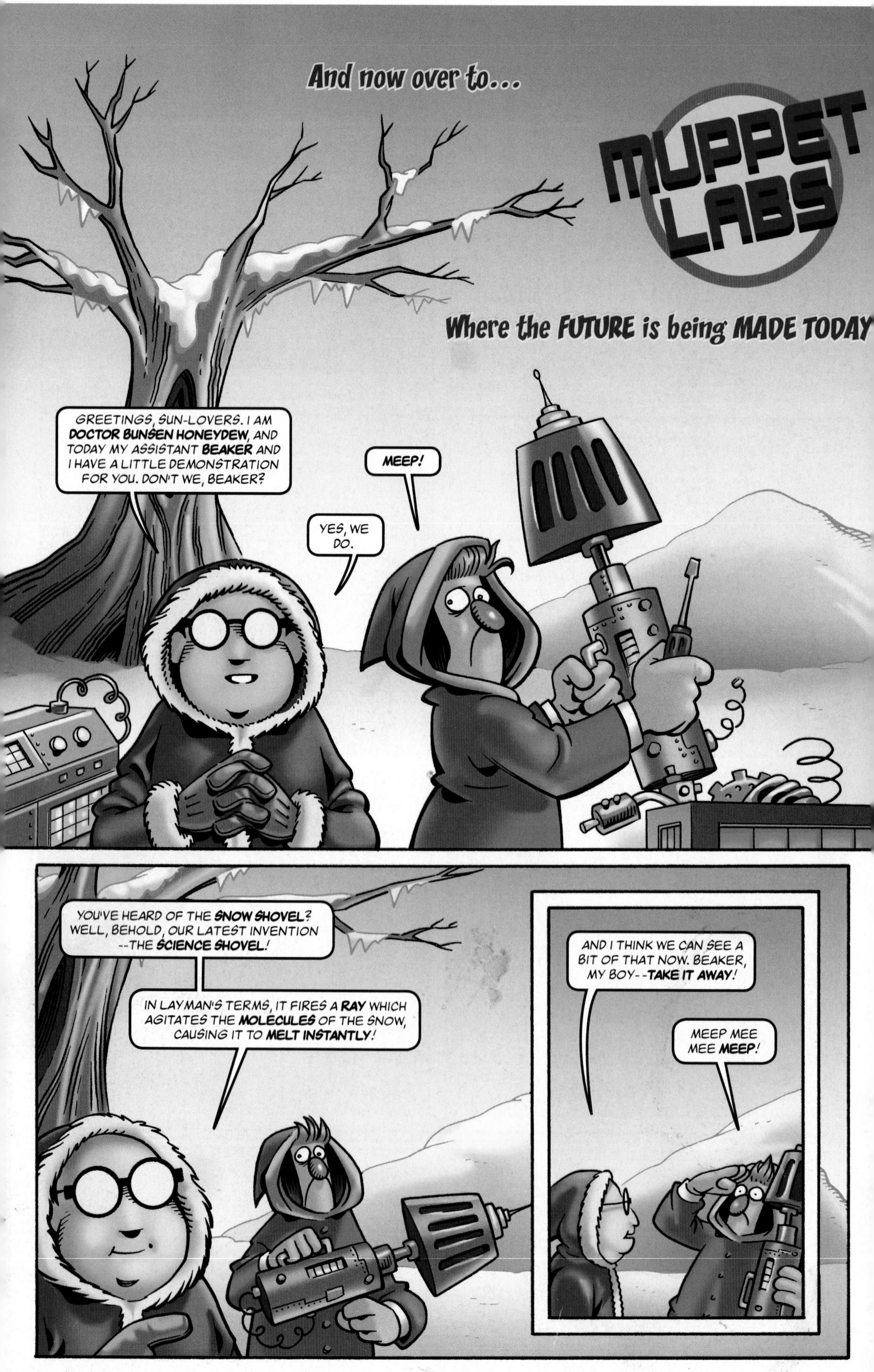
And now over to...
MUPPET LABS
Where the FUTURE is being MADE TODAY
GREETINGS, SUN-LOVERS. I AM DOCTOR BUNSEN HONEYDEW, AND TODAY MY ASSISTANT BEAKER AND I HAVE A LITTLE DEMONSTRATION FOR YOU. DON'T WE, BEAKER?
MEEP!
YES, WE DO.
YOU'VE HEARD OF THE SNOW SHOVEL? WELL, BEHOLD, OUR LATEST INVENTION --THE SCIENCE SHOVEL!
IN LAYMAN'S TERMS, IT FIRES A RAY WHICH AGITATES THE MOLECULES OF THE SNOW, CAUSING IT TO MELT INSTANTLY!
AND I THINK WE CAN SEE A BIT OF THAT NOW. BEAKER, MY BOY--TAKE IT AWAY!
MEEP MEE MEE MEEP!

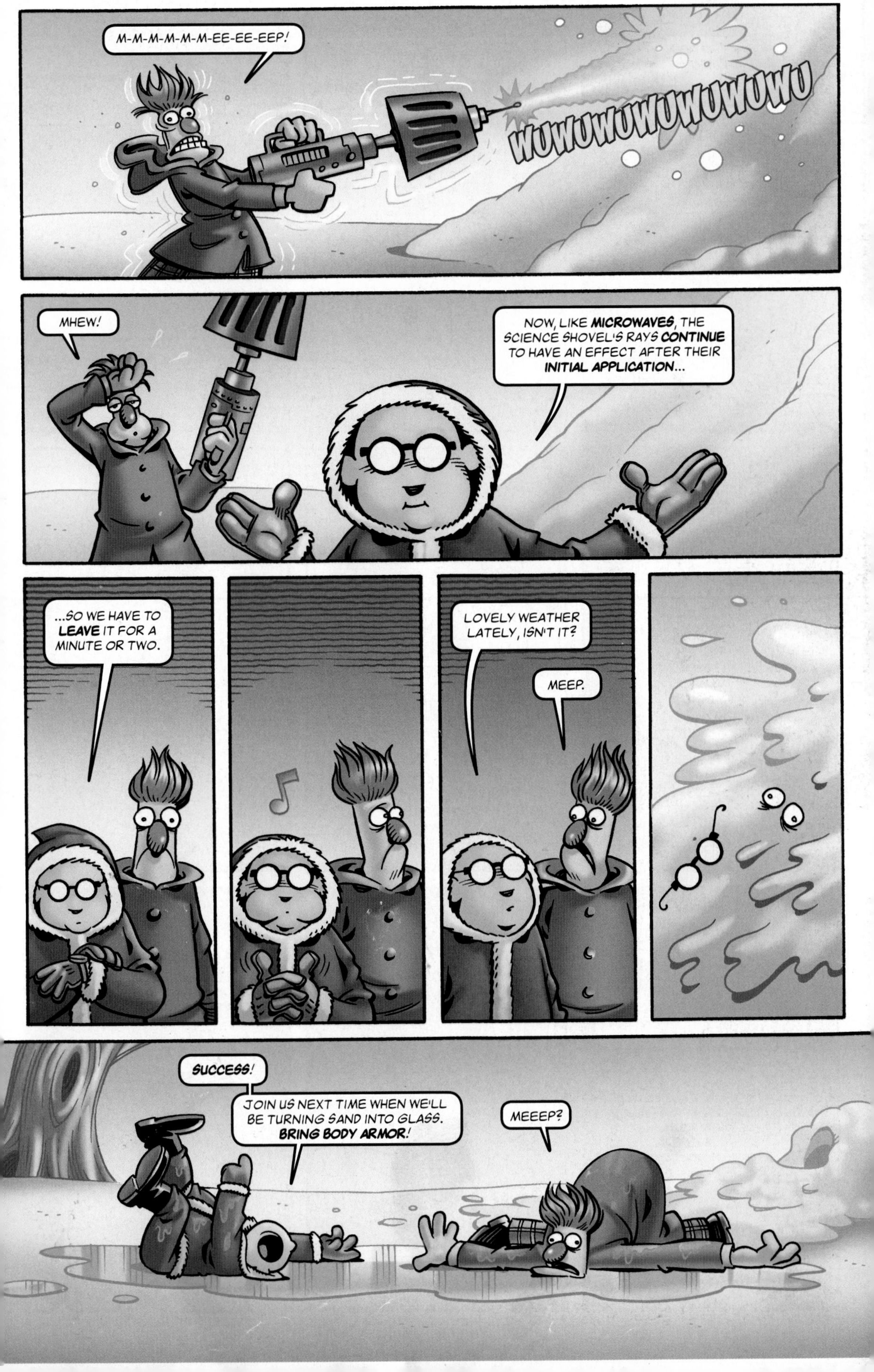
M-M-M-M-M-M-EE-EE-EEP!
WUWUWUWUWUWUWUWU
MHEW!
NOW, LIKE MICROWAVES, THE SCIENCE SHOVEL'S RAYS CONTINUE TO HAVE AN EFFECT AFTER THEIR INITIAL APPLICATION...
...SO WE HAVE TO LEAVE IT FOR A MINUTE OR TWO.
LOVELY WEATHER LATELY, ISN'T IT?
MEEP.
SUCCESS!
JOIN US NEXT TIME WHEN WE'LL BE TURNING SAND INTO GLASS. BRING BODY ARMOR!
MEEEP?

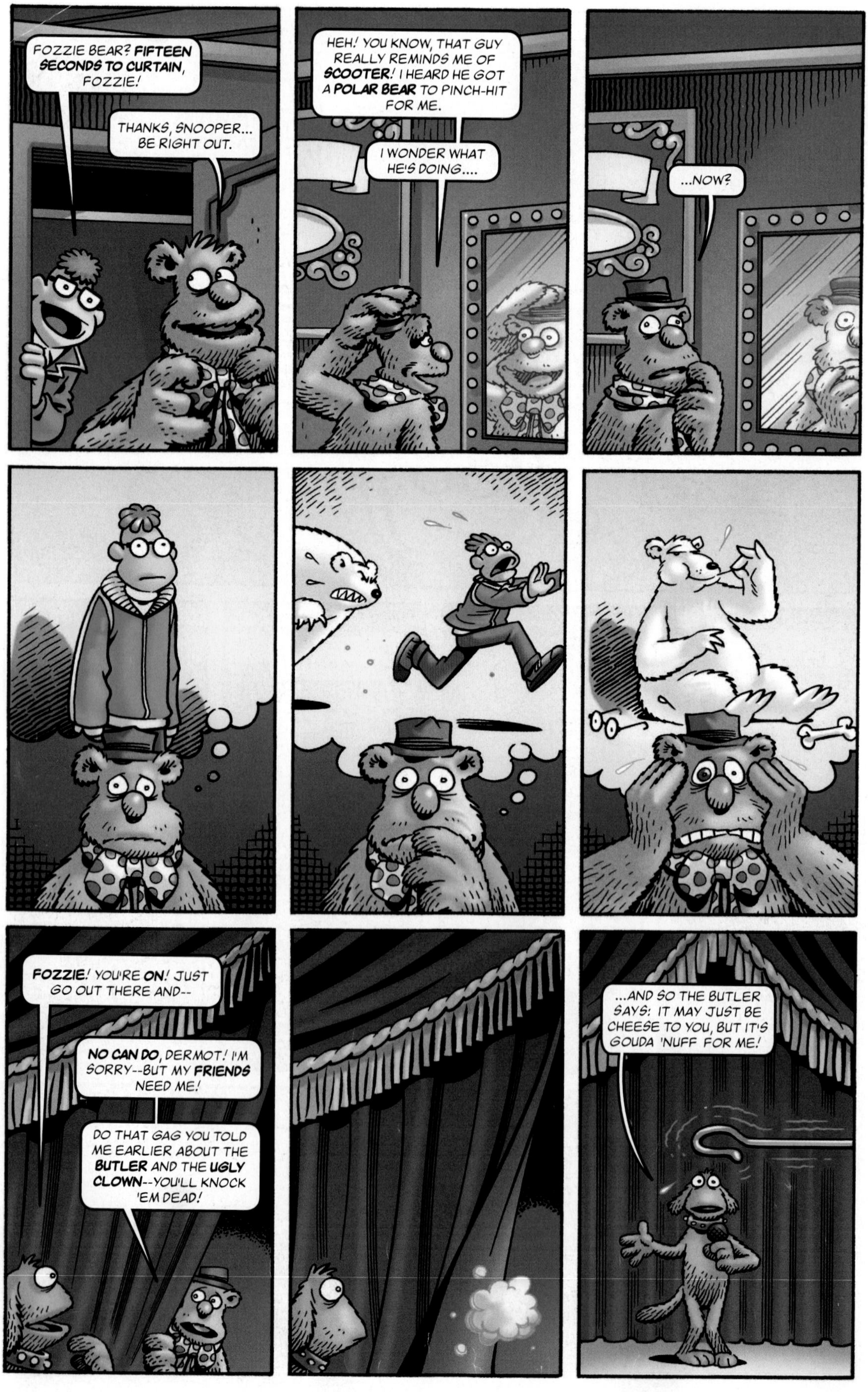
FOZZIE BEAR? FIFTEEN SECONDS TO CURTAIN, FOZZIE!
THANKS, SNOOPER... BE RIGHT OUT.
HEH! YOU KNOW, THAT GUY REALLY REMINDS ME OF SCOOTER! I HEARD HE GOT A POLAR BEAR TO PINCH-HIT FOR ME.
I WONDER WHAT HE'S DOING....
...NOW?
FOZZIE! YOU'RE ON! JUST GO OUT THERE AND--
NO CAN DO, DERMOT! I'M SORRY--BUT MY FRIENDS NEED ME!
DO THAT GAG YOU TOLD ME EARLIER ABOUT THE BUTLER AND THE UGLY CLOWN--YOU'LL KNOCK 'EM DEAD!
...AND SO THE BUTLER SAYS: IT MAY JUST BE CHEESE TO YOU, BUT IT'S GOUDA 'NUFF FOR ME!

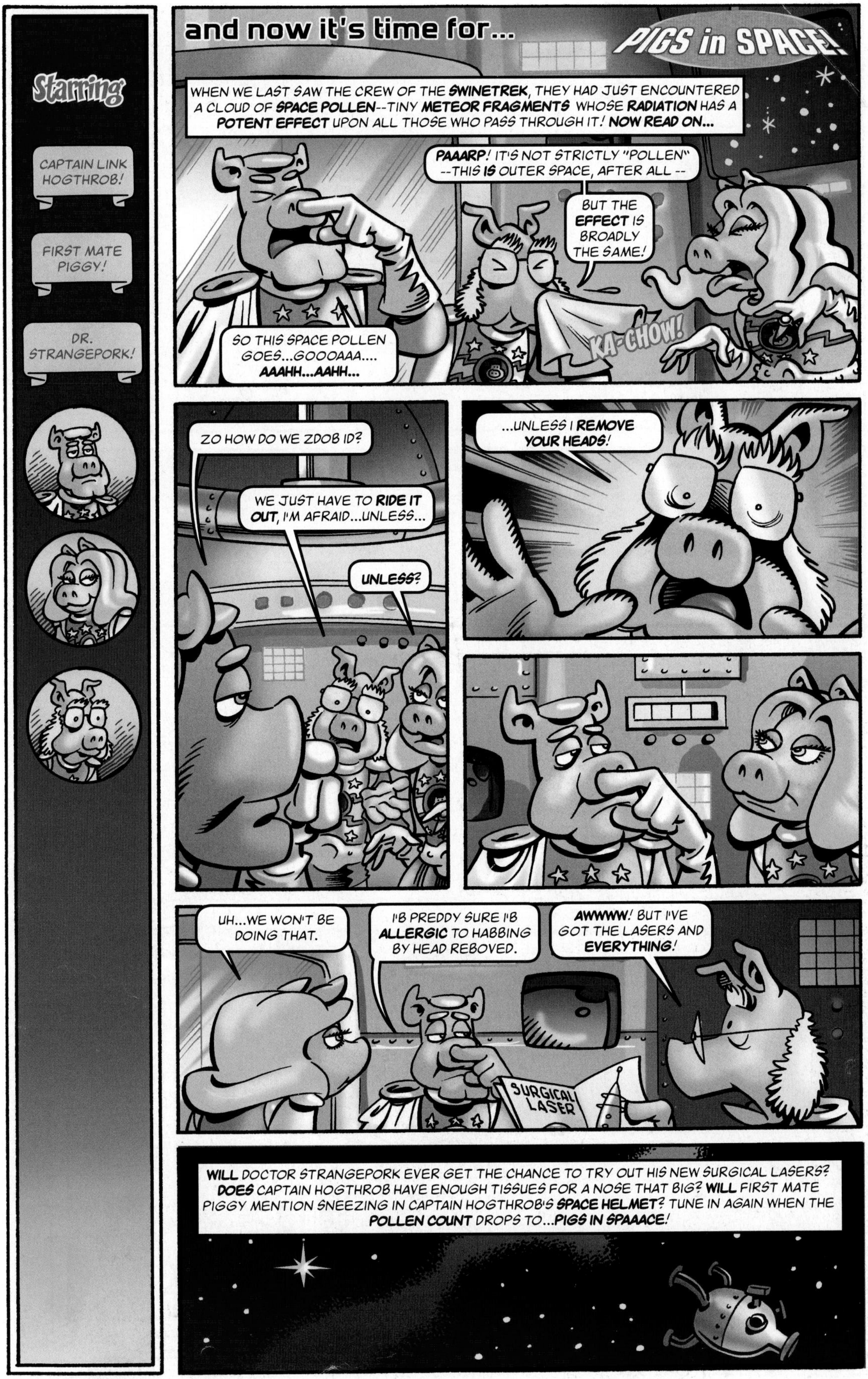

Starring
CAPTAIN LINK HOGTHROB!
FIRST MATE PIGGY!
DR. STRANGEPORK!
and now it's time for...
PIGS in SPACE!
WHEN WE LAST SAW THE CREW OF THE SWINETREK, THEY HAD JUST ENCOUNTERED A CLOUD OF SPACE POLLEN--TINY METEOR FRAGMENTS WHOSE RADIATION HAS A POTENT EFFECT UPON ALL THOSE WHO PASS THROUGH IT! NOW READ ON...
SO THIS SPACE POLLEN GOES...GOOOAAA.... AAAHH...AAHH...
PAAARP! IT'S NOT STRICTLY "POLLEN" --THIS IS OUTER SPACE, AFTER ALL --
BUT THE EFFECT IS BROADLY THE SAME!
KA-CHOW!
ZO HOW DO WE ZDOB ID?
WE JUST HAVE TO RIDE IT OUT, I'M AFRAID...UNLESS...
UNLESS?
...UNLESS I REMOVE YOUR HEADS!
UH...WE WON'T BE DOING THAT.
I'B PREDDY SURE I'B ALLERGIC TO HABBING BY HEAD REBOVED.
AWWWW! BUT I'VE GOT THE LASERS AND EVERYTHING!
SURGICAL LASER
WILL DOCTOR STRANGEPORK EVER GET THE CHANCE TO TRY OUT HIS NEW SURGICAL LASERS? DOES CAPTAIN HOGTHROB HAVE ENOUGH TISSUES FOR A NOSE THAT BIG? WILL FIRST MATE PIGGY MENTION SNEEZING IN CAPTAIN HOGTHROB'S SPACE HELMET? TUNE IN AGAIN WHEN THE POLLEN COUNT DROPS TO...PIGS IN SPAAACE!

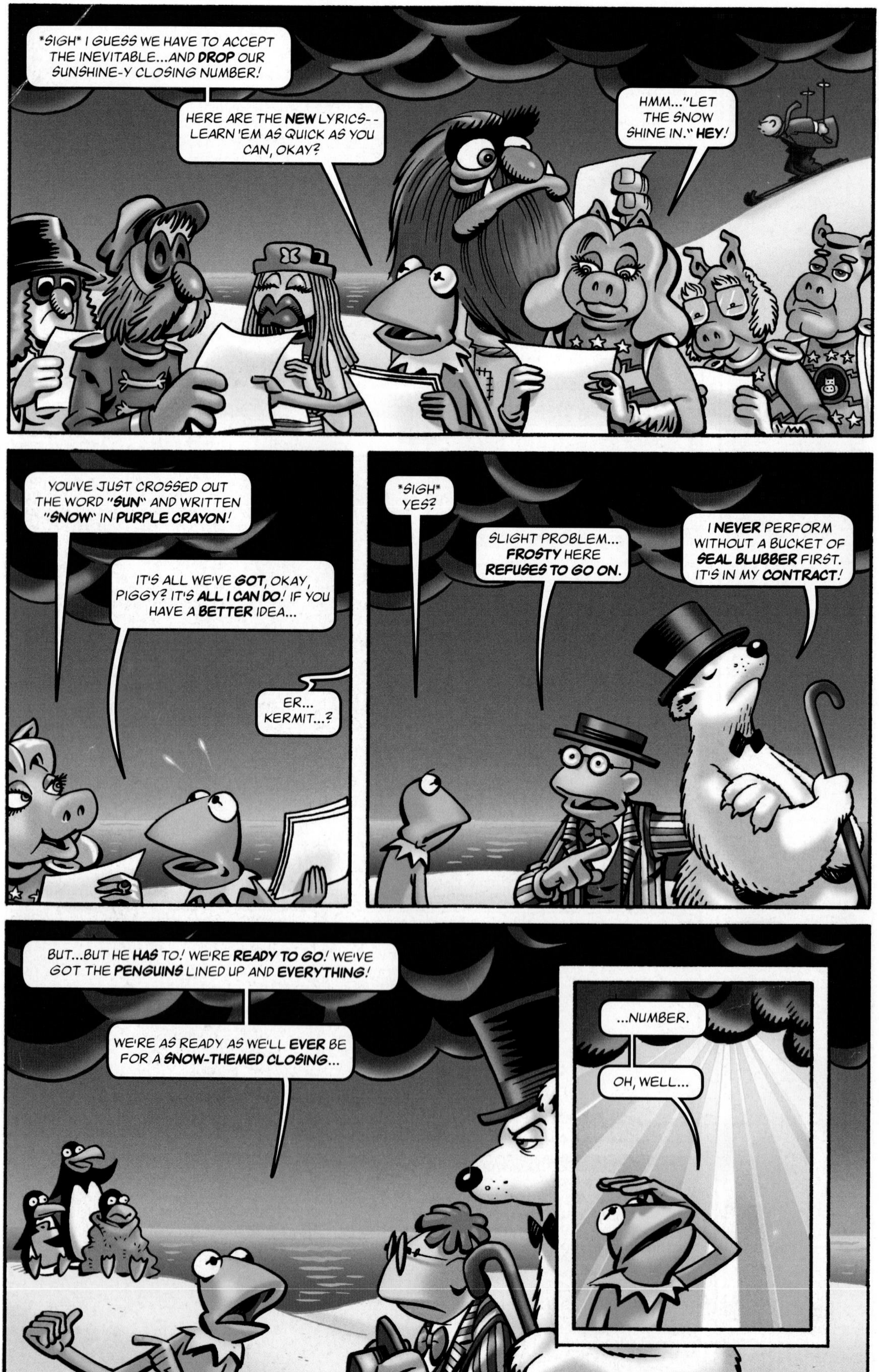
SIGH I GUESS WE HAVE TO ACCEPT THE INEVITABLE...AND DROP OUR SUNSHINE-Y CLOSING NUMBER!
HERE ARE THE NEW LYRICS--LEARN 'EM AS QUICK AS YOU CAN, OKAY?
HMM..."LET THE SNOW SHINE IN." HEY!
YOU'VE JUST CROSSED OUT THE WORD "SUN" AND WRITTEN "SNOW" IN PURPLE CRAYON!
IT'S ALL WE'VE GOT, OKAY, PIGGY? IT'S ALL I CAN DO! IF YOU HAVE A BETTER IDEA...
ER... KERMIT...?
SIGH YES?
SLIGHT PROBLEM... FROSTY HERE REFUSES TO GO ON.
I NEVER PERFORM WITHOUT A BUCKET OF SEAL BLUBBER FIRST. IT'S IN MY CONTRACT!
BUT...BUT HE HAS TO! WE'RE READY TO GO! WE'VE GOT THE PENGUINS LINED UP AND EVERYTHING!
WE'RE AS READY AS WE'LL EVER BE FOR A SNOW-THEMED CLOSING...
...NUMBER.
OH, WELL...

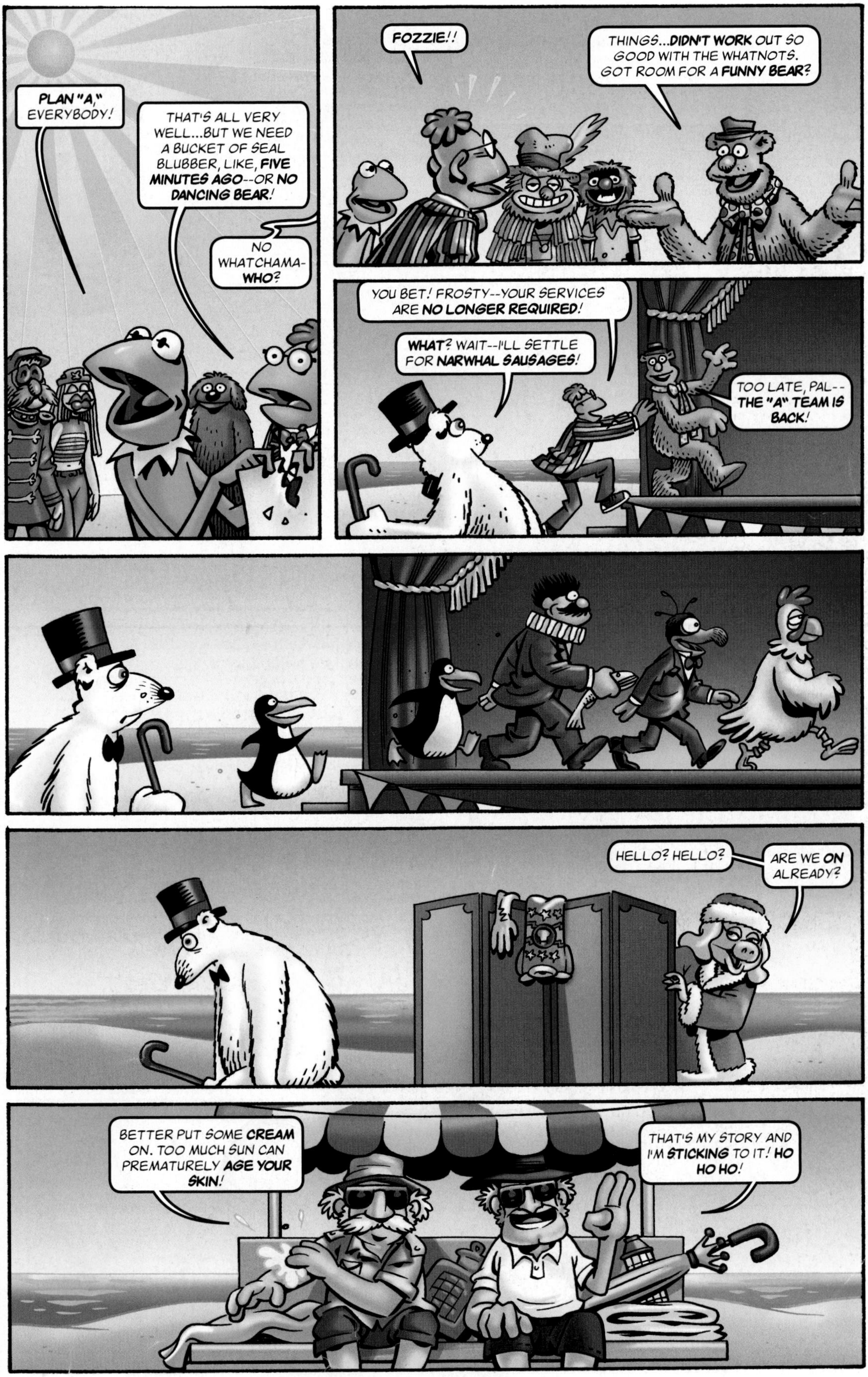
PLAN "A," EVERYBODY!
THAT'S ALL VERY WELL...BUT WE NEED A BUCKET OF SEAL BLUBBER, LIKE, FIVE MINUTES AGO--OR NO DANCING BEAR!
NO WHATCHAMA-WHO?
FOZZIE!!
THINGS...DIDN'T WORK OUT SO GOOD WITH THE WHATNOTS. GOT ROOM FOR A FUNNY BEAR?
YOU BET! FROSTY--YOUR SERVICES ARE NO LONGER REQUIRED!
WHAT? WAIT--I'LL SETTLE FOR NARWHAL SAUSAGES!
TOO LATE, PAL--THE "A" TEAM IS BACK!
HELLO? HELLO?
ARE WE ON ALREADY?
BETTER PUT SOME CREAM ON. TOO MUCH SUN CAN PREMATURELY AGE YOUR SKIN!
THAT'S MY STORY AND I'M STICKING TO IT! HO HO HO!

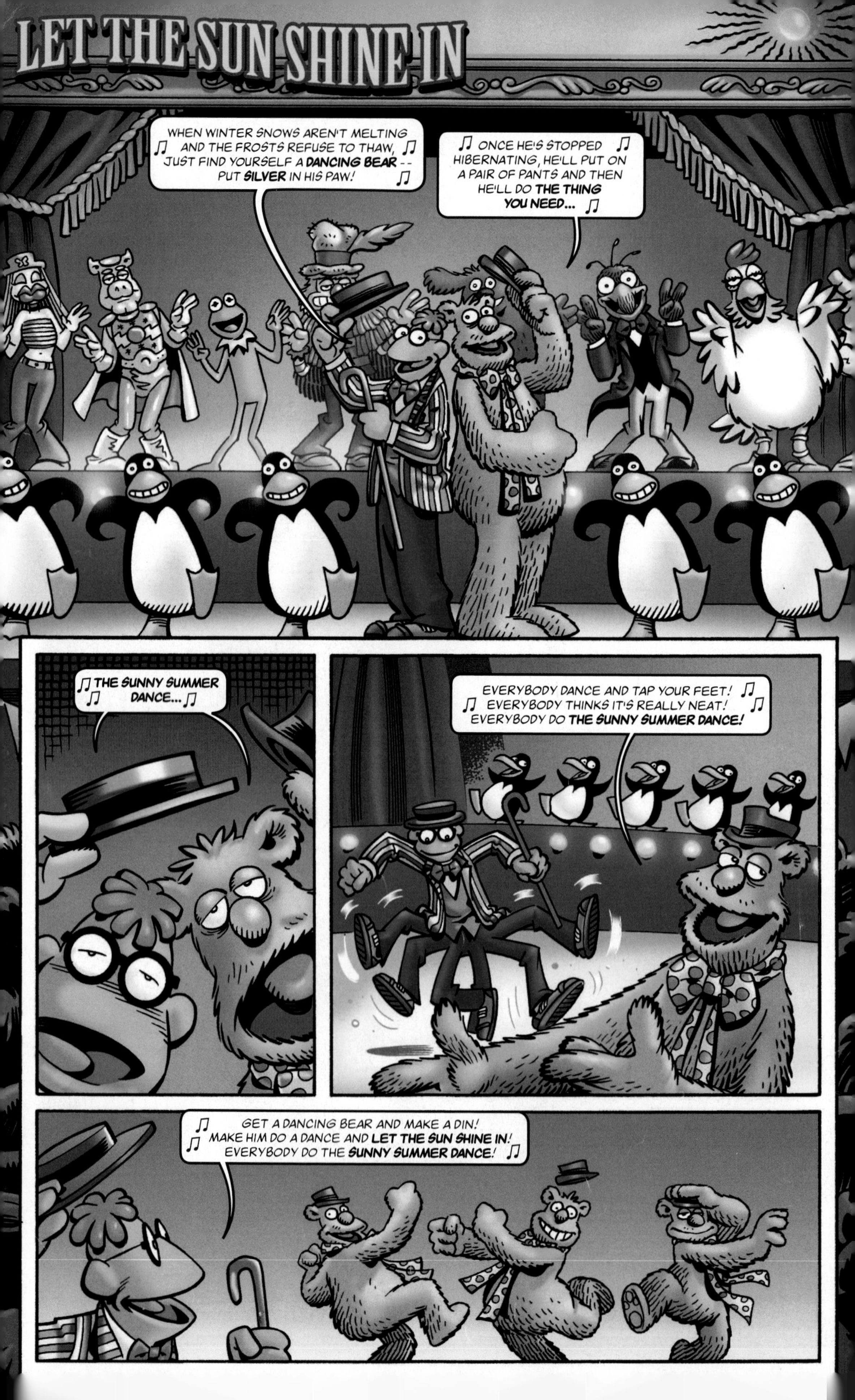
LET THE SUN SHINE IN
WHEN WINTER SNOWS AREN'T MELTING AND THE FROSTS REFUSE TO THAW, JUST FIND YOURSELF A DANCING BEAR -- PUT SILVER IN HIS PAW!
ONCE HE'S STOPPED HIBERNATING, HE'LL PUT ON A PAIR OF PANTS AND THEN HE'LL DO THE THING YOU NEED...
THE SUNNY SUMMER DANCE...
EVERYBODY DANCE AND TAP YOUR FEET! EVERYBODY THINKS IT'S REALLY NEAT! EVERYBODY DO THE SUNNY SUMMER DANCE!
GET A DANCING BEAR AND MAKE A DIN! MAKE HIM DO A DANCE AND LET THE SUN SHINE IN! EVERYBODY DO THE SUNNY SUMMER DANCE!

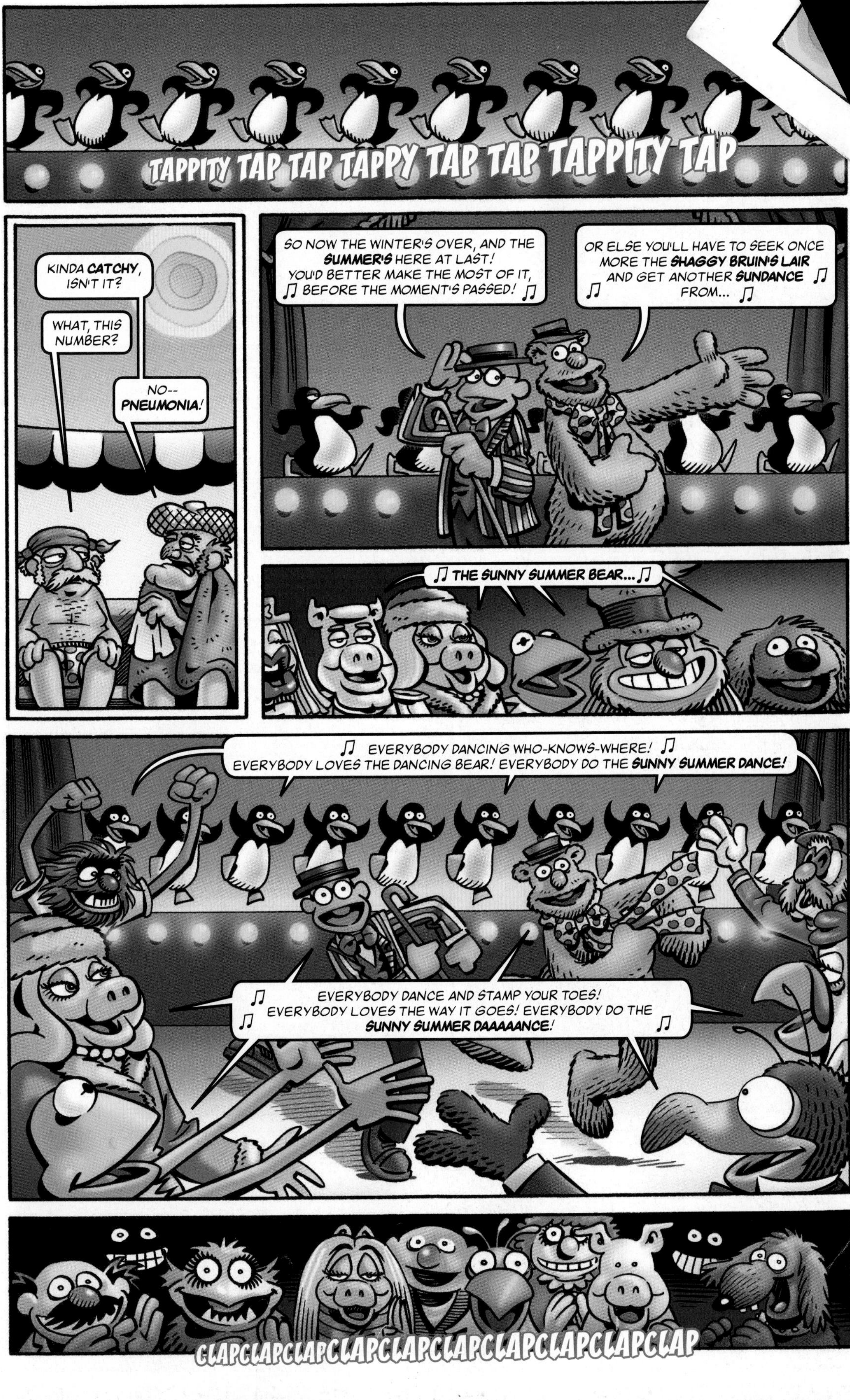
TAPPITY TAP TAP TAPPY TAP TAP TAPPITY TAP
KINDA CATCHY, ISN'T IT?
WHAT, THIS NUMBER?
NO-- PNEUMONIA!
SO NOW THE WINTER'S OVER, AND THE SUMMER'S HERE AT LAST! YOU'D BETTER MAKE THE MOST OF IT, ♫ BEFORE THE MOMENT'S PASSED! ♫
OR ELSE YOU'LL HAVE TO SEEK ONCE MORE THE SHAGGY BRUIN'S LAIR AND GET ANOTHER SUNDANCE ♫ ♫ FROM... ♫
♫ THE SUNNY SUMMER BEAR... ♫
♫ EVERYBODY DANCING WHO-KNOWS-WHERE! ♫ EVERYBODY LOVES THE DANCING BEAR! EVERYBODY DO THE SUNNY SUMMER DANCE!
♫ EVERYBODY DANCE AND STAMP YOUR TOES! ♫ EVERYBODY LOVES THE WAY IT GOES! EVERYBODY DO THE SUNNY SUMMER DAAAAANCE! ♫
CLAPCLAPCLAPCLAPCLAPCLAPCLAPCLAPCLAPCLAP

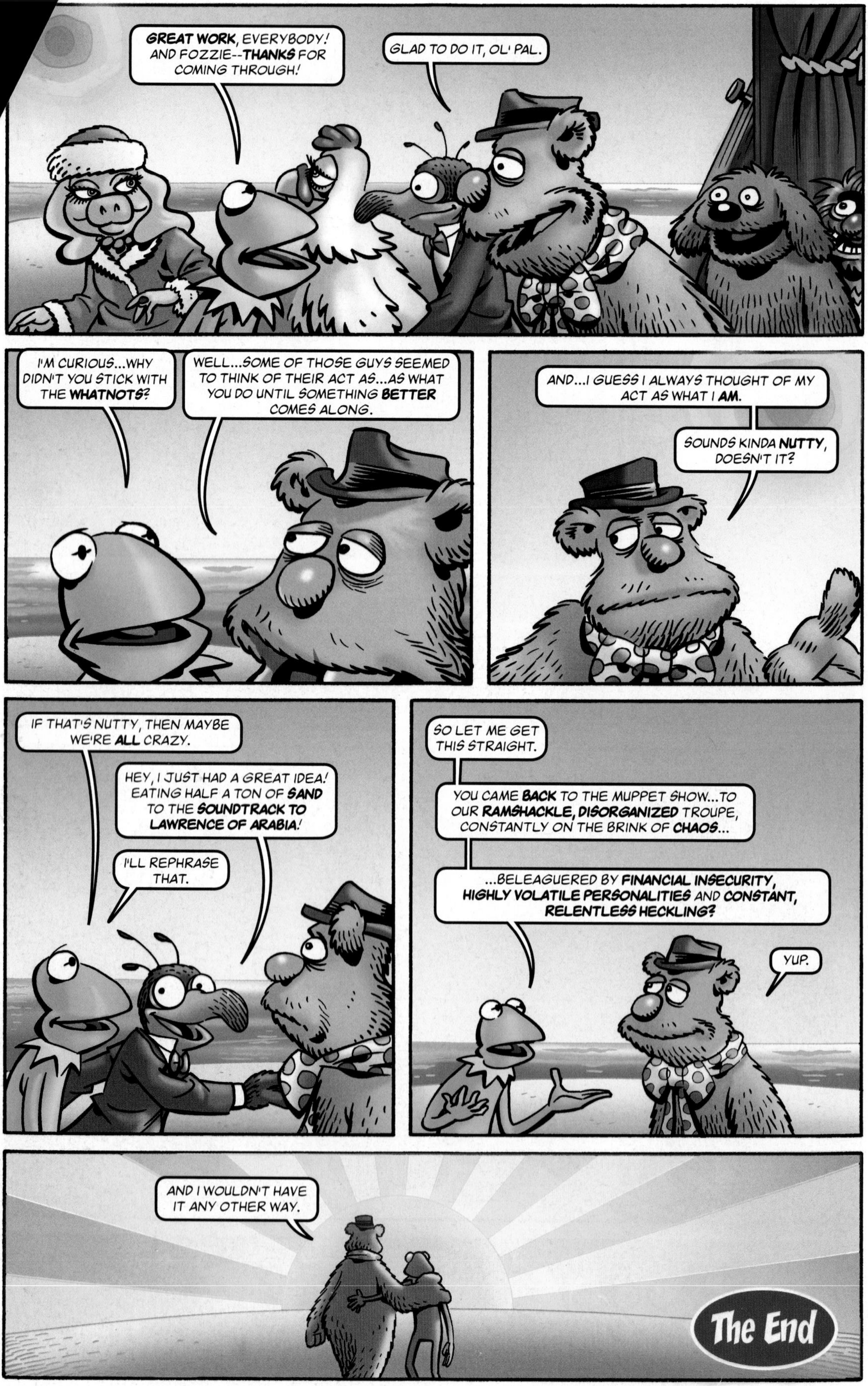
GREAT WORK, EVERYBODY! AND FOZZIE--THANKS FOR COMING THROUGH!
GLAD TO DO IT, OL' PAL.
I'M CURIOUS...WHY DIDN'T YOU STICK WITH THE WHATNOTS?
WELL...SOME OF THOSE GUYS SEEMED TO THINK OF THEIR ACT AS...AS WHAT YOU DO UNTIL SOMETHING BETTER COMES ALONG.
AND...I GUESS I ALWAYS THOUGHT OF MY ACT AS WHAT I AM.
SOUNDS KINDA NUTTY, DOESN'T IT?
IF THAT'S NUTTY, THEN MAYBE WE'RE ALL CRAZY.
HEY, I JUST HAD A GREAT IDEA! EATING HALF A TON OF SAND TO THE SOUNDTRACK TO LAWRENCE OF ARABIA!
I'LL REPHRASE THAT.
SO LET ME GET THIS STRAIGHT.
YOU CAME BACK TO THE MUPPET SHOW...TO OUR RAMSHACKLE, DISORGANIZED TROUPE, CONSTANTLY ON THE BRINK OF CHAOS...
...BELEAGUERED BY FINANCIAL INSECURITY, HIGHLY VOLATILE PERSONALITIES AND CONSTANT, RELENTLESS HECKLING?
YUP.
AND I WOULDN'T HAVE IT ANY OTHER WAY.
The End

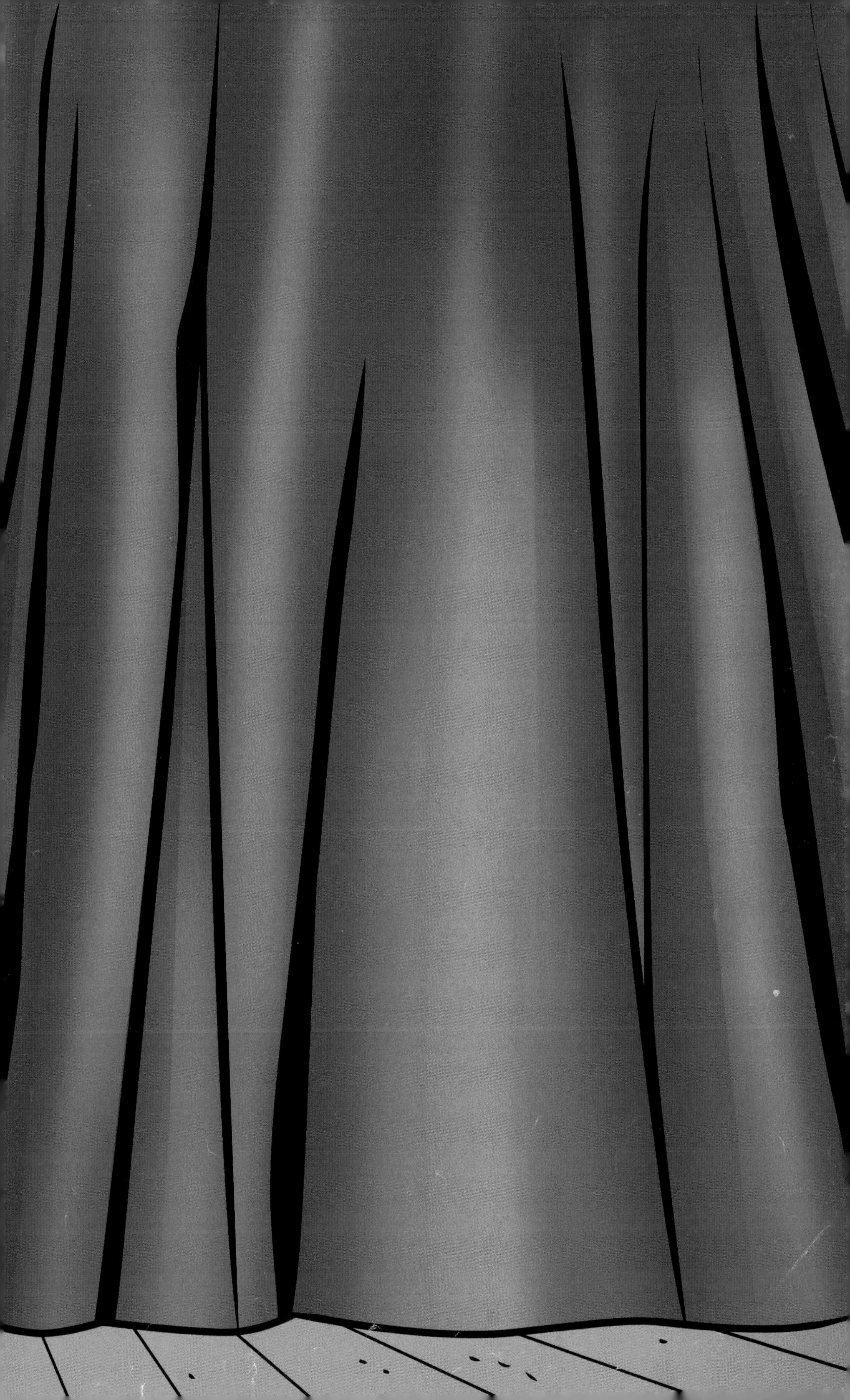

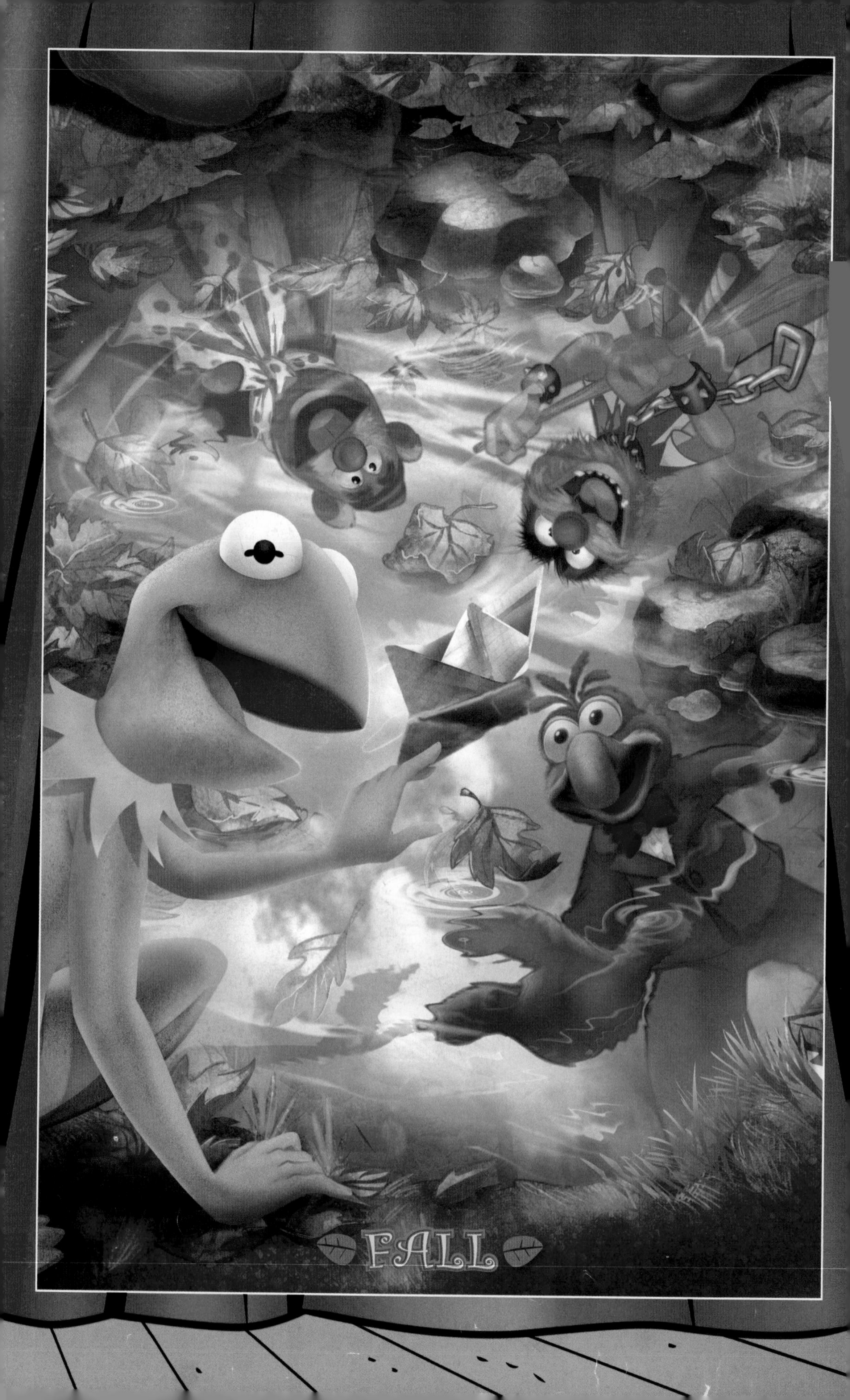
FALL

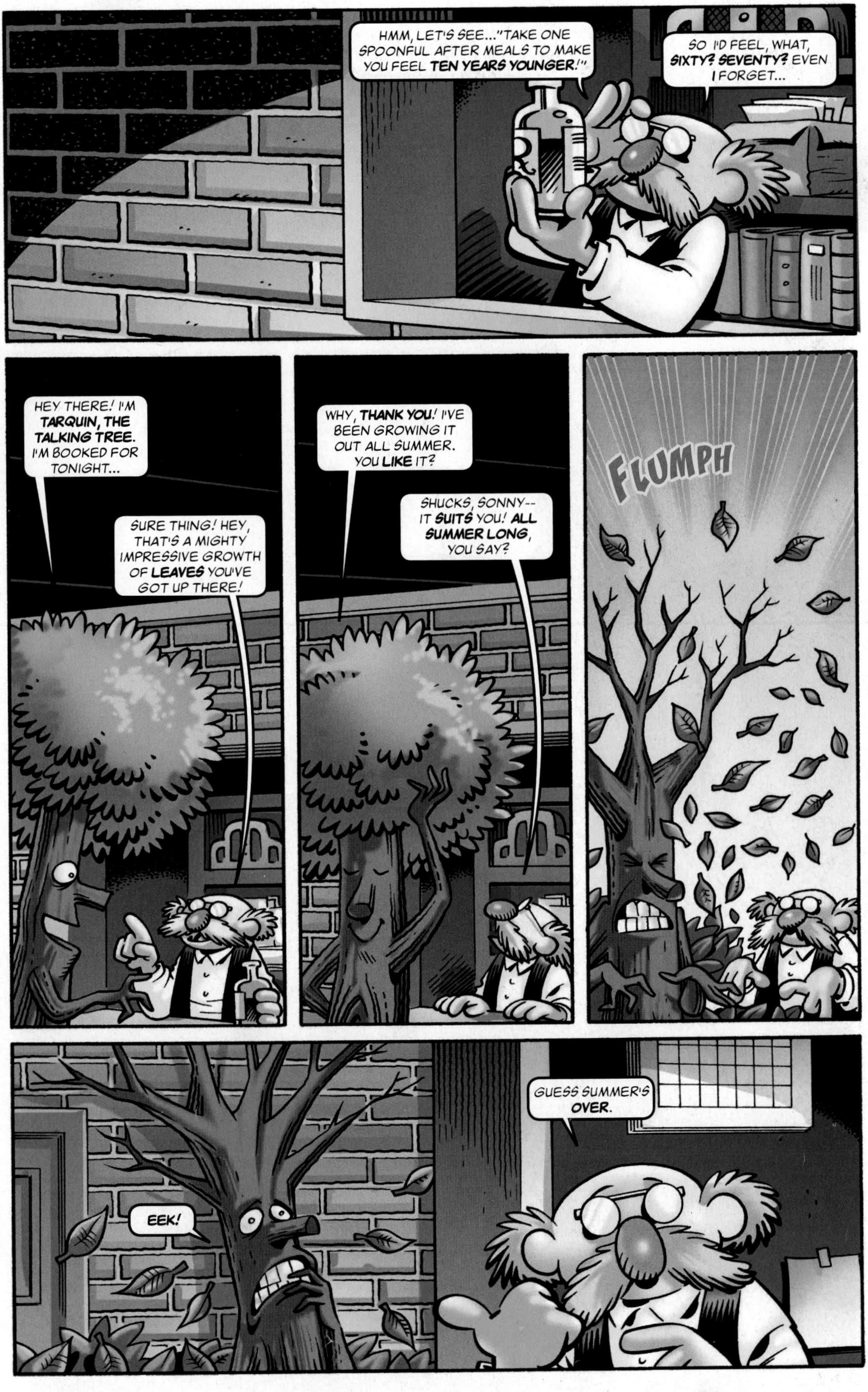

HMM, LET'S SEE..."TAKE ONE SPOONFUL AFTER MEALS TO MAKE YOU FEEL **TEN YEARS YOUNGER**."
SO I'D FEEL, WHAT, **SIXTY? SEVENTY?** EVEN I FORGET...
HEY THERE! I'M **TARQUIN, THE TALKING TREE**. I'M BOOKED FOR TONIGHT...
SURE THING! HEY, THAT'S A MIGHTY IMPRESSIVE GROWTH OF **LEAVES** YOU'VE GOT UP THERE!
WHY, **THANK YOU**! I'VE BEEN GROWING IT OUT ALL SUMMER. YOU **LIKE** IT?
SHUCKS, SONNY-- IT **SUITS** YOU! **ALL SUMMER LONG**, YOU SAY?
FLUMPH
EEK!
GUESS SUMMER'S **OVER**.

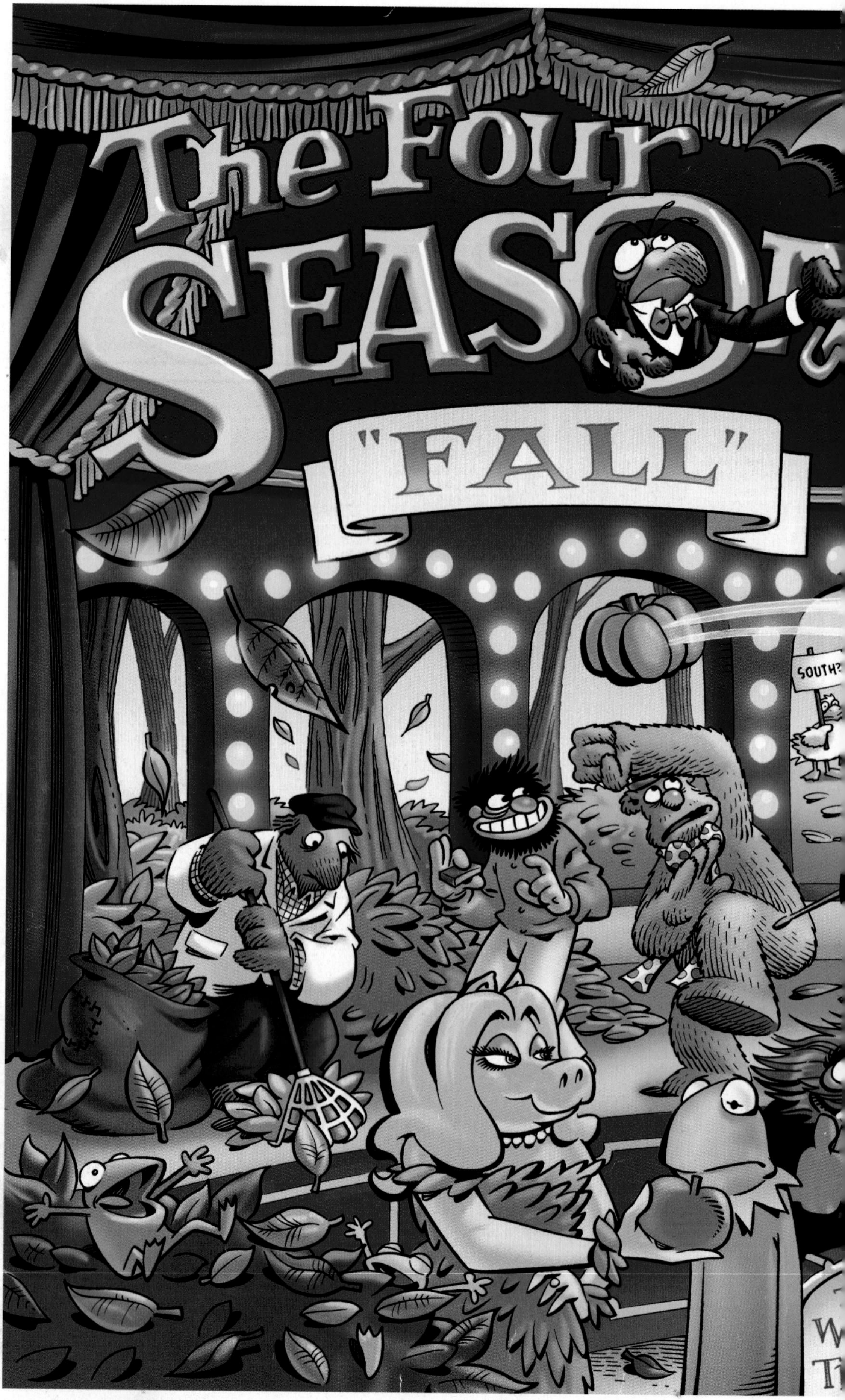

The Four
SEASO
"FALL"
SOUTH?

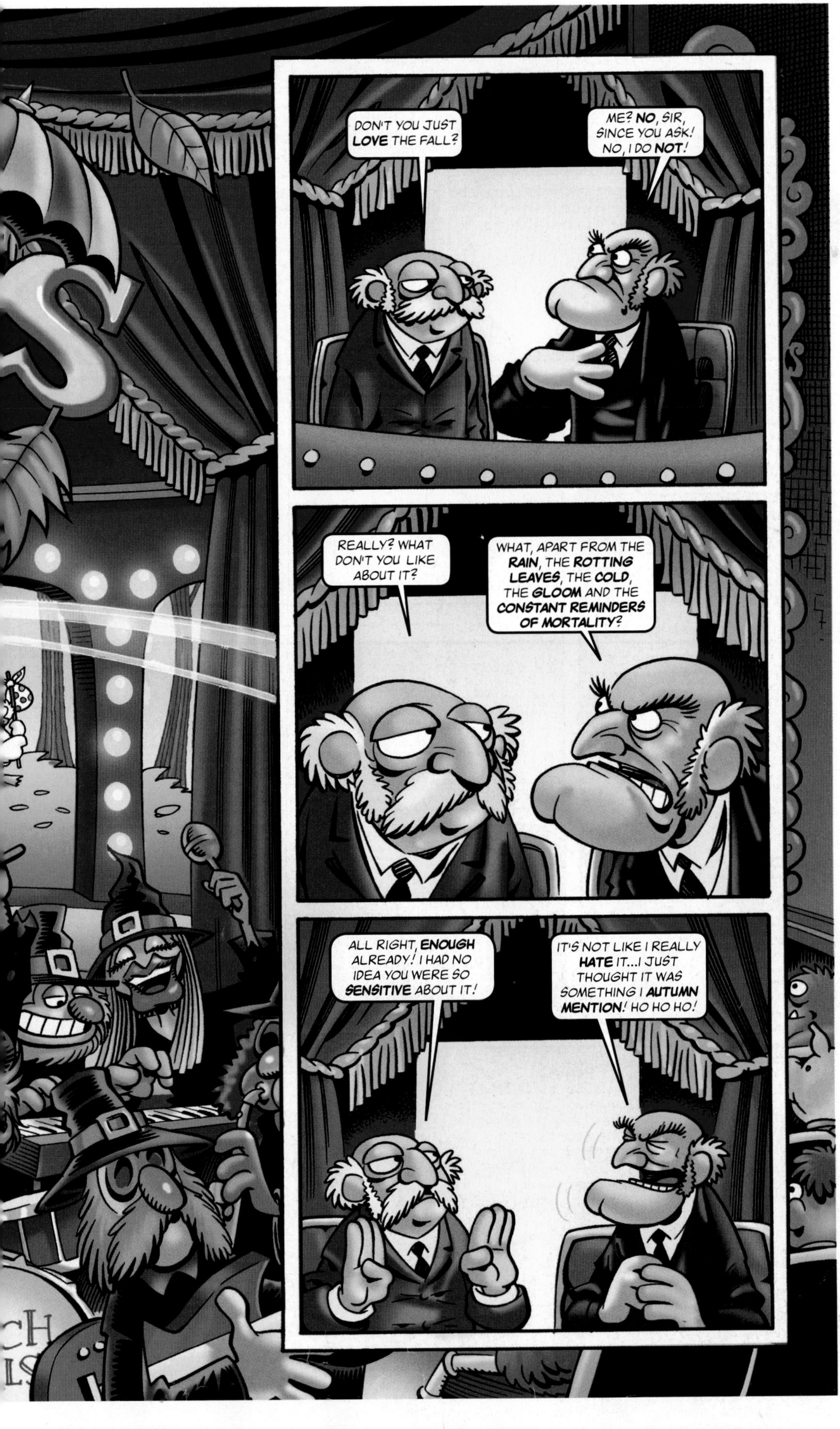
DON'T YOU JUST LOVE THE FALL?
ME? NO, SIR, SINCE YOU ASK! NO, I DO NOT!
REALLY? WHAT DON'T YOU LIKE ABOUT IT?
WHAT, APART FROM THE RAIN, THE ROTTING LEAVES, THE COLD, THE GLOOM AND THE CONSTANT REMINDERS OF MORTALITY?
ALL RIGHT, ENOUGH ALREADY! I HAD NO IDEA YOU WERE SO SENSITIVE ABOUT IT!
IT'S NOT LIKE I REALLY HATE IT...I JUST THOUGHT IT WAS SOMETHING I AUTUMN MENTION! HO HO HO!

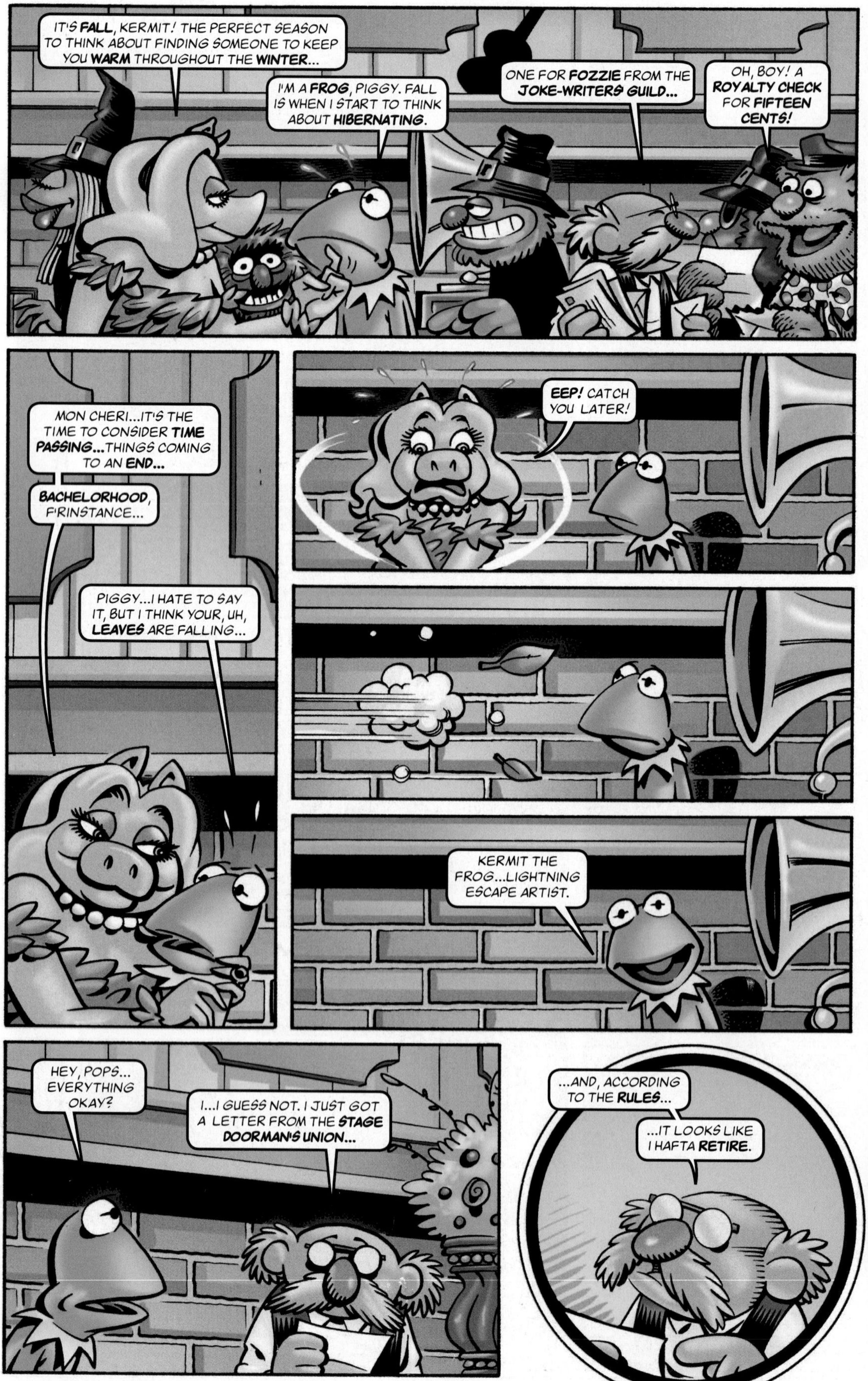
IT'S FALL, KERMIT! THE PERFECT SEASON TO THINK ABOUT FINDING SOMEONE TO KEEP YOU WARM THROUGHOUT THE WINTER...
I'M A FROG, PIGGY. FALL IS WHEN I START TO THINK ABOUT HIBERNATING.
ONE FOR FOZZIE FROM THE JOKE-WRITERS GUILD...
OH, BOY! A ROYALTY CHECK FOR FIFTEEN CENTS!
MON CHERI...IT'S THE TIME TO CONSIDER TIME PASSING...THINGS COMING TO AN END...
BACHELORHOOD, F'RINSTANCE...
PIGGY...I HATE TO SAY IT, BUT I THINK YOUR, UH, LEAVES ARE FALLING...
EEP! CATCH YOU LATER!
KERMIT THE FROG...LIGHTNING ESCAPE ARTIST.
HEY, POPS... EVERYTHING OKAY?
I...I GUESS NOT. I JUST GOT A LETTER FROM THE STAGE DOORMAN'S UNION...
...AND, ACCORDING TO THE RULES...
...IT LOOKS LIKE I HAFTA RETIRE.

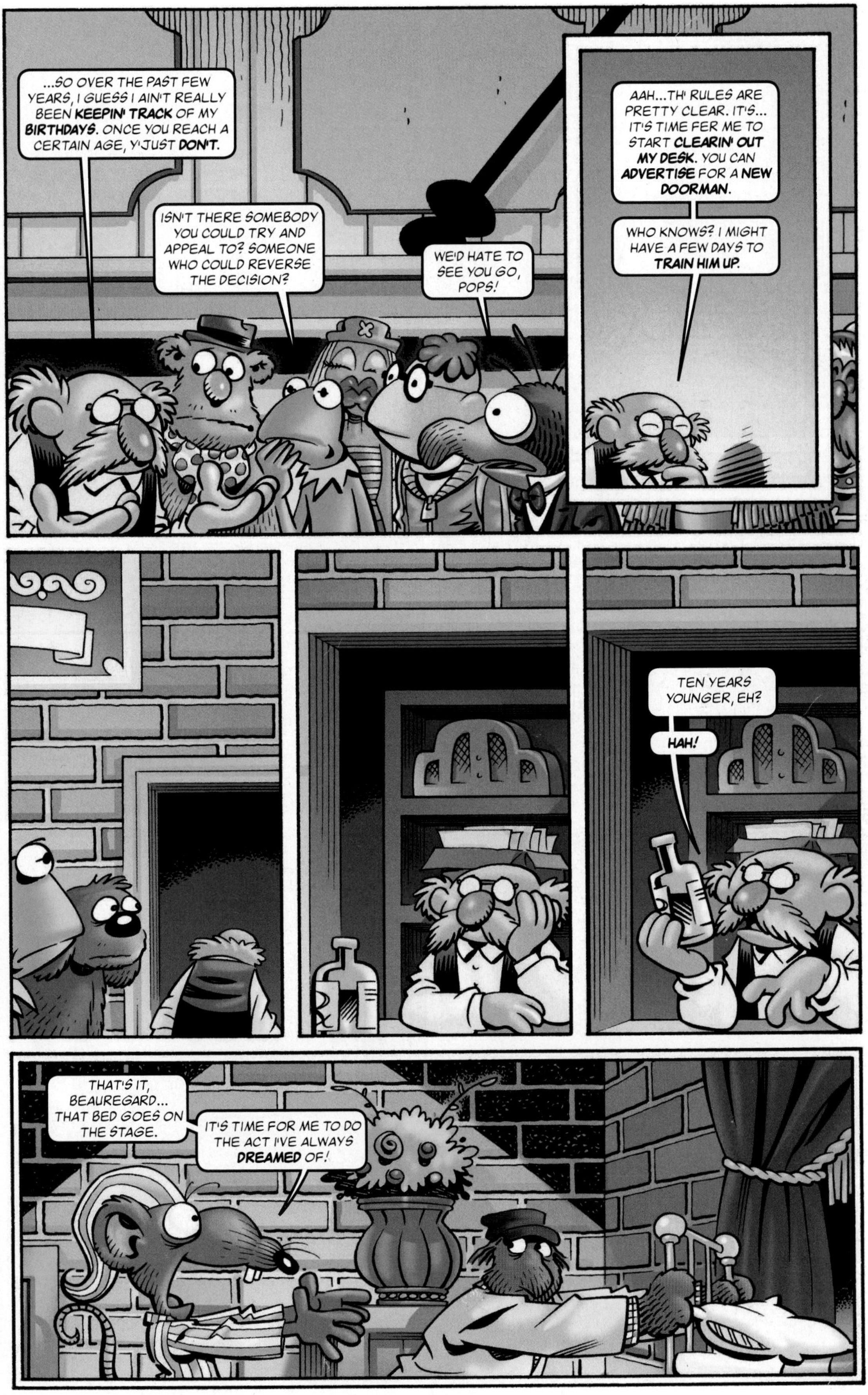
...SO OVER THE PAST FEW YEARS, I GUESS I AIN'T REALLY BEEN **KEEPIN' TRACK** OF MY **BIRTHDAYS**. ONCE YOU REACH A CERTAIN AGE, Y'JUST **DON'T**.
ISN'T THERE SOMEBODY YOU COULD TRY AND APPEAL TO? SOMEONE WHO COULD REVERSE THE DECISION?
WE'D HATE TO SEE YOU GO, POPS!
AAH...TH' RULES ARE PRETTY CLEAR. IT'S... IT'S TIME FER ME TO START **CLEARIN' OUT MY DESK**. YOU CAN **ADVERTISE** FOR A **NEW DOORMAN**.
WHO KNOWS? I MIGHT HAVE A FEW DAYS TO **TRAIN HIM UP**.
TEN YEARS YOUNGER, EH?
HAH!
THAT'S IT, BEAUREGARD... THAT BED GOES ON THE STAGE.
IT'S TIME FOR ME TO DO THE ACT I'VE ALWAYS **DREAMED** OF!

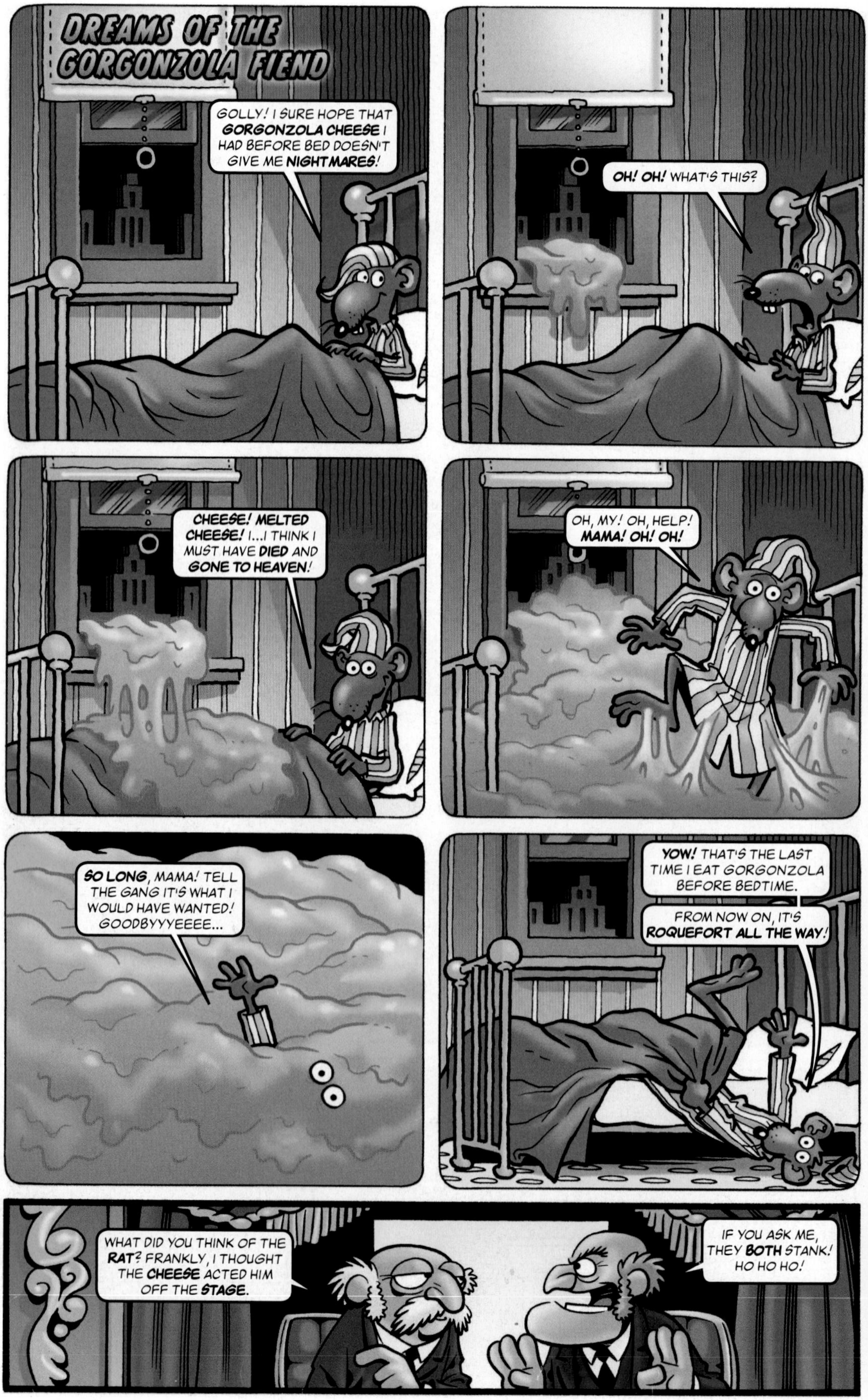
DREAMS OF THE GORGONZOLA FIEND
GOLLY! I SURE HOPE THAT GORGONZOLA CHEESE I HAD BEFORE BED DOESN'T GIVE ME NIGHTMARES!
OH! OH! WHAT'S THIS?
CHEESE! MELTED CHEESE! I...I THINK I MUST HAVE DIED AND GONE TO HEAVEN!
OH, MY! OH, HELP! MAMA! OH! OH!
SO LONG, MAMA! TELL THE GANG IT'S WHAT I WOULD HAVE WANTED! GOODBYYYEEEE...
YOW! THAT'S THE LAST TIME I EAT GORGONZOLA BEFORE BEDTIME.
FROM NOW ON, IT'S ROQUEFORT ALL THE WAY!
WHAT DID YOU THINK OF THE RAT? FRANKLY, I THOUGHT THE CHEESE ACTED HIM OFF THE STAGE.
IF YOU ASK ME, THEY BOTH STANK! HO HO HO!

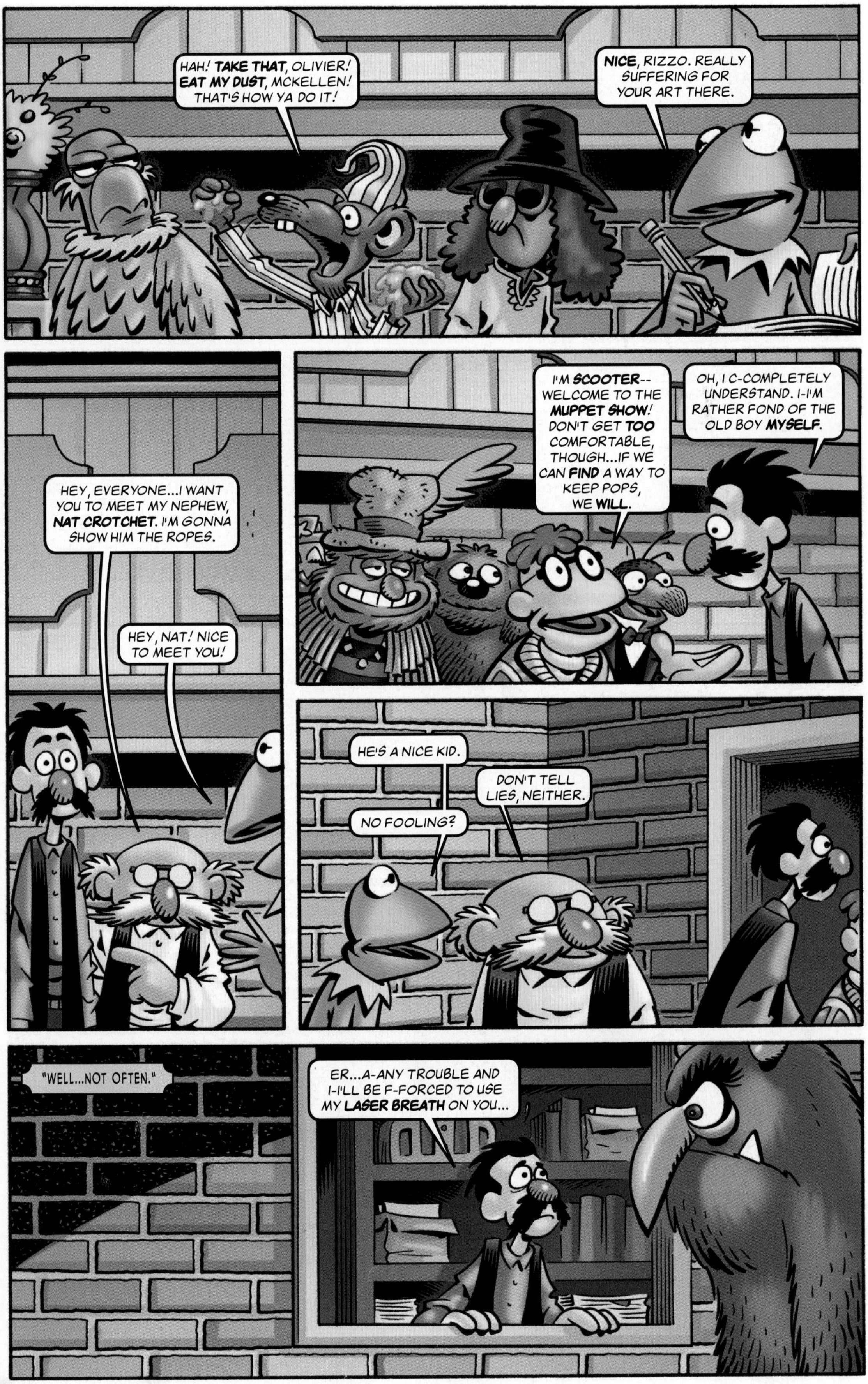
HAH! TAKE THAT, OLIVIER! EAT MY DUST, MCKELLEN! THAT'S HOW YA DO IT!
NICE, RIZZO. REALLY SUFFERING FOR YOUR ART THERE.
HEY, EVERYONE...I WANT YOU TO MEET MY NEPHEW, NAT CROTCHET. I'M GONNA SHOW HIM THE ROPES.
HEY, NAT! NICE TO MEET YOU!
I'M SCOOTER-- WELCOME TO THE MUPPET SHOW! DON'T GET TOO COMFORTABLE, THOUGH...IF WE CAN FIND A WAY TO KEEP POPS, WE WILL.
OH, I C-COMPLETELY UNDERSTAND. I-I'M RATHER FOND OF THE OLD BOY MYSELF.
HE'S A NICE KID.
NO FOOLING?
DON'T TELL LIES, NEITHER.
"WELL...NOT OFTEN."
ER...A-ANY TROUBLE AND I-I'LL BE F-FORCED TO USE MY LASER BREATH ON YOU...

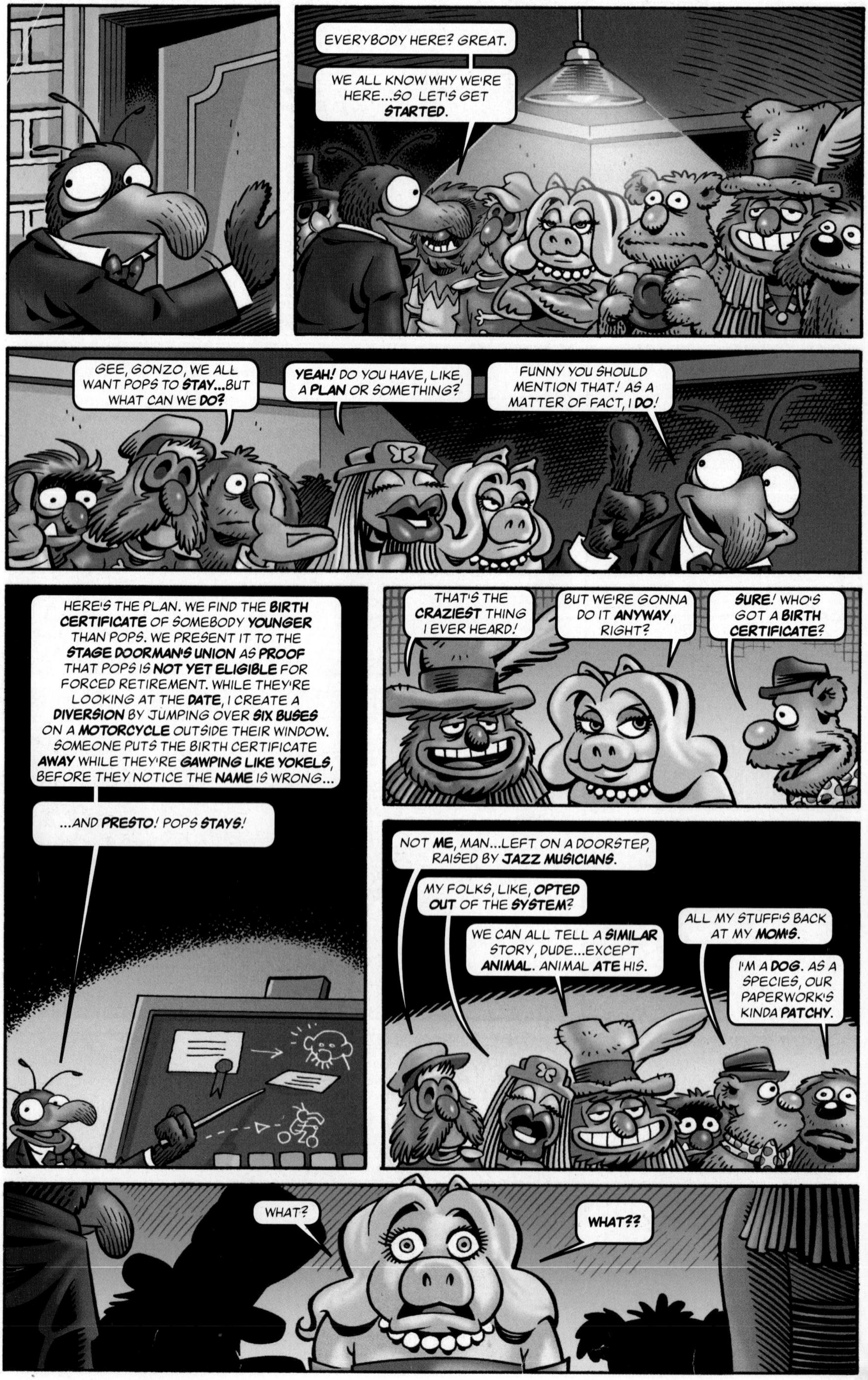
EVERYBODY HERE? GREAT.
WE ALL KNOW WHY WE'RE HERE...SO LET'S GET STARTED.
GEE, GONZO, WE ALL WANT POPS TO STAY...BUT WHAT CAN WE DO?
YEAH! DO YOU HAVE, LIKE, A PLAN OR SOMETHING?
FUNNY YOU SHOULD MENTION THAT! AS A MATTER OF FACT, I DO!
HERE'S THE PLAN. WE FIND THE BIRTH CERTIFICATE OF SOMEBODY YOUNGER THAN POPS. WE PRESENT IT TO THE STAGE DOORMAN'S UNION AS PROOF THAT POPS IS NOT YET ELIGIBLE FOR FORCED RETIREMENT. WHILE THEY'RE LOOKING AT THE DATE, I CREATE A DIVERSION BY JUMPING OVER SIX BUSES ON A MOTORCYCLE OUTSIDE THEIR WINDOW. SOMEONE PUTS THE BIRTH CERTIFICATE AWAY WHILE THEY'RE GAWPING LIKE YOKELS, BEFORE THEY NOTICE THE NAME IS WRONG...
...AND PRESTO! POPS STAYS!
THAT'S THE CRAZIEST THING I EVER HEARD!
BUT WE'RE GONNA DO IT ANYWAY, RIGHT?
SURE! WHO'S GOT A BIRTH CERTIFICATE?
NOT ME, MAN...LEFT ON A DOORSTEP, RAISED BY JAZZ MUSICIANS.
MY FOLKS, LIKE, OPTED OUT OF THE SYSTEM?
WE CAN ALL TELL A SIMILAR STORY, DUDE...EXCEPT ANIMAL. ANIMAL ATE HIS.
ALL MY STUFF'S BACK AT MY MOM'S.
I'M A DOG. AS A SPECIES, OUR PAPERWORK'S KINDA PATCHY.
WHAT?
WHAT??

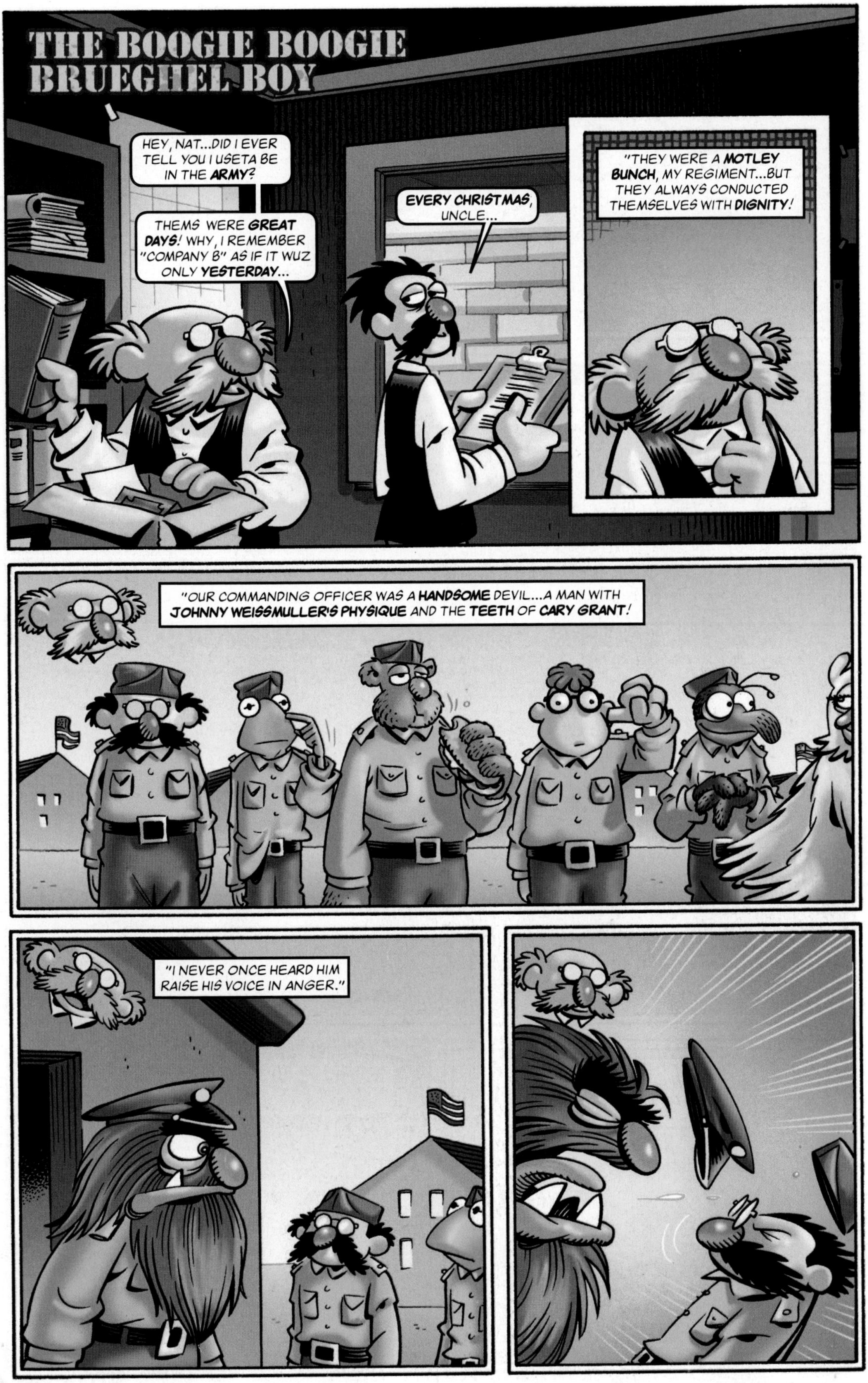
THE BOOGIE BOOGIE BRUEGHEL BOY
HEY, NAT...DID I EVER TELL YOU I USETA BE IN THE ARMY?
THEMS WERE GREAT DAYS! WHY, I REMEMBER "COMPANY B" AS IF IT WUZ ONLY YESTERDAY...
EVERY CHRISTMAS, UNCLE...
"THEY WERE A MOTLEY BUNCH, MY REGIMENT...BUT THEY ALWAYS CONDUCTED THEMSELVES WITH DIGNITY!
"OUR COMMANDING OFFICER WAS A HANDSOME DEVIL...A MAN WITH JOHNNY WEISSMULLER'S PHYSIQUE AND THE TEETH OF CARY GRANT!
"I NEVER ONCE HEARD HIM RAISE HIS VOICE IN ANGER."

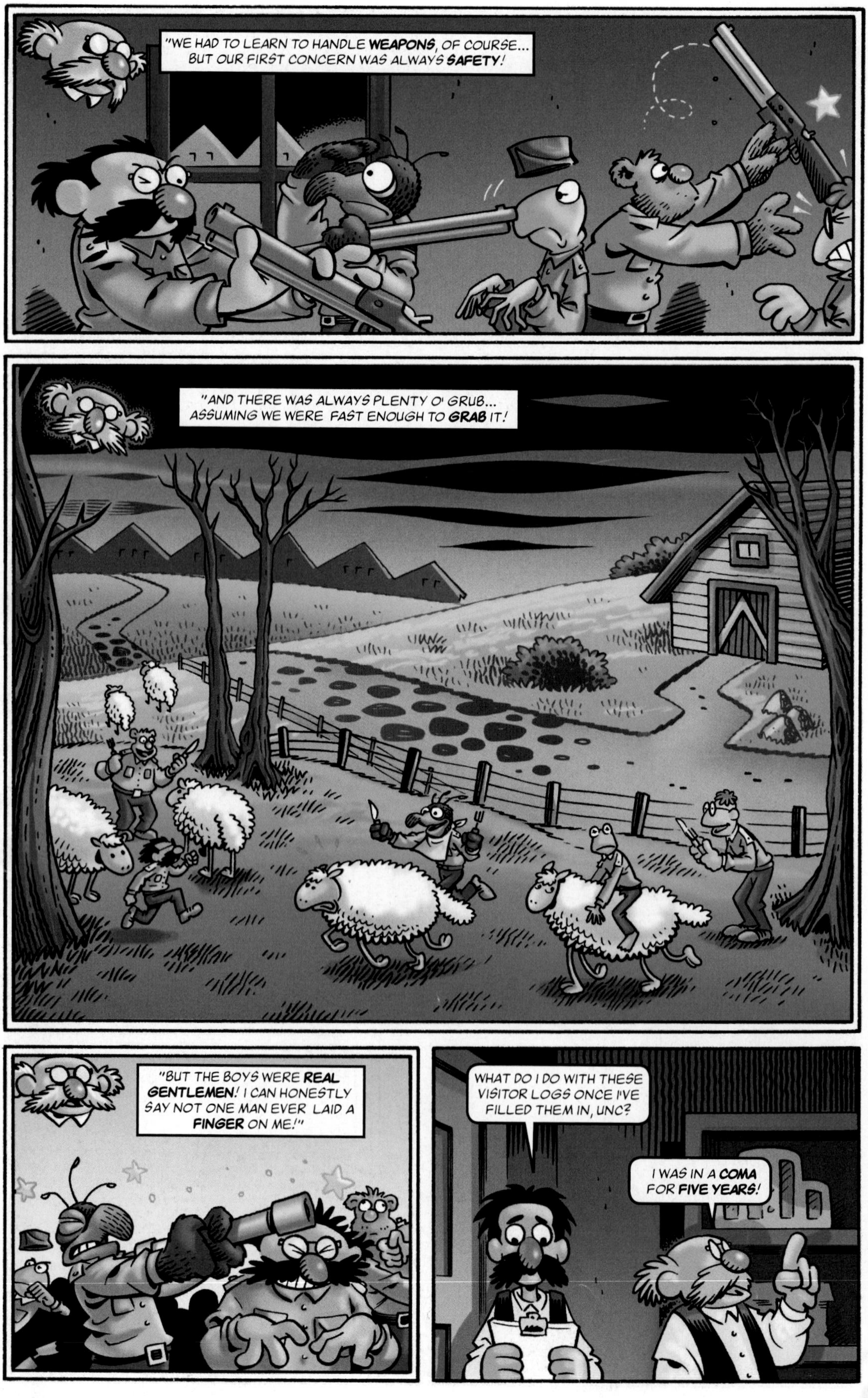
"WE HAD TO LEARN TO HANDLE WEAPONS, OF COURSE... BUT OUR FIRST CONCERN WAS ALWAYS SAFETY!
"AND THERE WAS ALWAYS PLENTY O' GRUB... ASSUMING WE WERE FAST ENOUGH TO GRAB IT!
"BUT THE BOYS WERE REAL GENTLEMEN! I CAN HONESTLY SAY NOT ONE MAN EVER LAID A FINGER ON ME!"
WHAT DO I DO WITH THESE VISITOR LOGS ONCE I'VE FILLED THEM IN, UNC?
I WAS IN A COMA FOR FIVE YEARS!

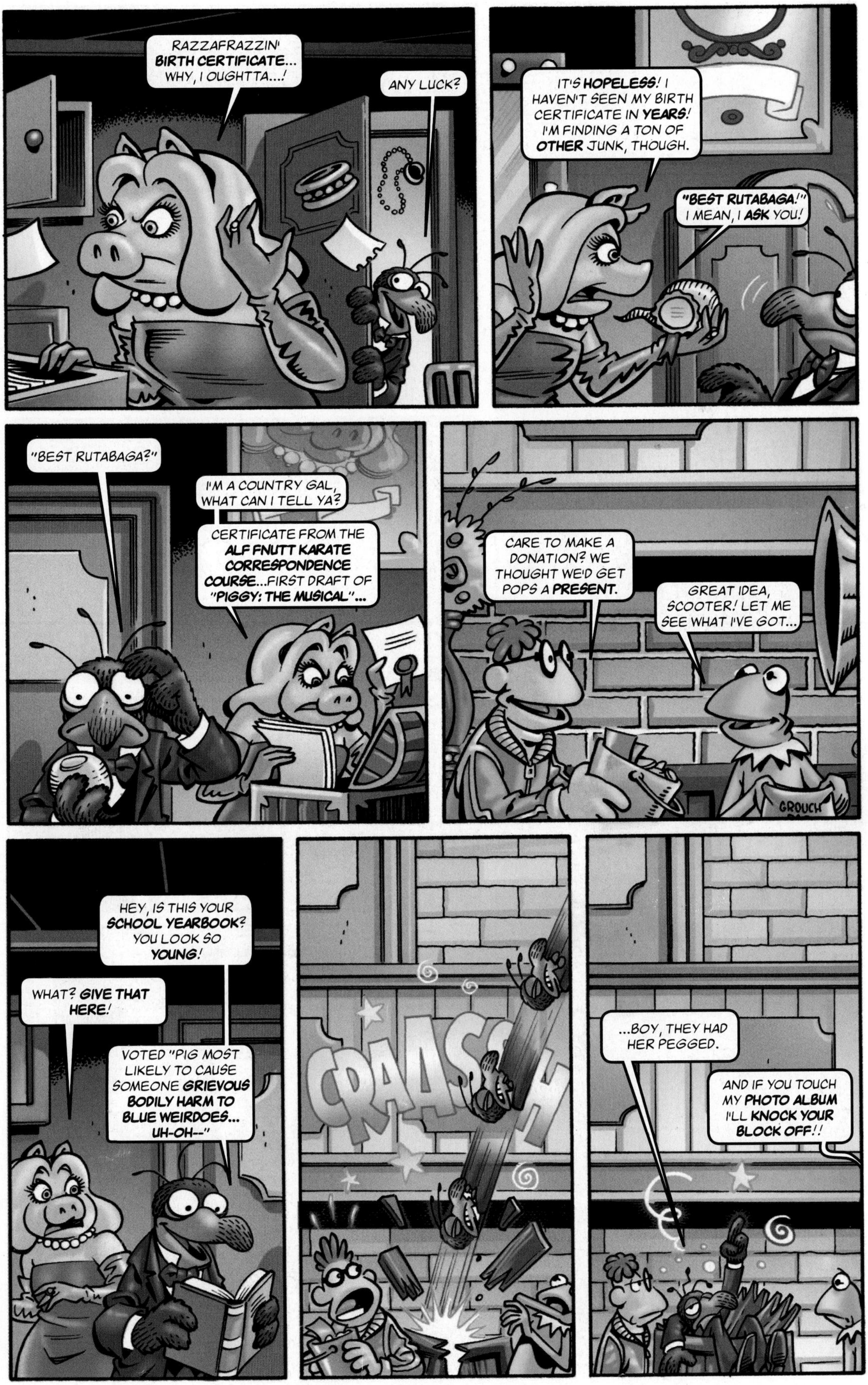
RAZZAFRAZZIN' BIRTH CERTIFICATE... WHY, I OUGHTTA...!
ANY LUCK?
IT'S HOPELESS! I HAVEN'T SEEN MY BIRTH CERTIFICATE IN YEARS! I'M FINDING A TON OF OTHER JUNK, THOUGH.
"BEST RUTABAGA!" I MEAN, I ASK YOU!
"BEST RUTABAGA?"
I'M A COUNTRY GAL, WHAT CAN I TELL YA?
CERTIFICATE FROM THE ALF FNUTT KARATE CORRESPONDENCE COURSE...FIRST DRAFT OF "PIGGY: THE MUSICAL"...
CARE TO MAKE A DONATION? WE THOUGHT WE'D GET POPS A PRESENT.
GREAT IDEA, SCOOTER! LET ME SEE WHAT I'VE GOT...
GROUCH
HEY, IS THIS YOUR SCHOOL YEARBOOK? YOU LOOK SO YOUNG!
WHAT? GIVE THAT HERE!
VOTED "PIG MOST LIKELY TO CAUSE SOMEONE GRIEVOUS BODILY HARM TO BLUE WEIRDOES... UH-OH--"
CRAASSH
...BOY, THEY HAD HER PEGGED.
AND IF YOU TOUCH MY PHOTO ALBUM I'LL KNOCK YOUR BLOCK OFF!!

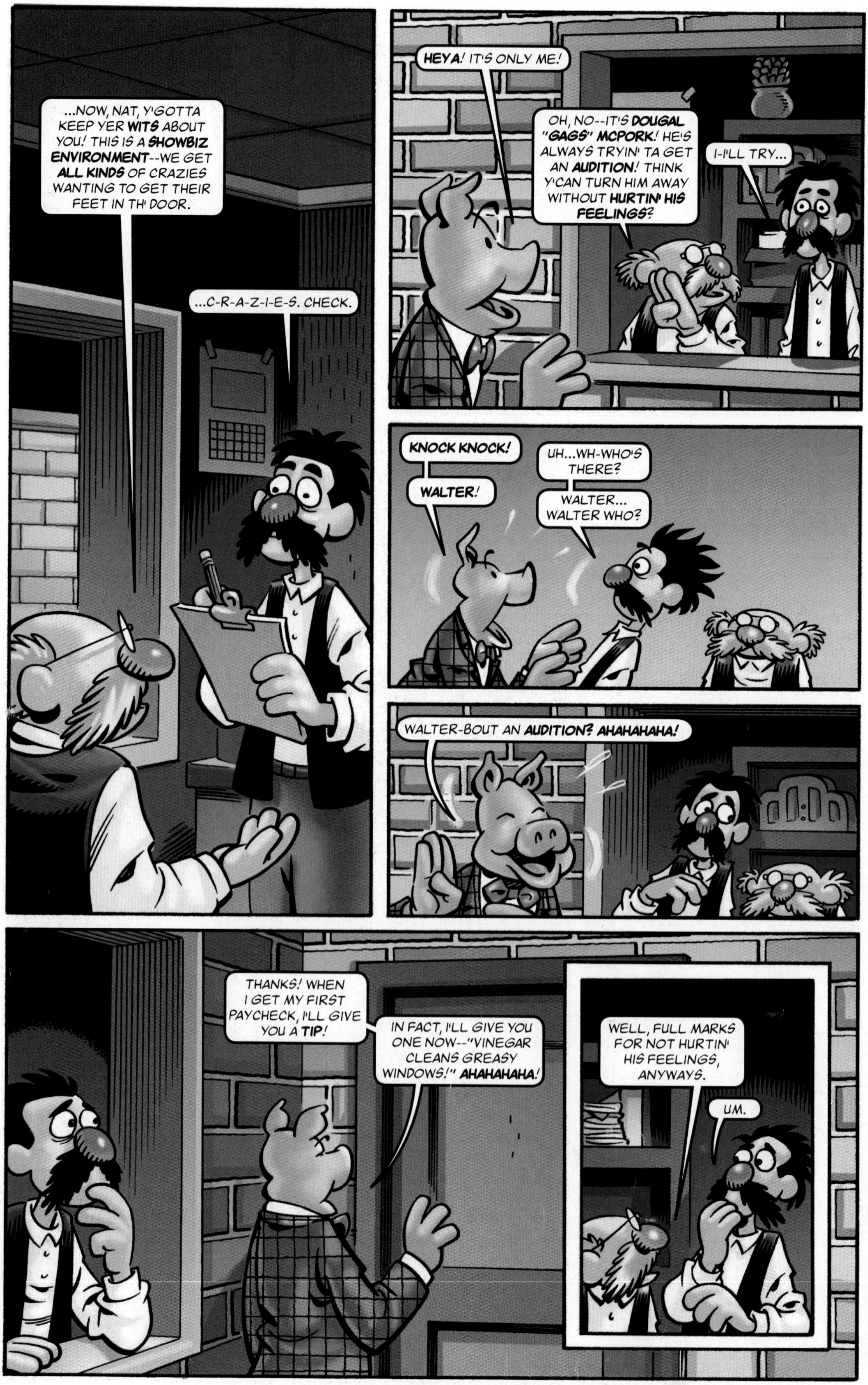
...NOW, NAT, Y'GOTTA KEEP YER WITS ABOUT YOU! THIS IS A SHOWBIZ ENVIRONMENT--WE GET ALL KINDS OF CRAZIES WANTING TO GET THEIR FEET IN TH' DOOR.
...C-R-A-Z-I-E-S. CHECK.
HEYA! IT'S ONLY ME!
OH, NO--IT'S DOUGAL "GAGS" MCPORK! HE'S ALWAYS TRYIN' TA GET AN AUDITION! THINK Y'CAN TURN HIM AWAY WITHOUT HURTIN' HIS FEELINGS?
I-I'LL TRY...
KNOCK KNOCK!
UH...WH-WHO'S THERE?
WALTER!
WALTER... WALTER WHO?
WALTER-BOUT AN AUDITION? AHAHAHAHA!
THANKS! WHEN I GET MY FIRST PAYCHECK, I'LL GIVE YOU A TIP!
IN FACT, I'LL GIVE YOU ONE NOW--"VINEGAR CLEANS GREASY WINDOWS!" AHAHAHAHA!
WELL, FULL MARKS FOR NOT HURTIN' HIS FEELINGS, ANYWAYS.
UM.

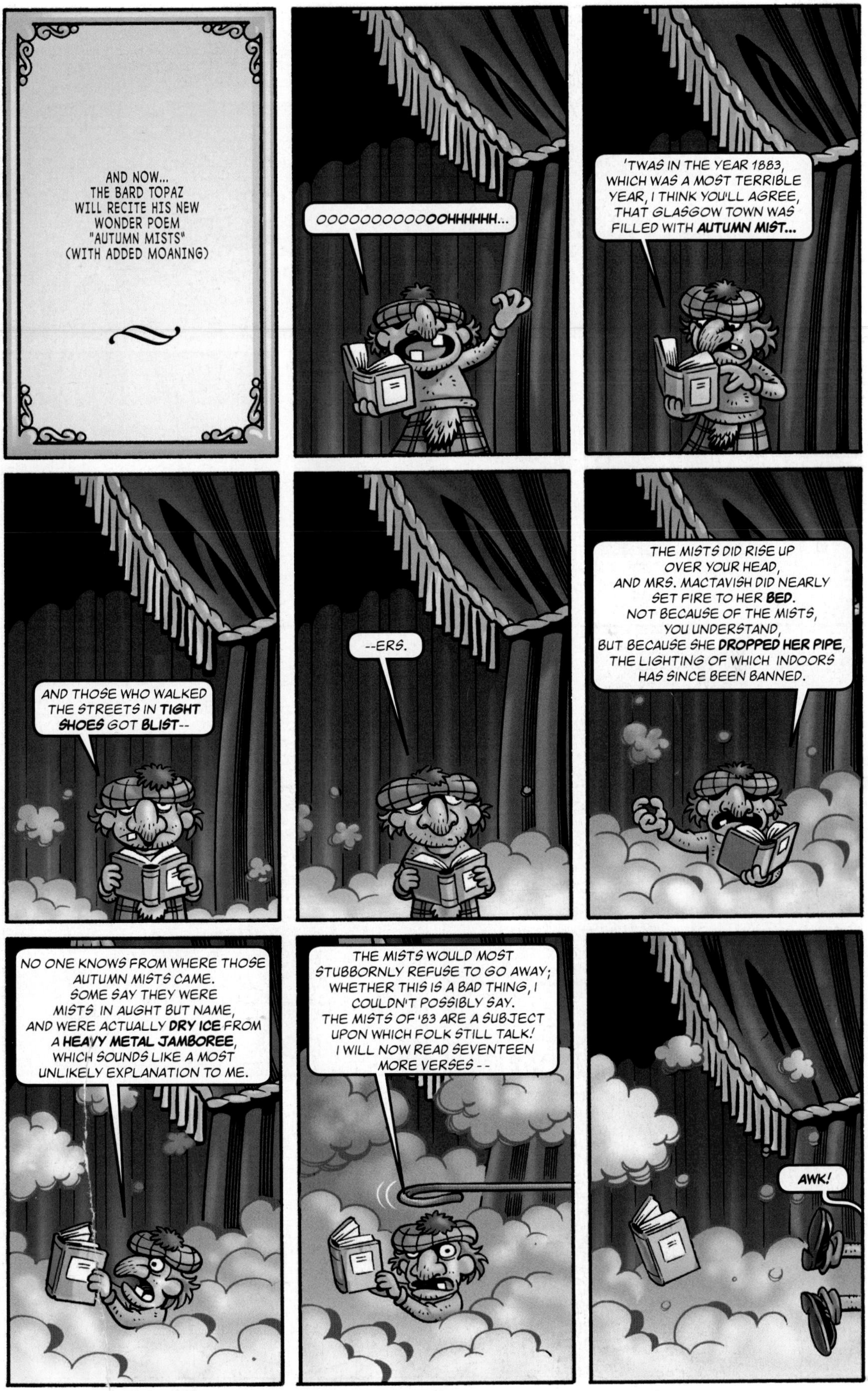
AND NOW...
THE BARD TOPAZ
WILL RECITE HIS NEW
WONDER POEM
"AUTUMN MISTS"
(WITH ADDED MOANING)
OOOOOOOOOOOHHHHHH...
'TWAS IN THE YEAR 1883,
WHICH WAS A MOST TERRIBLE
YEAR, I THINK YOU'LL AGREE,
THAT GLASGOW TOWN WAS
FILLED WITH AUTUMN MIST...
AND THOSE WHO WALKED
THE STREETS IN TIGHT
SHOES GOT BLIST--
--ERS.
THE MISTS DID RISE UP
OVER YOUR HEAD,
AND MRS. MACTAVISH DID NEARLY
SET FIRE TO HER BED.
NOT BECAUSE OF THE MISTS,
YOU UNDERSTAND,
BUT BECAUSE SHE DROPPED HER PIPE,
THE LIGHTING OF WHICH INDOORS
HAS SINCE BEEN BANNED.
NO ONE KNOWS FROM WHERE THOSE
AUTUMN MISTS CAME.
SOME SAY THEY WERE
MISTS IN AUGHT BUT NAME,
AND WERE ACTUALLY DRY ICE FROM
A HEAVY METAL JAMBOREE,
WHICH SOUNDS LIKE A MOST
UNLIKELY EXPLANATION TO ME.
THE MISTS WOULD MOST
STUBBORNLY REFUSE TO GO AWAY;
WHETHER THIS IS A BAD THING, I
COULDN'T POSSIBLY SAY.
THE MISTS OF '83 ARE A SUBJECT
UPON WHICH FOLK STILL TALK!
I WILL NOW READ SEVENTEEN
MORE VERSES --
AWK!

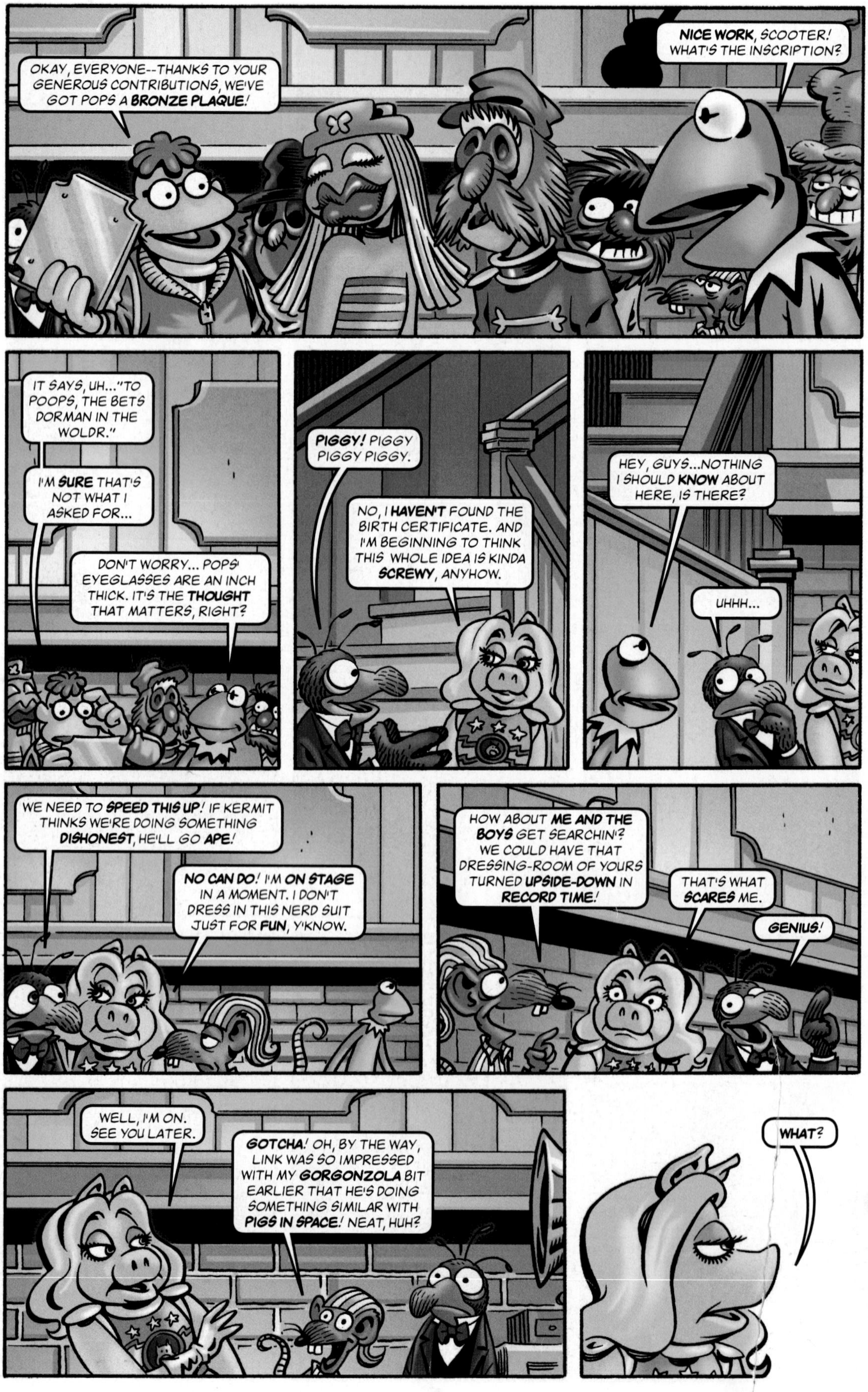
OKAY, EVERYONE--THANKS TO YOUR GENEROUS CONTRIBUTIONS, WE'VE GOT POPS A BRONZE PLAQUE!
NICE WORK, SCOOTER! WHAT'S THE INSCRIPTION?
IT SAYS, UH..."TO POOPS, THE BETS DORMAN IN THE WOLDR."
I'M SURE THAT'S NOT WHAT I ASKED FOR...
DON'T WORRY... POPS' EYEGLASSES ARE AN INCH THICK. IT'S THE THOUGHT THAT MATTERS, RIGHT?
PIGGY! PIGGY PIGGY PIGGY.
NO, I HAVEN'T FOUND THE BIRTH CERTIFICATE. AND I'M BEGINNING TO THINK THIS WHOLE IDEA IS KINDA SCREWY, ANYHOW.
HEY, GUYS...NOTHING I SHOULD KNOW ABOUT HERE, IS THERE?
UHHH...
WE NEED TO SPEED THIS UP! IF KERMIT THINKS WE'RE DOING SOMETHING DISHONEST, HE'LL GO APE!
NO CAN DO! I'M ON STAGE IN A MOMENT. I DON'T DRESS IN THIS NERD SUIT JUST FOR FUN, Y'KNOW.
HOW ABOUT ME AND THE BOYS GET SEARCHIN'? WE COULD HAVE THAT DRESSING-ROOM OF YOURS TURNED UPSIDE-DOWN IN RECORD TIME!
THAT'S WHAT SCARES ME.
GENIUS!
WELL, I'M ON. SEE YOU LATER.
GOTCHA! OH, BY THE WAY, LINK WAS SO IMPRESSED WITH MY GORGONZOLA BIT EARLIER THAT HE'S DOING SOMETHING SIMILAR WITH PIGS IN SPACE! NEAT, HUH?
WHAT?

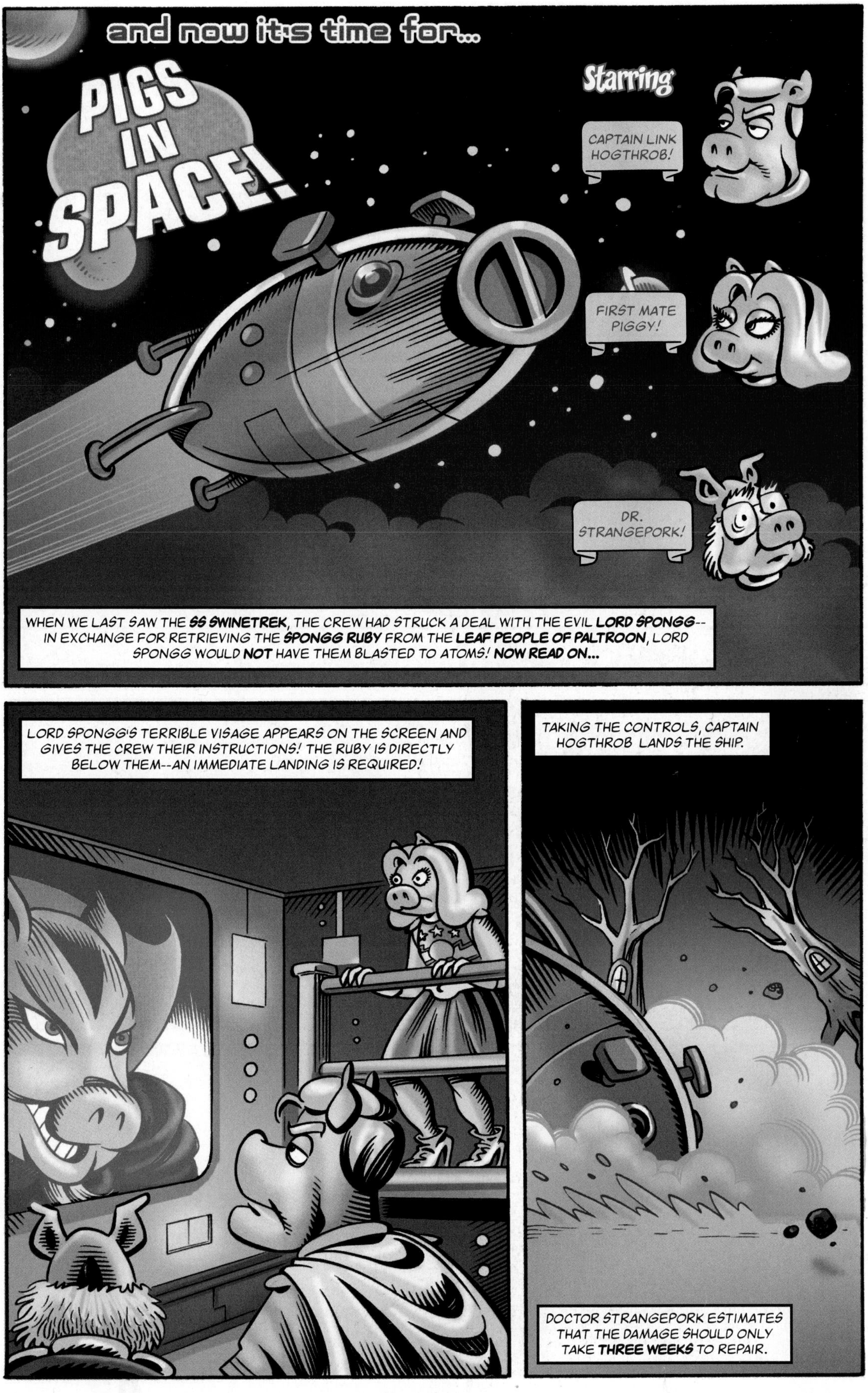

and now it's time for...
PIGS IN SPACE!
Starring
CAPTAIN LINK HOGTHROB!
FIRST MATE PIGGY!
DR. STRANGEPORK!
WHEN WE LAST SAW THE SS SWINETREK, THE CREW HAD STRUCK A DEAL WITH THE EVIL LORD SPONGG-- IN EXCHANGE FOR RETRIEVING THE SPONGG RUBY FROM THE LEAF PEOPLE OF PALTROON, LORD SPONGG WOULD NOT HAVE THEM BLASTED TO ATOMS! NOW READ ON...
LORD SPONGG'S TERRIBLE VISAGE APPEARS ON THE SCREEN AND GIVES THE CREW THEIR INSTRUCTIONS! THE RUBY IS DIRECTLY BELOW THEM--AN IMMEDIATE LANDING IS REQUIRED!
TAKING THE CONTROLS, CAPTAIN HOGTHROB LANDS THE SHIP.
DOCTOR STRANGEPORK ESTIMATES THAT THE DAMAGE SHOULD ONLY TAKE THREE WEEKS TO REPAIR.

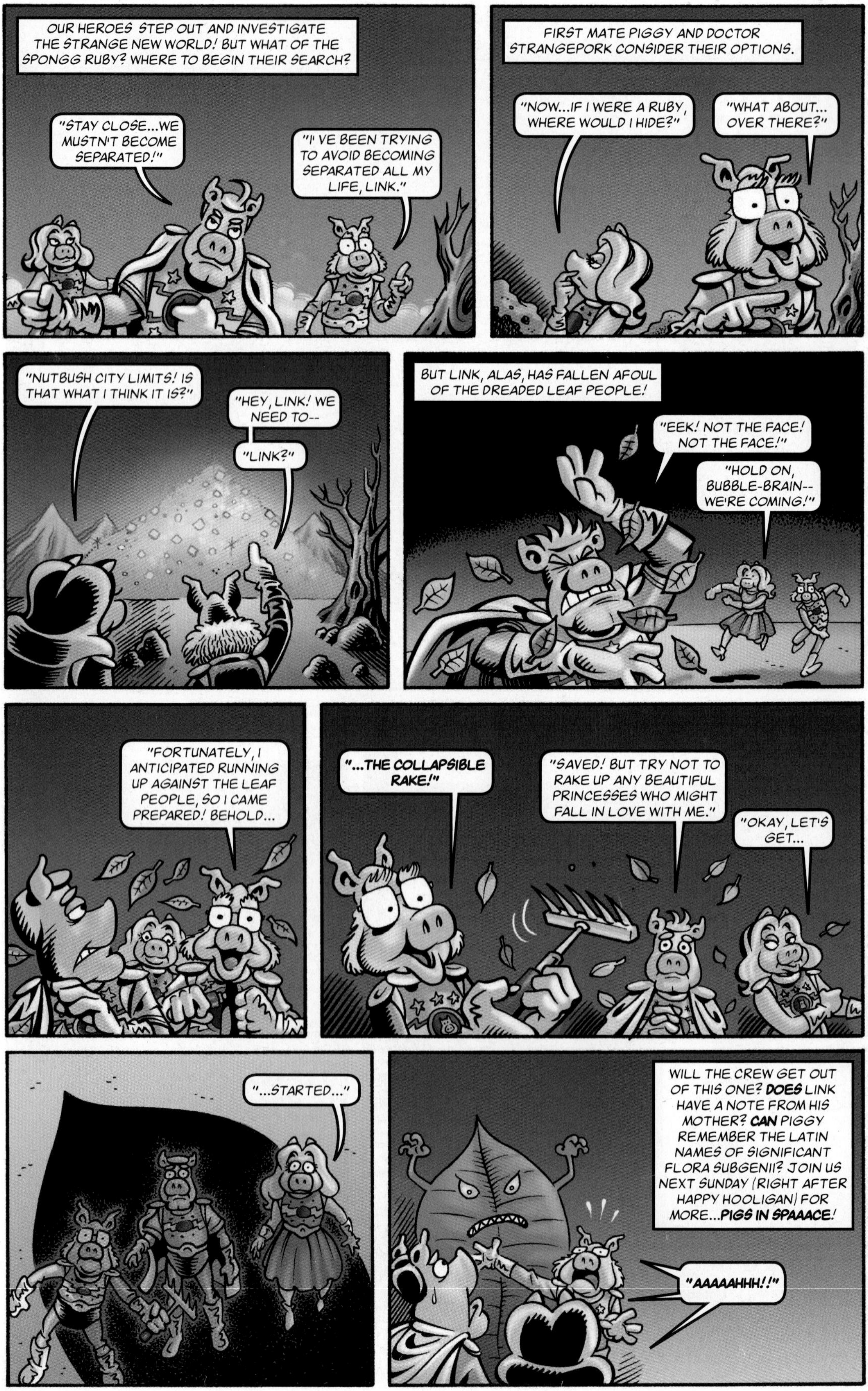
OUR HEROES STEP OUT AND INVESTIGATE THE STRANGE NEW WORLD! BUT WHAT OF THE SPONGG RUBY? WHERE TO BEGIN THEIR SEARCH?
"STAY CLOSE...WE MUSTN'T BECOME SEPARATED!"
"I'VE BEEN TRYING TO AVOID BECOMING SEPARATED ALL MY LIFE, LINK."
FIRST MATE PIGGY AND DOCTOR STRANGEPORK CONSIDER THEIR OPTIONS.
"NOW...IF I WERE A RUBY, WHERE WOULD I HIDE?"
"WHAT ABOUT... OVER THERE?"
"NUTBUSH CITY LIMITS! IS THAT WHAT I THINK IT IS?"
"HEY, LINK! WE NEED TO--
"LINK?"
BUT LINK, ALAS, HAS FALLEN AFOUL OF THE DREADED LEAF PEOPLE!
"EEK! NOT THE FACE! NOT THE FACE!"
"HOLD ON, BUBBLE-BRAIN-- WE'RE COMING!"
"FORTUNATELY, I ANTICIPATED RUNNING UP AGAINST THE LEAF PEOPLE, SO I CAME PREPARED! BEHOLD...
"...THE COLLAPSIBLE RAKE!"
"SAVED! BUT TRY NOT TO RAKE UP ANY BEAUTIFUL PRINCESSES WHO MIGHT FALL IN LOVE WITH ME."
"OKAY, LET'S GET...
"...STARTED..."
WILL THE CREW GET OUT OF THIS ONE? DOES LINK HAVE A NOTE FROM HIS MOTHER? CAN PIGGY REMEMBER THE LATIN NAMES OF SIGNIFICANT FLORA SUBGENII? JOIN US NEXT SUNDAY (RIGHT AFTER HAPPY HOOLIGAN) FOR MORE...PIGS IN SPAAACE!
"AAAAAHHH!!"

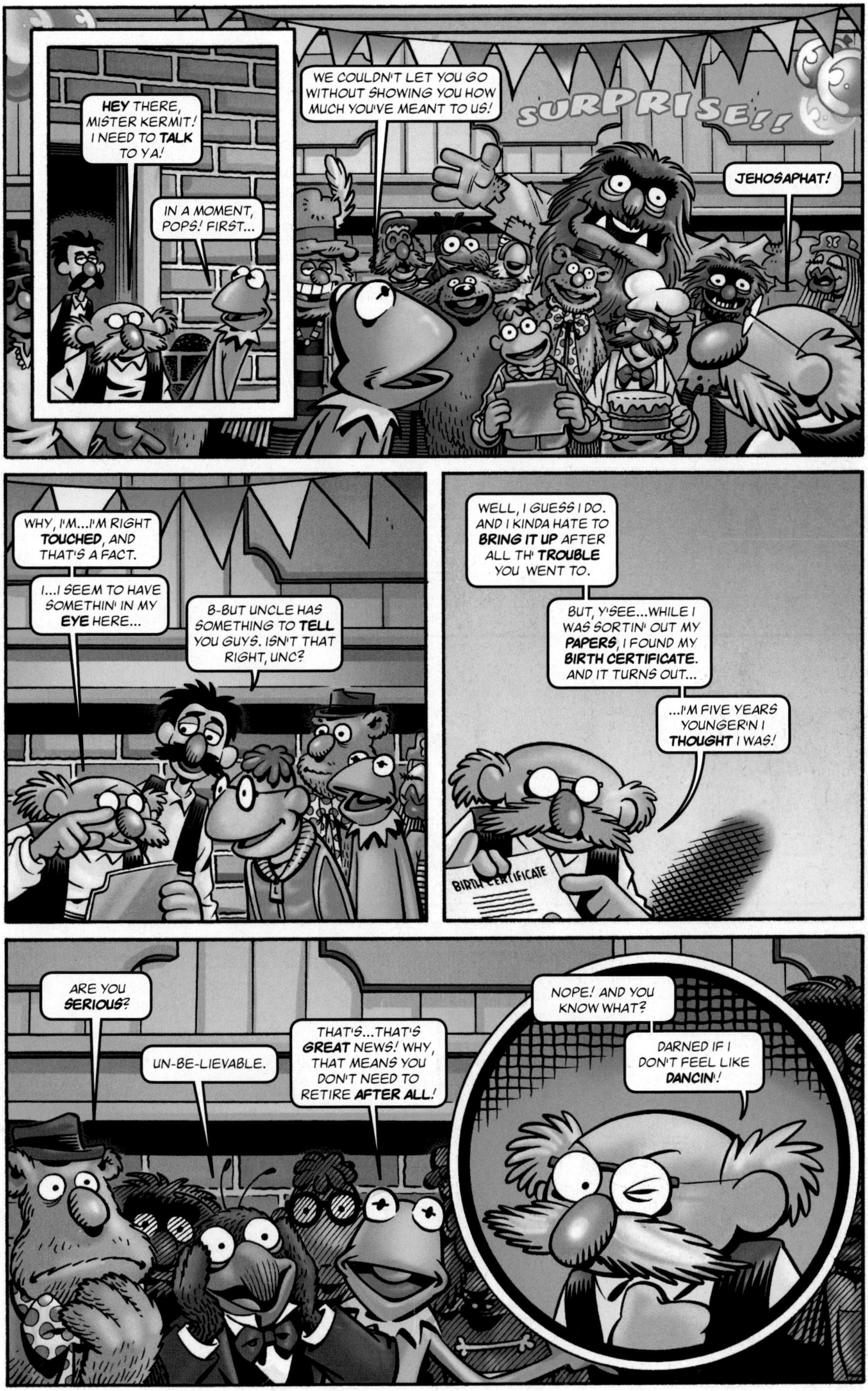
HEY THERE, MISTER KERMIT! I NEED TO TALK TO YA!
IN A MOMENT, POPS! FIRST...
WE COULDN'T LET YOU GO WITHOUT SHOWING YOU HOW MUCH YOU'VE MEANT TO US!
SURPRISE!!
JEHOSAPHAT!
WHY, I'M...I'M RIGHT TOUCHED, AND THAT'S A FACT.
I...I SEEM TO HAVE SOMETHIN' IN MY EYE HERE...
B-BUT UNCLE HAS SOMETHING TO TELL YOU GUYS. ISN'T THAT RIGHT, UNC?
WELL, I GUESS I DO. AND I KINDA HATE TO BRING IT UP AFTER ALL TH' TROUBLE YOU WENT TO.
BUT, Y'SEE...WHILE I WAS SORTIN' OUT MY PAPERS, I FOUND MY BIRTH CERTIFICATE. AND IT TURNS OUT...
...I'M FIVE YEARS YOUNGER'N I THOUGHT I WAS!
BIRTH CERTIFICATE
ARE YOU SERIOUS?
UN-BE-LIEVABLE.
THAT'S...THAT'S GREAT NEWS! WHY, THAT MEANS YOU DON'T NEED TO RETIRE AFTER ALL!
NOPE! AND YOU KNOW WHAT?
DARNED IF I DON'T FEEL LIKE DANCIN'!

AUTUMN SHMAUTUMN

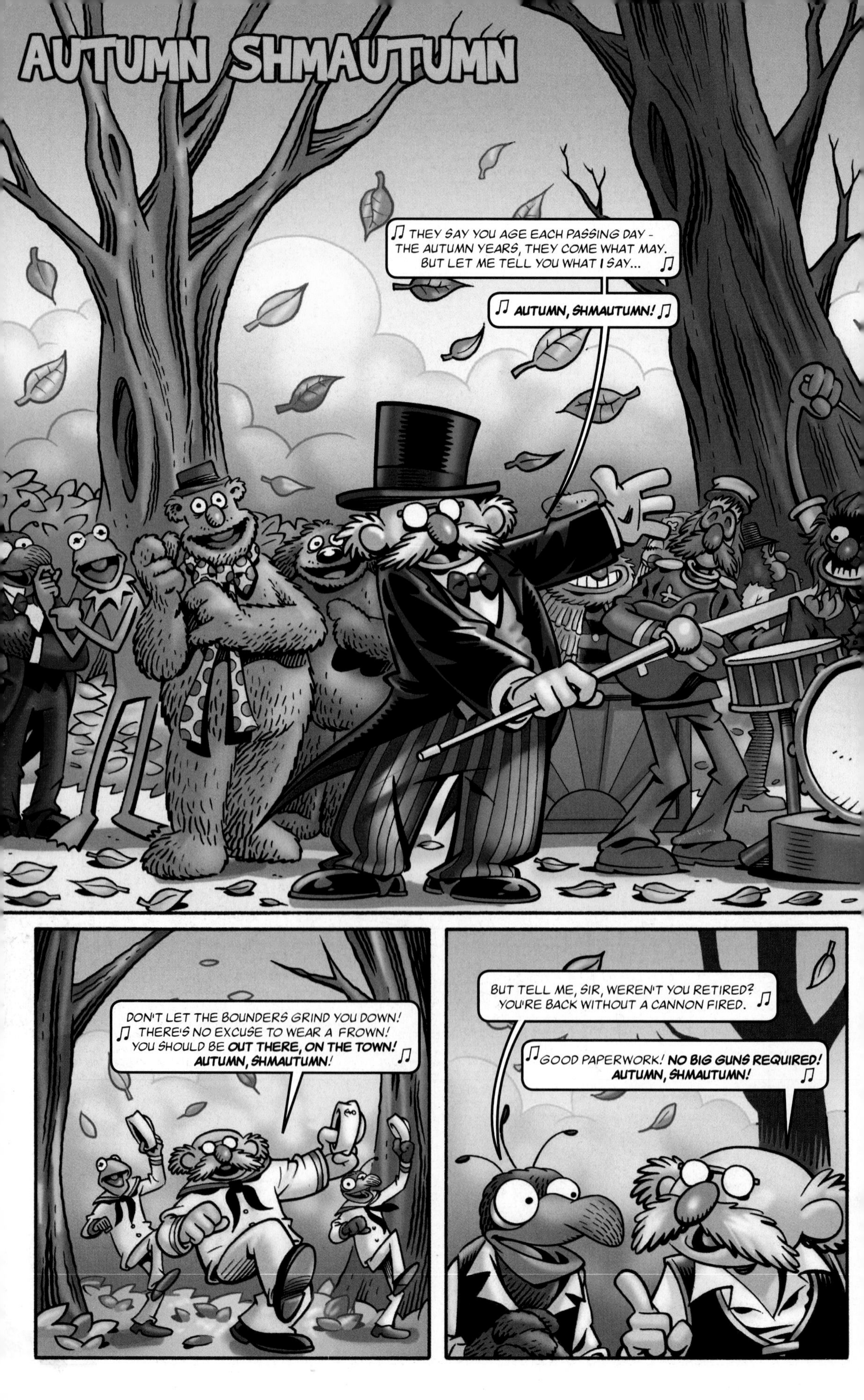
THEY SAY YOU AGE EACH PASSING DAY - THE AUTUMN YEARS, THEY COME WHAT MAY. BUT LET ME TELL YOU WHAT I SAY...
AUTUMN, SHMAUTUMN!
DON'T LET THE BOUNDERS GRIND YOU DOWN! THERE'S NO EXCUSE TO WEAR A FROWN! YOU SHOULD BE OUT THERE, ON THE TOWN! AUTUMN, SHMAUTUMN!
BUT TELL ME, SIR, WEREN'T YOU RETIRED? YOU'RE BACK WITHOUT A CANNON FIRED.
GOOD PAPERWORK! NO BIG GUNS REQUIRED! AUTUMN, SHMAUTUMN!

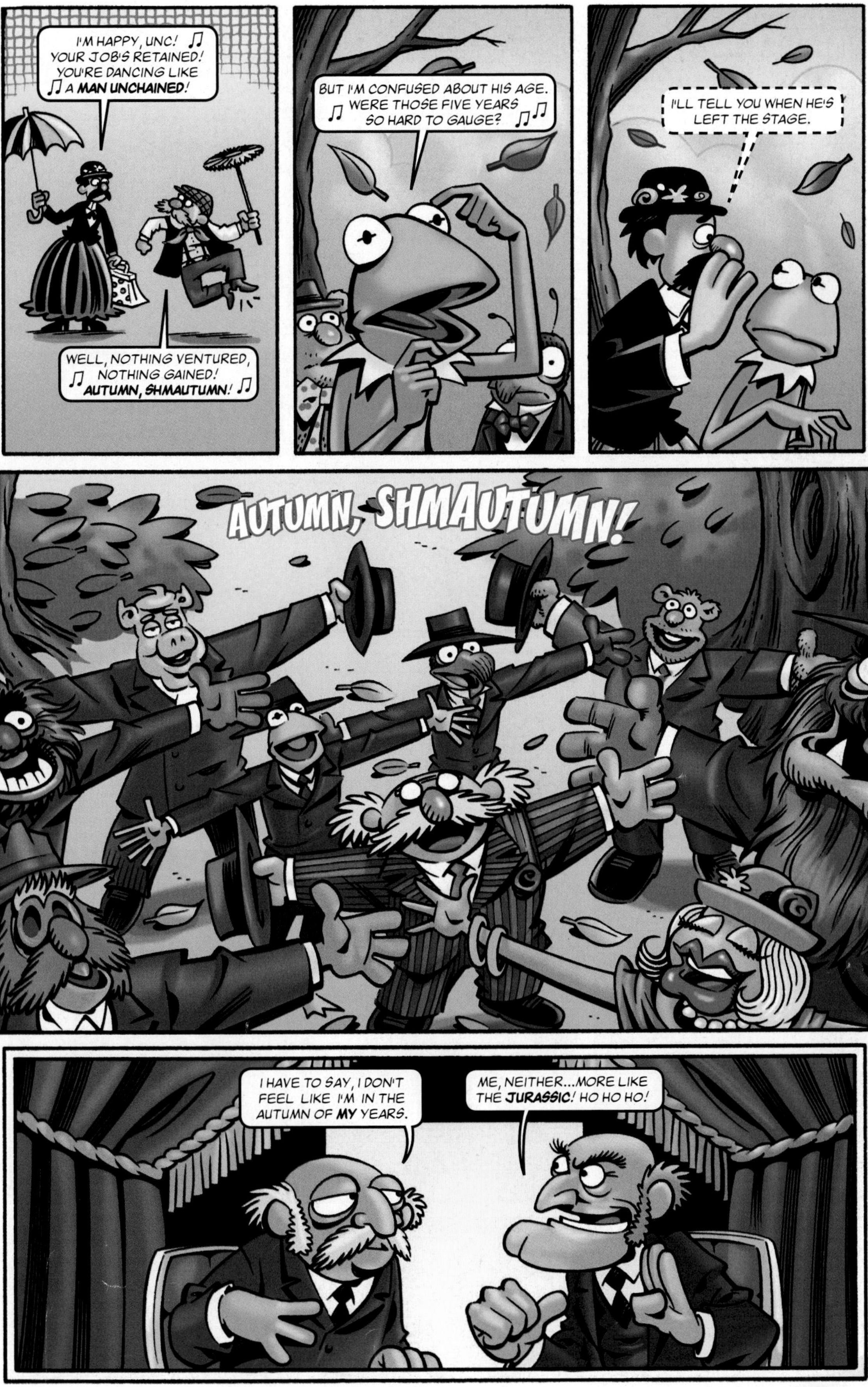
I'M HAPPY, UNC! ♫ YOUR JOB'S RETAINED! YOU'RE DANCING LIKE ♫ A **MAN UNCHAINED**!
WELL, NOTHING VENTURED, ♫ NOTHING GAINED! **AUTUMN, SHMAUTUMN**! ♫
BUT I'M CONFUSED ABOUT HIS AGE. ♫ WERE THOSE FIVE YEARS SO HARD TO GAUGE? ♫♫
I'LL TELL YOU WHEN HE'S LEFT THE STAGE.
AUTUMN, SHMAUTUMN!
I HAVE TO SAY, I DON'T FEEL LIKE I'M IN THE AUTUMN OF **MY** YEARS.
ME, NEITHER...MORE LIKE THE **JURASSIC**! HO HO HO!

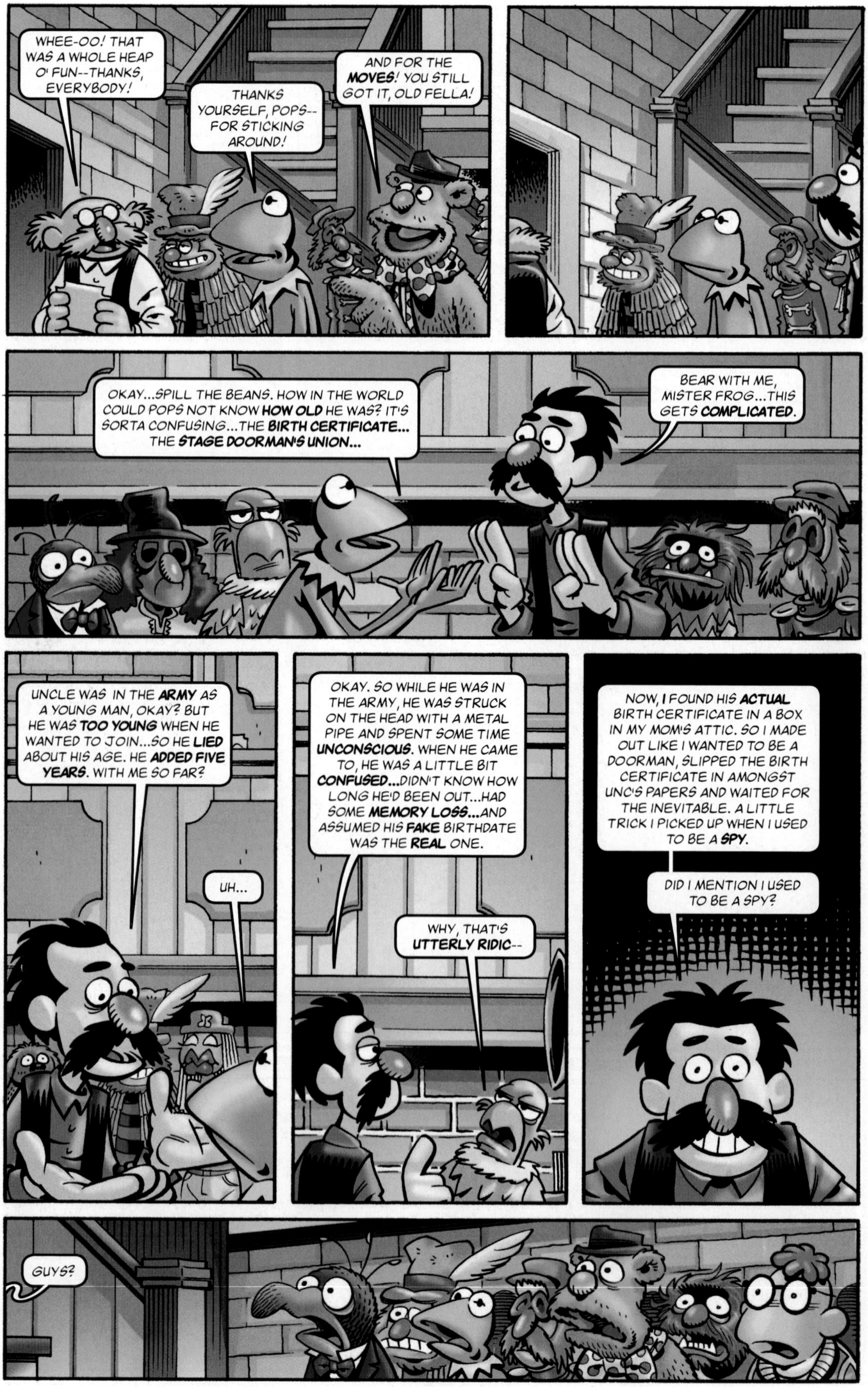
WHEE-OO! THAT WAS A WHOLE HEAP O' FUN--THANKS, EVERYBODY!
THANKS YOURSELF, POPS--FOR STICKING AROUND!
AND FOR THE MOVES! YOU STILL GOT IT, OLD FELLA!
OKAY...SPILL THE BEANS. HOW IN THE WORLD COULD POPS NOT KNOW HOW OLD HE WAS? IT'S SORTA CONFUSING...THE BIRTH CERTIFICATE... THE STAGE DOORMAN'S UNION...
BEAR WITH ME, MISTER FROG...THIS GETS COMPLICATED.
UNCLE WAS IN THE ARMY AS A YOUNG MAN, OKAY? BUT HE WAS TOO YOUNG WHEN HE WANTED TO JOIN...SO HE LIED ABOUT HIS AGE. HE ADDED FIVE YEARS. WITH ME SO FAR?
UH...
OKAY. SO WHILE HE WAS IN THE ARMY, HE WAS STRUCK ON THE HEAD WITH A METAL PIPE AND SPENT SOME TIME UNCONSCIOUS. WHEN HE CAME TO, HE WAS A LITTLE BIT CONFUSED...DIDN'T KNOW HOW LONG HE'D BEEN OUT...HAD SOME MEMORY LOSS...AND ASSUMED HIS FAKE BIRTHDATE WAS THE REAL ONE.
WHY, THAT'S UTTERLY RIDIC--
NOW, I FOUND HIS ACTUAL BIRTH CERTIFICATE IN A BOX IN MY MOM'S ATTIC. SO I MADE OUT LIKE I WANTED TO BE A DOORMAN, SLIPPED THE BIRTH CERTIFICATE IN AMONGST UNC'S PAPERS AND WAITED FOR THE INEVITABLE. A LITTLE TRICK I PICKED UP WHEN I USED TO BE A SPY.
DID I MENTION I USED TO BE A SPY?
GUYS?

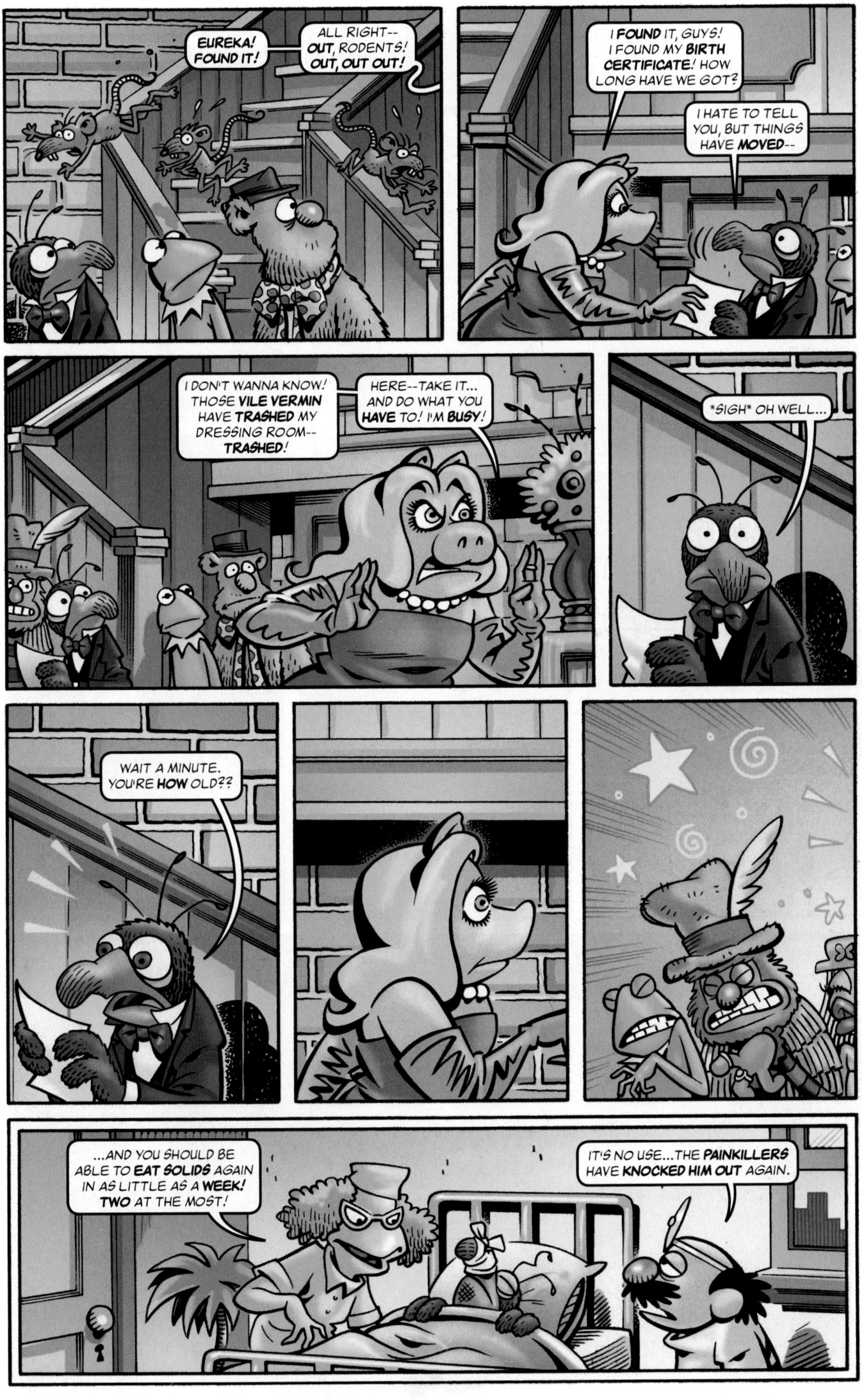
EUREKA! FOUND IT!
ALL RIGHT-- OUT, RODENTS! OUT, OUT OUT!
I FOUND IT, GUYS! I FOUND MY BIRTH CERTIFICATE! HOW LONG HAVE WE GOT?
I HATE TO TELL YOU, BUT THINGS HAVE MOVED--
I DON'T WANNA KNOW! THOSE VILE VERMIN HAVE TRASHED MY DRESSING ROOM-- TRASHED!
HERE--TAKE IT... AND DO WHAT YOU HAVE TO! I'M BUSY!
SIGH OH WELL...
WAIT A MINUTE. YOU'RE HOW OLD??
...AND YOU SHOULD BE ABLE TO EAT SOLIDS AGAIN IN AS LITTLE AS A WEEK! TWO AT THE MOST!
IT'S NO USE...THE PAINKILLERS HAVE KNOCKED HIM OUT AGAIN.

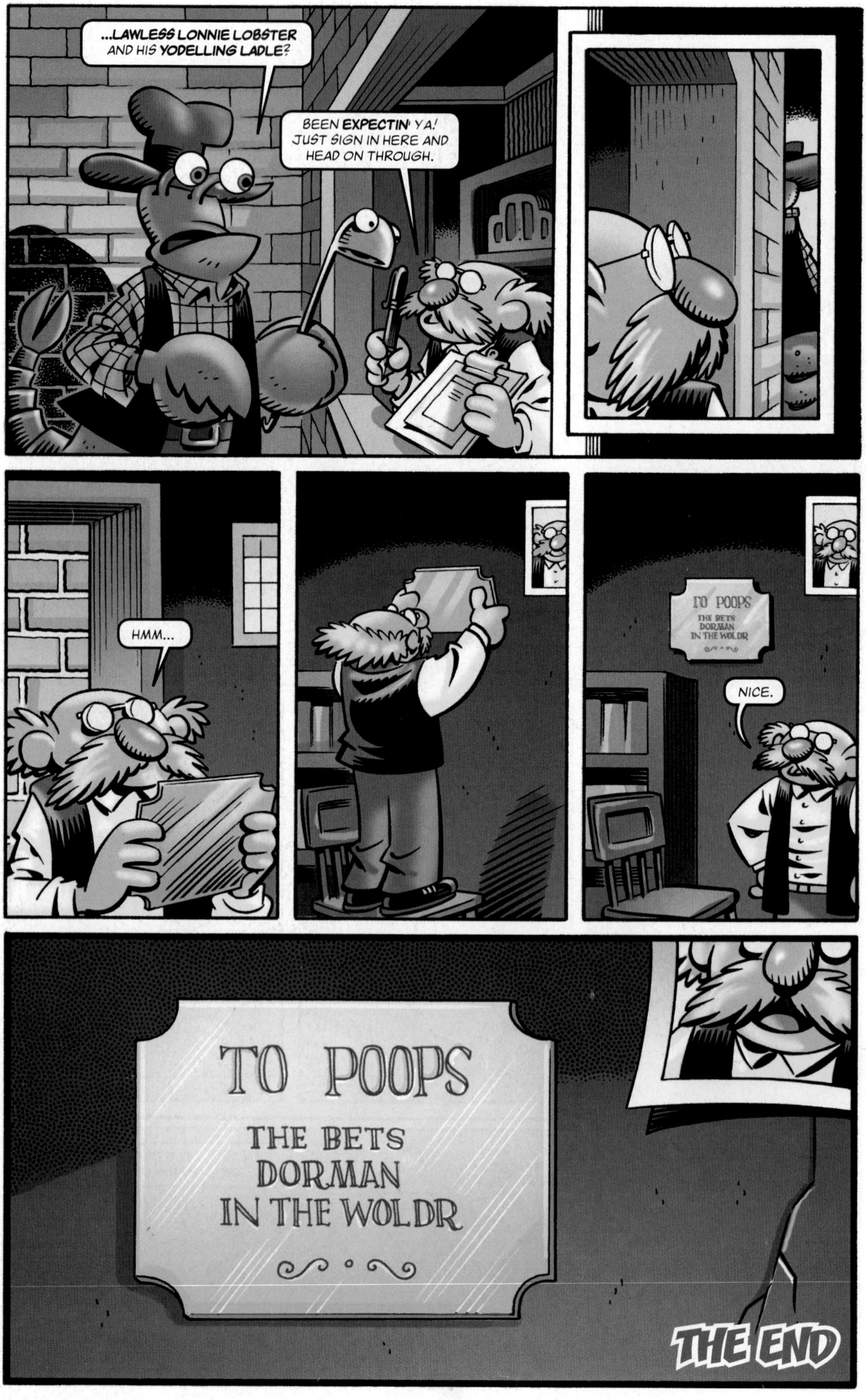
...LAWLESS LONNIE LOBSTER AND HIS YODELLING LADLE?
BEEN EXPECTIN' YA! JUST SIGN IN HERE AND HEAD ON THROUGH.
HMM...
TO POOPS THE BETS DORMAN IN THE WOLDR
NICE.
TO POOPS
THE BETS
DORMAN
IN THE WOLDR
THE END

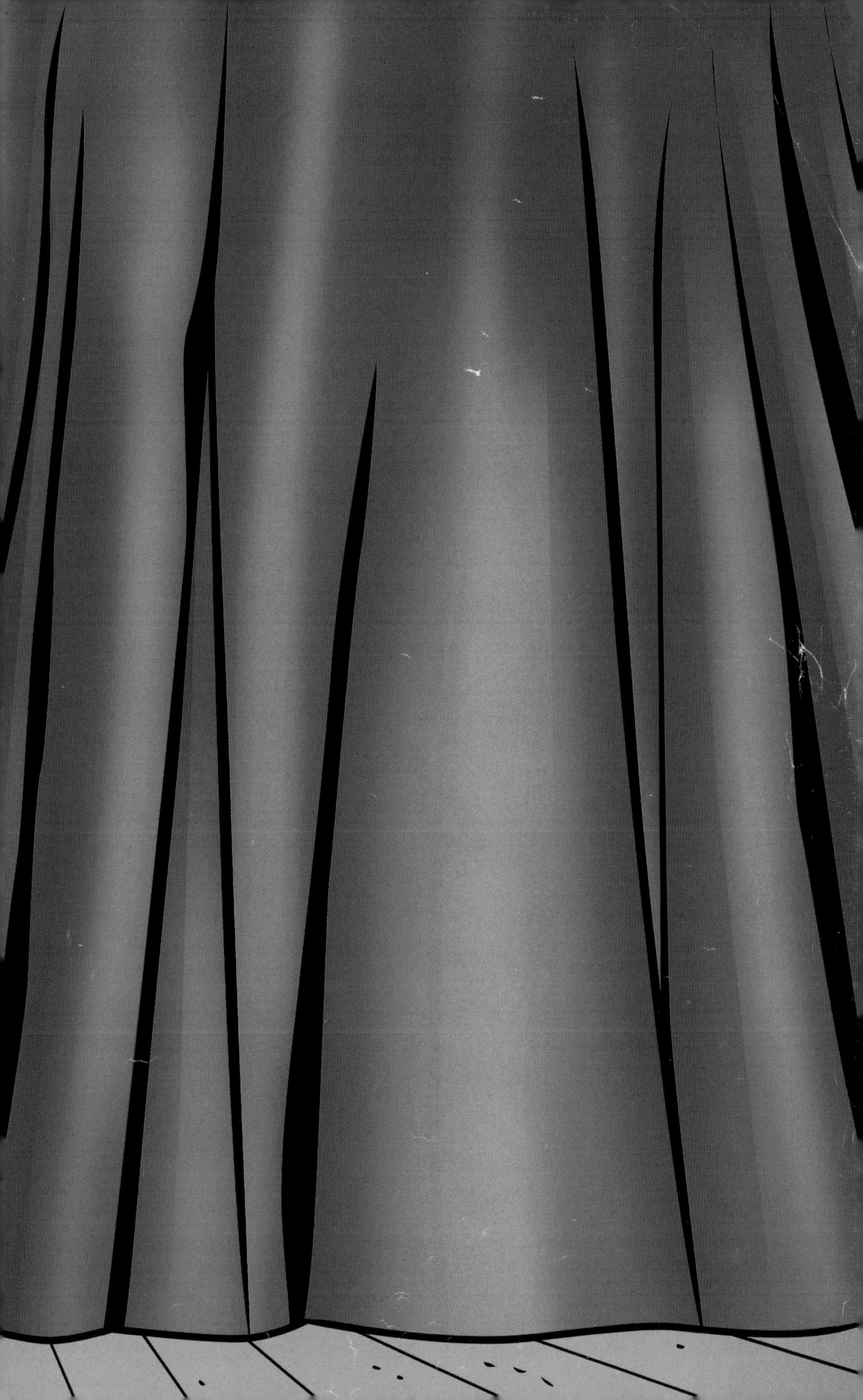

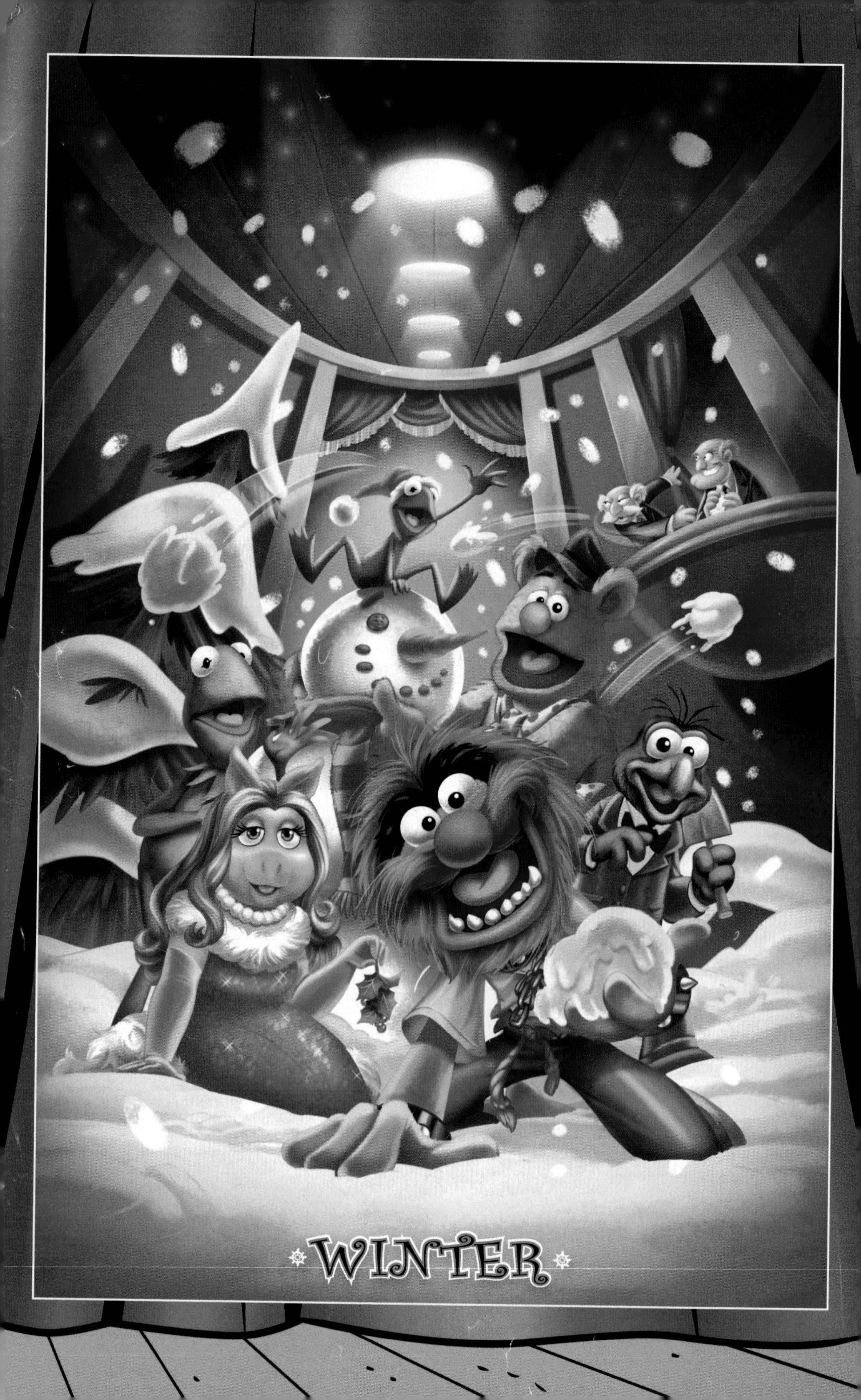
WINTER

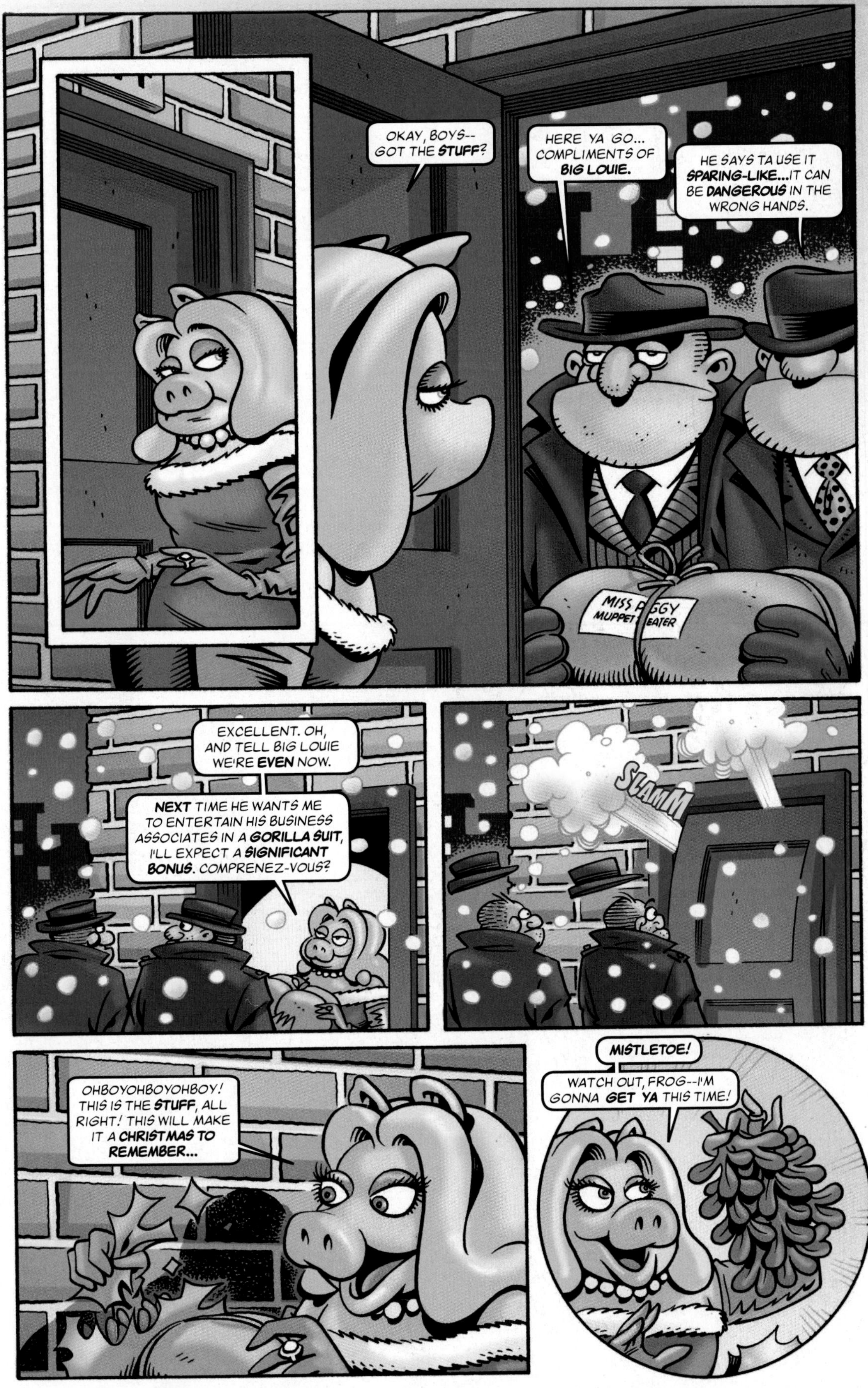

OKAY, BOYS-- GOT THE STUFF?
HERE YA GO... COMPLIMENTS OF BIG LOUIE.
HE SAYS TA USE IT SPARING-LIKE... IT CAN BE DANGEROUS IN THE WRONG HANDS.
EXCELLENT. OH, AND TELL BIG LOUIE WE'RE EVEN NOW.
NEXT TIME HE WANTS ME TO ENTERTAIN HIS BUSINESS ASSOCIATES IN A GORILLA SUIT, I'LL EXPECT A SIGNIFICANT BONUS. COMPRENEZ-VOUS?
SLAMM
OHBOYOHBOYOHBOY! THIS IS THE STUFF, ALL RIGHT! THIS WILL MAKE IT A CHRISTMAS TO REMEMBER...
MISTLETOE!
WATCH OUT, FROG--I'M GONNA GET YA THIS TIME!

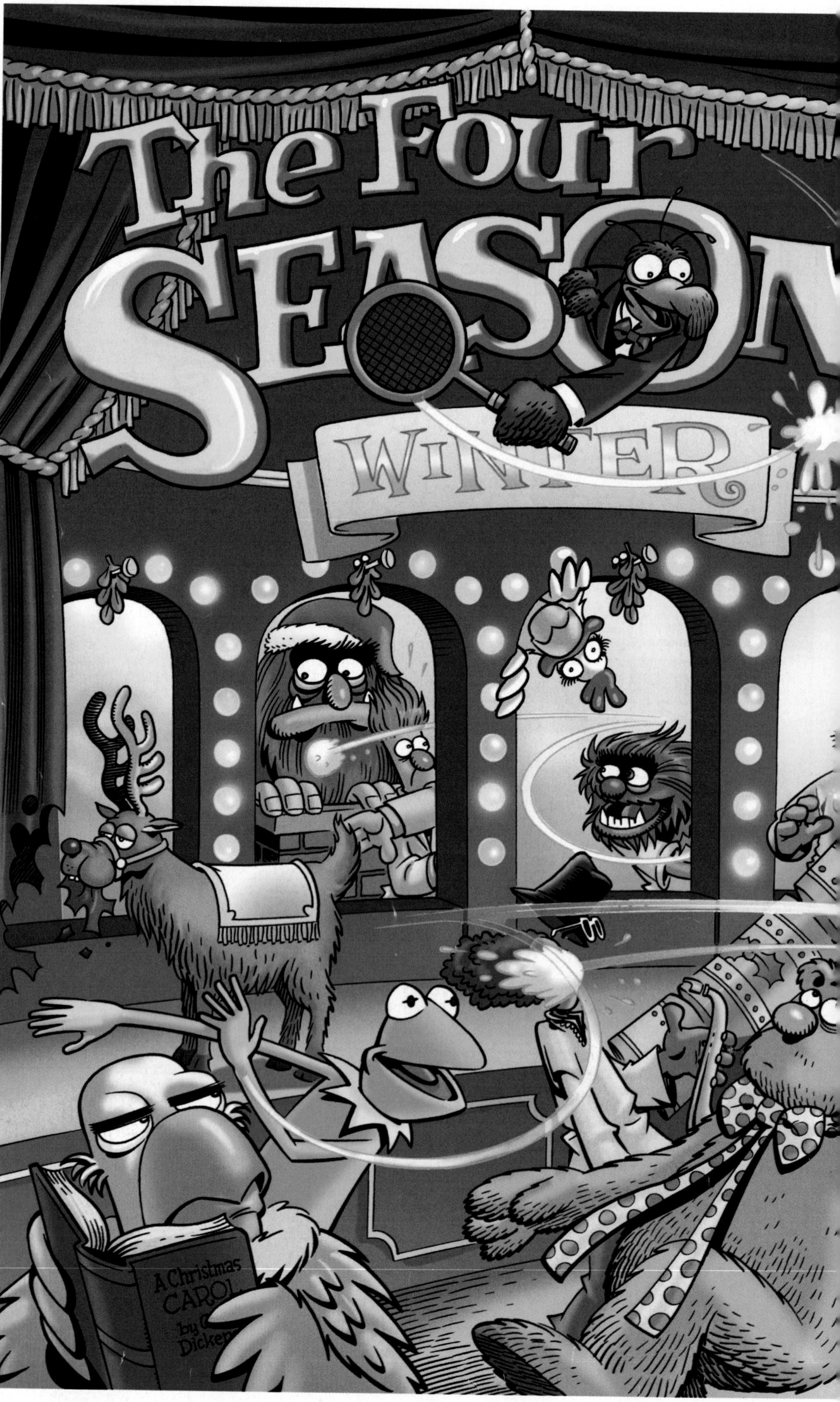

The Four
SEASO
WINTER
A Christmas
CAROL

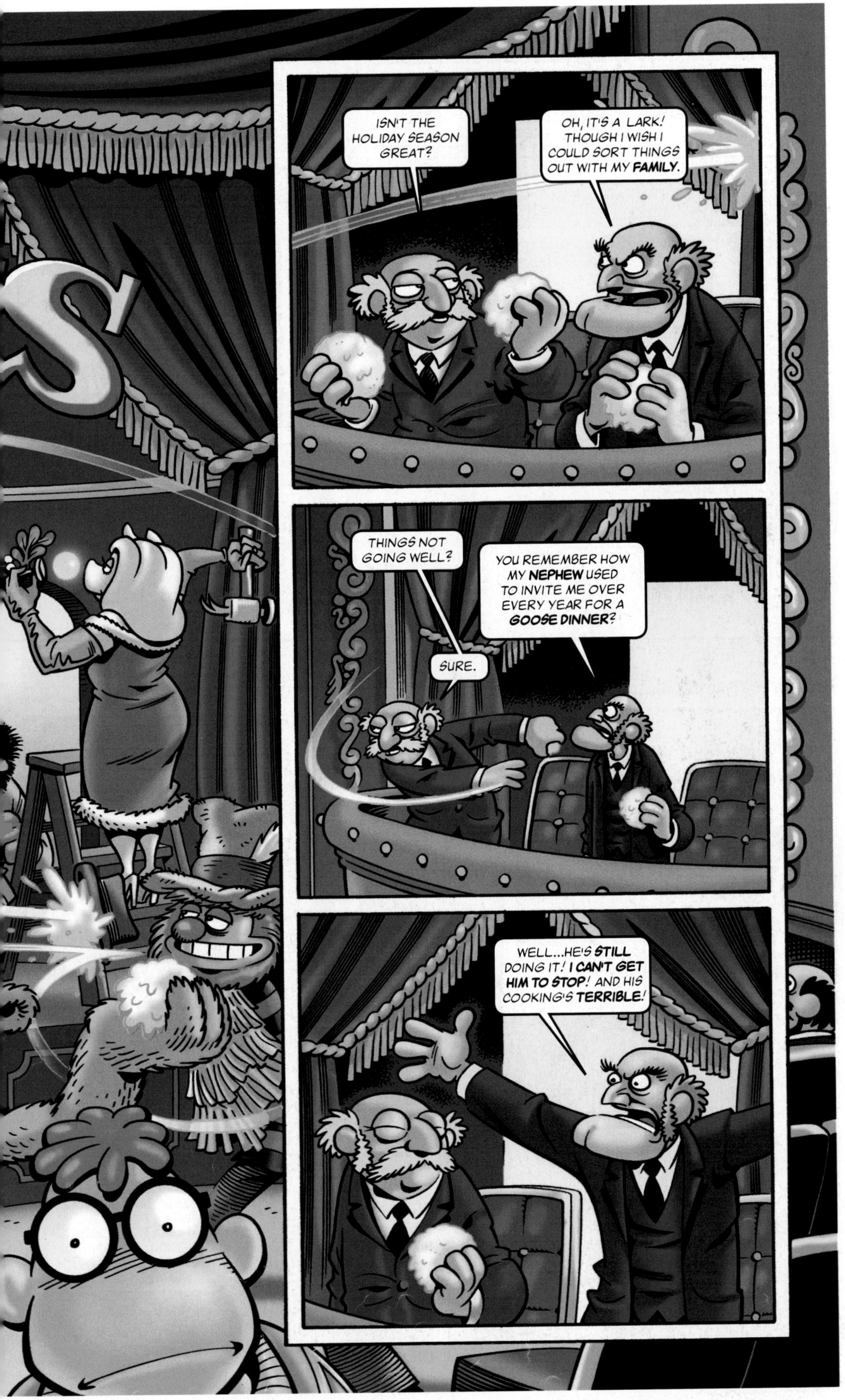
ISN'T THE HOLIDAY SEASON GREAT?
OH, IT'S A LARK! THOUGH I WISH I COULD SORT THINGS OUT WITH MY FAMILY.
THINGS NOT GOING WELL?
YOU REMEMBER HOW MY NEPHEW USED TO INVITE ME OVER EVERY YEAR FOR A GOOSE DINNER?
SURE.
WELL...HE'S STILL DOING IT! I CAN'T GET HIM TO STOP! AND HIS COOKING'S TERRIBLE!

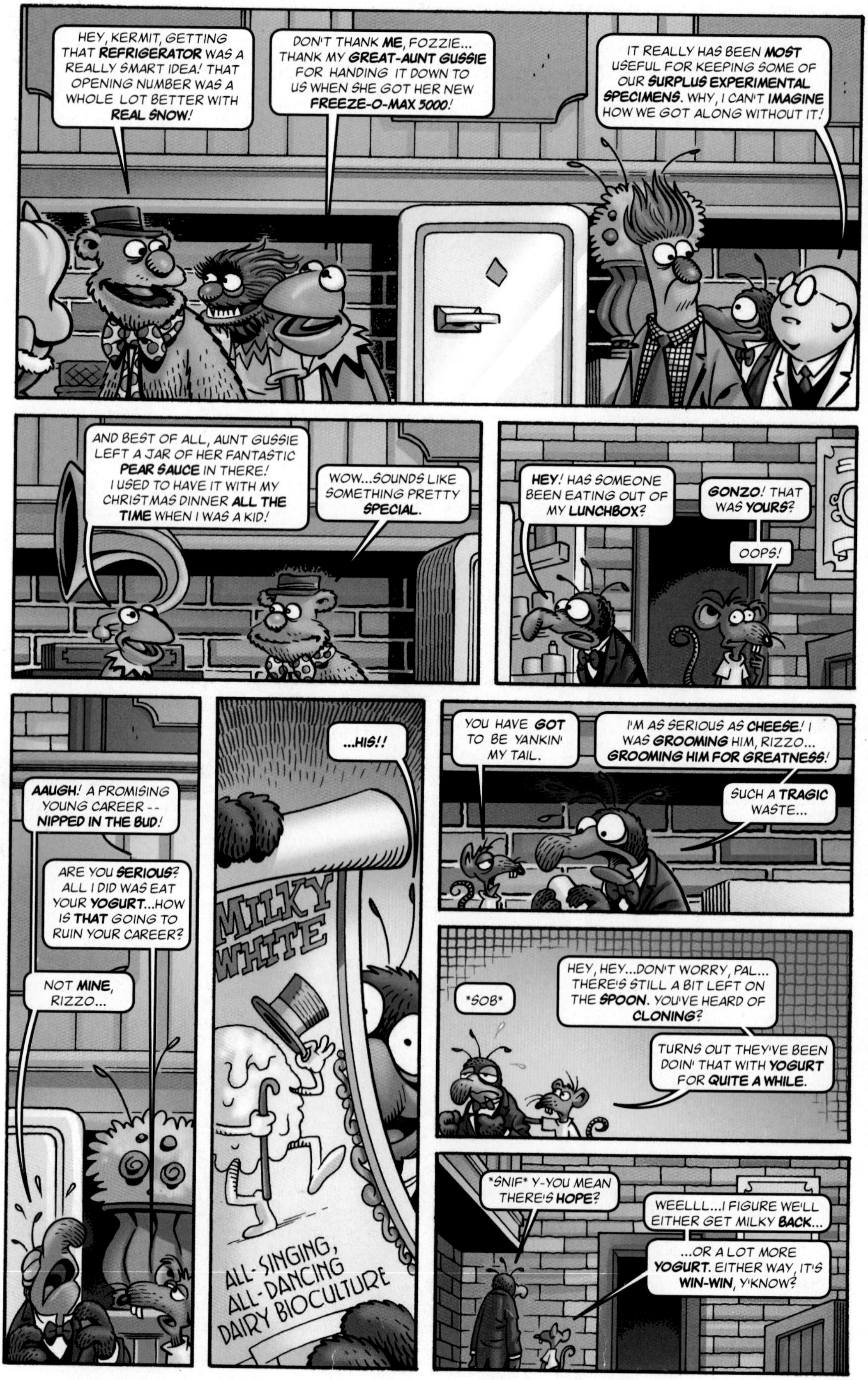

HEY, KERMIT, GETTING THAT REFRIGERATOR WAS A REALLY SMART IDEA! THAT OPENING NUMBER WAS A WHOLE LOT BETTER WITH REAL SNOW!
DON'T THANK ME, FOZZIE... THANK MY GREAT-AUNT GUSSIE FOR HANDING IT DOWN TO US WHEN SHE GOT HER NEW FREEZE-O-MAX 5000!
IT REALLY HAS BEEN MOST USEFUL FOR KEEPING SOME OF OUR SURPLUS EXPERIMENTAL SPECIMENS. WHY, I CAN'T IMAGINE HOW WE GOT ALONG WITHOUT IT!
AND BEST OF ALL, AUNT GUSSIE LEFT A JAR OF HER FANTASTIC PEAR SAUCE IN THERE! I USED TO HAVE IT WITH MY CHRISTMAS DINNER ALL THE TIME WHEN I WAS A KID!
WOW...SOUNDS LIKE SOMETHING PRETTY SPECIAL.
HEY! HAS SOMEONE BEEN EATING OUT OF MY LUNCHBOX?
GONZO! THAT WAS YOURS?
OOPS!
AAUGH! A PROMISING YOUNG CAREER -- NIPPED IN THE BUD!
ARE YOU SERIOUS? ALL I DID WAS EAT YOUR YOGURT...HOW IS THAT GOING TO RUIN YOUR CAREER?
NOT MINE, RIZZO...
...HIS!!
MILKY WHITE
ALL-SINGING, ALL-DANCING DAIRY BIOCULTURE
YOU HAVE GOT TO BE YANKIN' MY TAIL.
I'M AS SERIOUS AS CHEESE! I WAS GROOMING HIM, RIZZO... GROOMING HIM FOR GREATNESS!
SUCH A TRAGIC WASTE...
SOB
HEY, HEY...DON'T WORRY, PAL... THERE'S STILL A BIT LEFT ON THE SPOON. YOU'VE HEARD OF CLONING?
TURNS OUT THEY'VE BEEN DOIN' THAT WITH YOGURT FOR QUITE A WHILE.
SNIF Y-YOU MEAN THERE'S HOPE?
WEELLL...I FIGURE WE'LL EITHER GET MILKY BACK...
...OR A LOT MORE YOGURT. EITHER WAY, IT'S WIN-WIN, Y'KNOW?

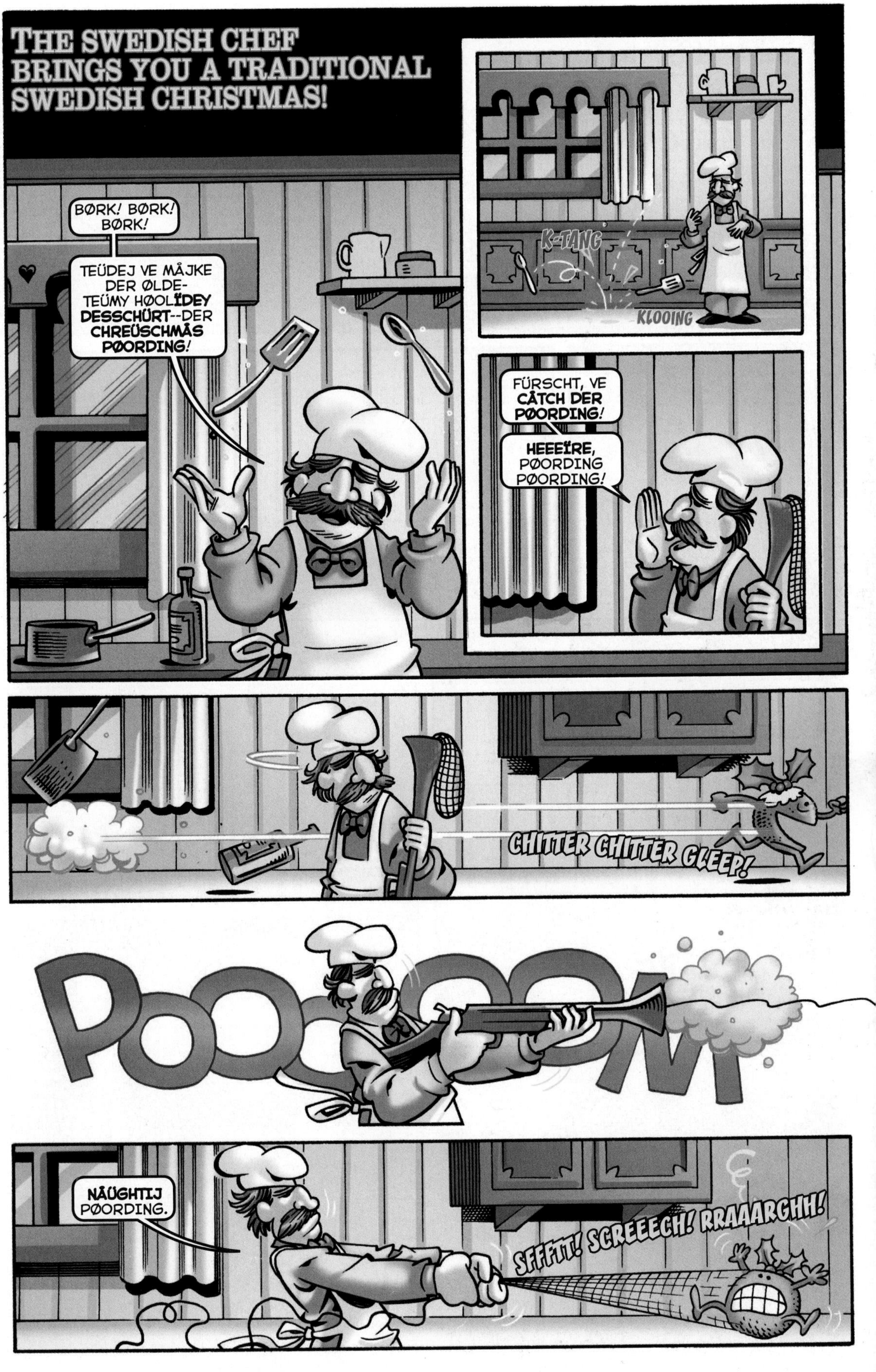
THE SWEDISH CHEF BRINGS YOU A TRADITIONAL SWEDISH CHRISTMAS!
BØRK! BØRK! BØRK!
TEÜDEJ VE MÅJKE DER ØLDE-TEÜMY HØOLÏDEY DESSCHÜRT--DER CHREÜSCHMÅS PØORDING!
K-TANG
KLOOING
FÜRSCHT, VE CÅTCH DER PØORDING!
HEEEÏRE, PØORDING PØORDING!
CHITTER CHITTER GLEEP!
POOOOM
NÅÜGHTIJ PØORDING.
SFFFTT! SCREEECH! RRAAARGHH!

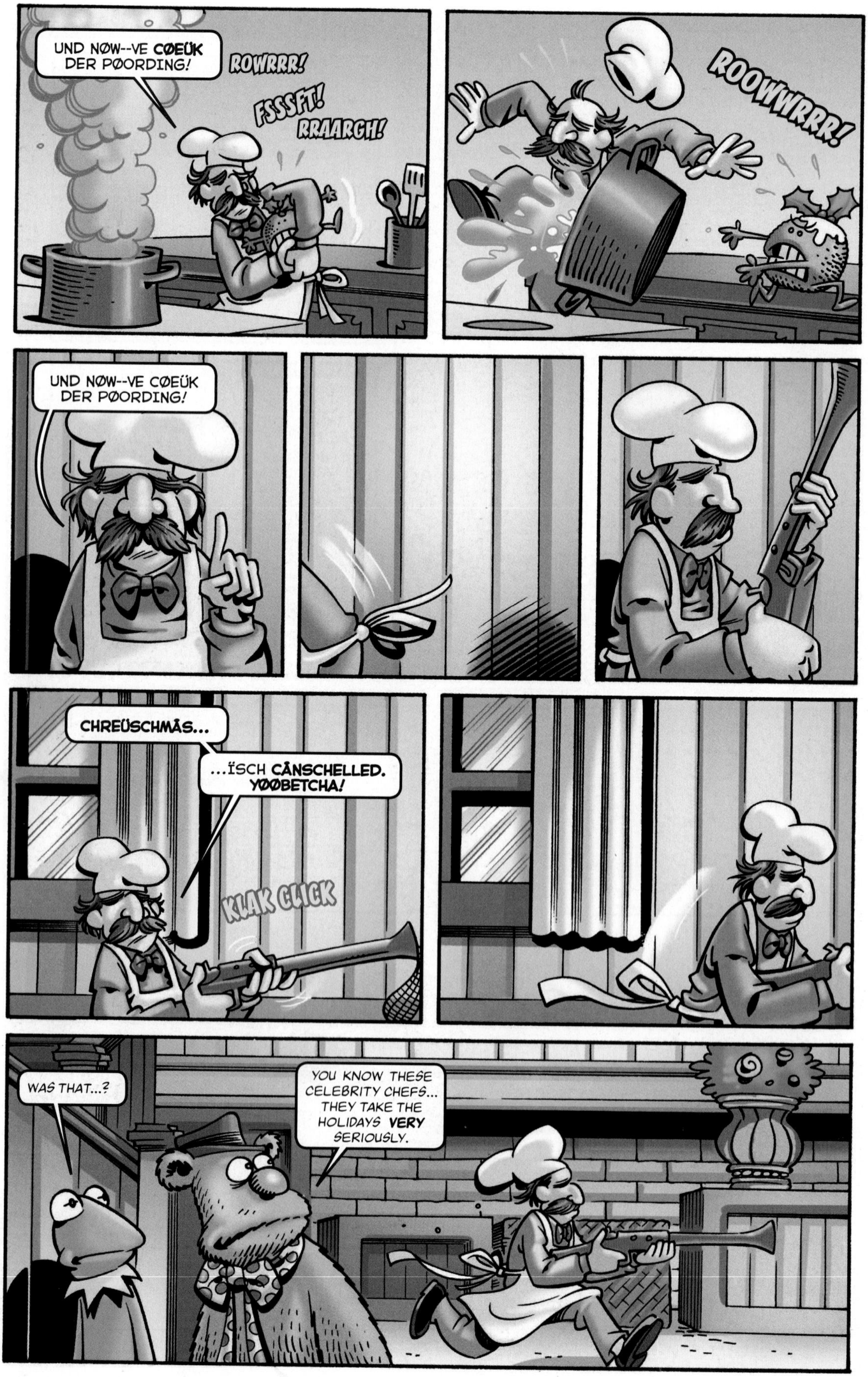
UND NØW--VE CØEÜK DER PØORDING!
ROWRRR!
FSSSFT!
RRAARGH!
ROOWWRRR!
UND NØW--VE CØEÜK DER PØORDING!
CHREÜSCHMÅS...
...ÏSCH CÅNSCHELLED. YØØBETCHA!
KLAK CLICK
WAS THAT...?
YOU KNOW THESE CELEBRITY CHEFS... THEY TAKE THE HOLIDAYS VERY SERIOUSLY.

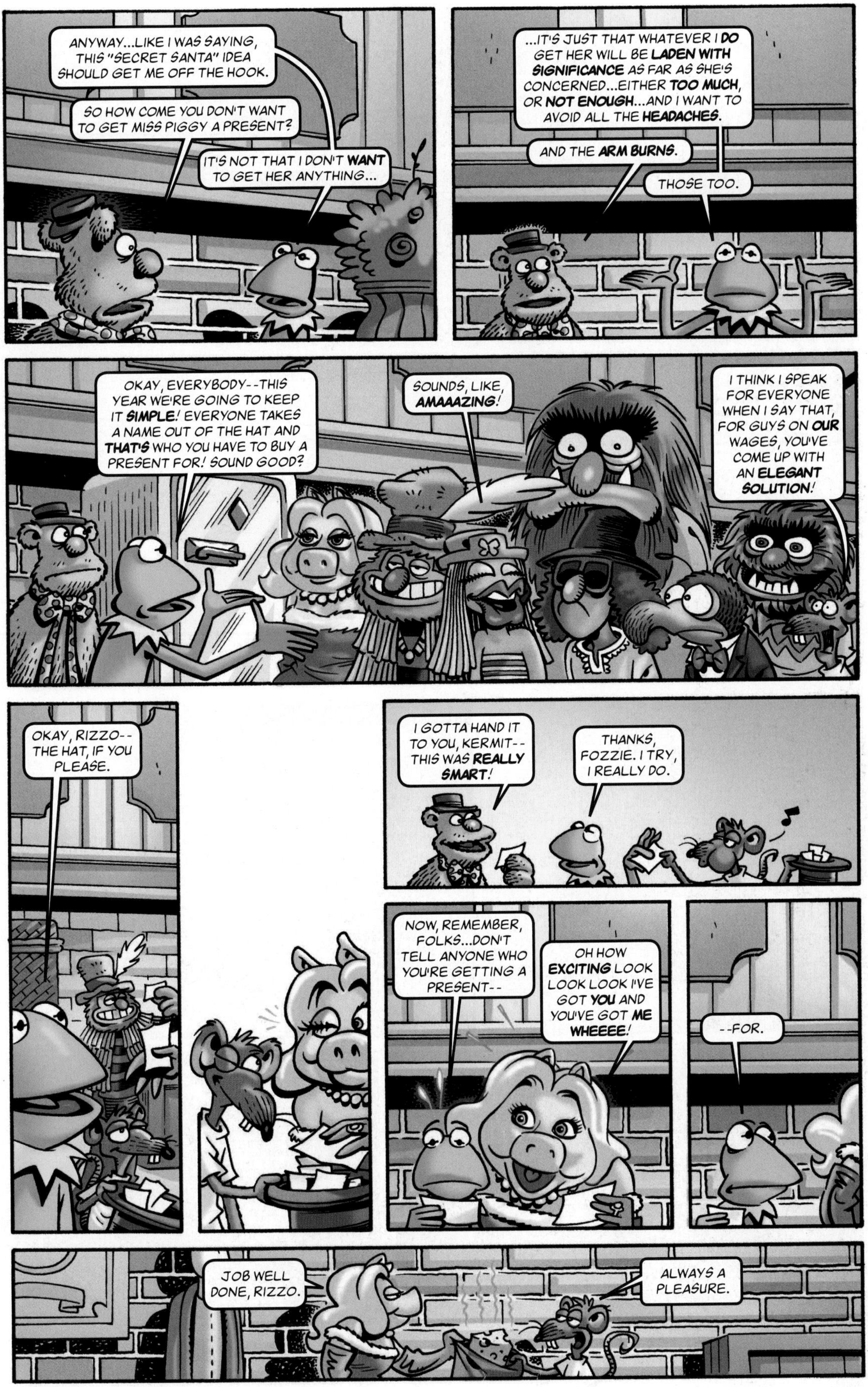

ANYWAY...LIKE I WAS SAYING, THIS "SECRET SANTA" IDEA SHOULD GET ME OFF THE HOOK.
SO HOW COME YOU DON'T WANT TO GET MISS PIGGY A PRESENT?
IT'S NOT THAT I DON'T **WANT** TO GET HER ANYTHING...
...IT'S JUST THAT WHATEVER I **DO** GET HER WILL BE **LADEN WITH SIGNIFICANCE** AS FAR AS SHE'S CONCERNED...EITHER **TOO MUCH**, OR **NOT ENOUGH**...AND I WANT TO AVOID ALL THE **HEADACHES**.
AND THE **ARM BURNS**.
THOSE TOO.
OKAY, EVERYBODY--THIS YEAR WE'RE GOING TO KEEP IT **SIMPLE**! EVERYONE TAKES A NAME OUT OF THE HAT AND **THAT'S** WHO YOU HAVE TO BUY A PRESENT FOR! SOUND GOOD?
SOUNDS, LIKE, **AMAAAZING**!
I THINK I SPEAK FOR EVERYONE WHEN I SAY THAT, FOR GUYS ON **OUR** WAGES, YOU'VE COME UP WITH AN **ELEGANT SOLUTION**!
OKAY, RIZZO--THE HAT, IF YOU PLEASE.
I GOTTA HAND IT TO YOU, KERMIT--THIS WAS **REALLY SMART**!
THANKS, FOZZIE. I TRY, I REALLY DO.
NOW, REMEMBER, FOLKS...DON'T TELL ANYONE WHO YOU'RE GETTING A PRESENT--
OH HOW **EXCITING** LOOK LOOK LOOK I'VE GOT **YOU** AND YOU'VE GOT **ME** **WHEEEE**!
--FOR.
JOB WELL DONE, RIZZO.
ALWAYS A PLEASURE.

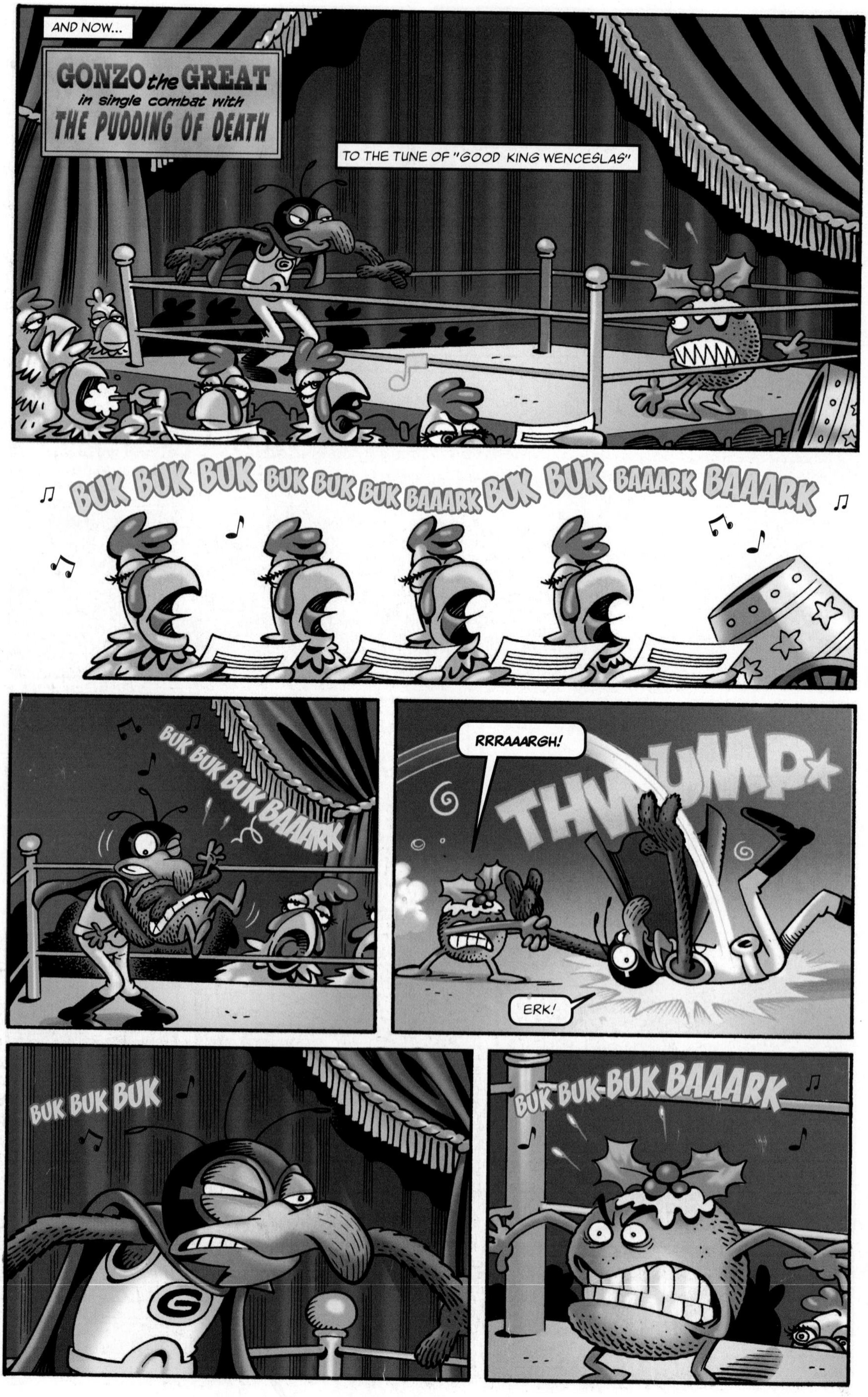

AND NOW...
GONZO the GREAT
in single combat with
THE PUDDING OF DEATH
TO THE TUNE OF "GOOD KING WENCESLAS"
BUK BUK BUK BUK BUK BUK BAAARK BUK BUK BAAARK BAAARK
BUK BUK BUK BAAARK
RRRAAARGH!
THWUMP
ERK!
BUK BUK BUK
BUK BUK-BUK BAAARK

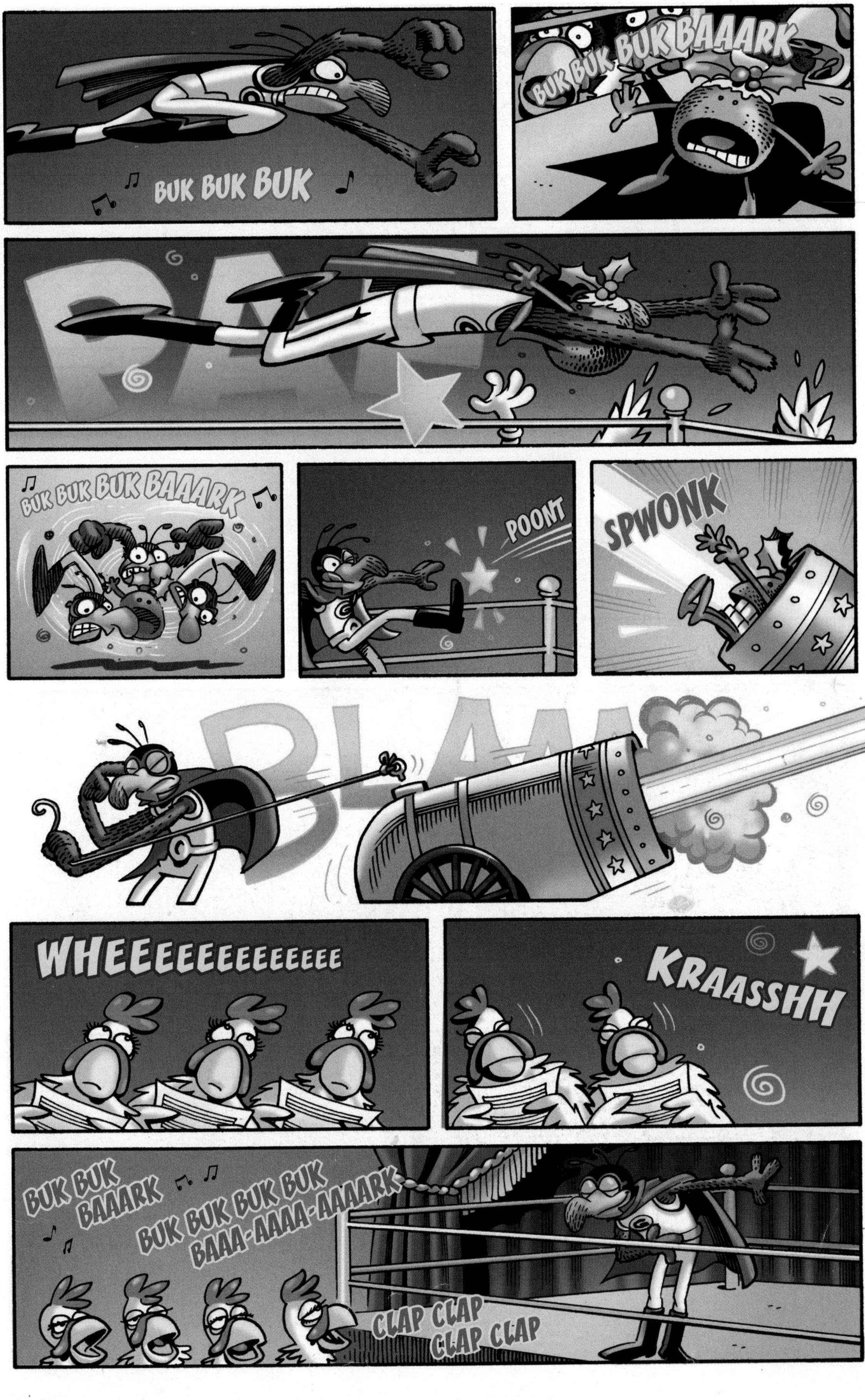
BUK BUK BUK
BUK BUK BUK BAAARK
BUK BUK BUK BAAARK
POONT
SPWONK
WHEEEEEEEEEEEE
KRAASSHH
BUK BUK BAAARK
BUK BUK BUK BUK BAAA-AAAA-AAAARK
CLAP CLAP CLAP CLAP

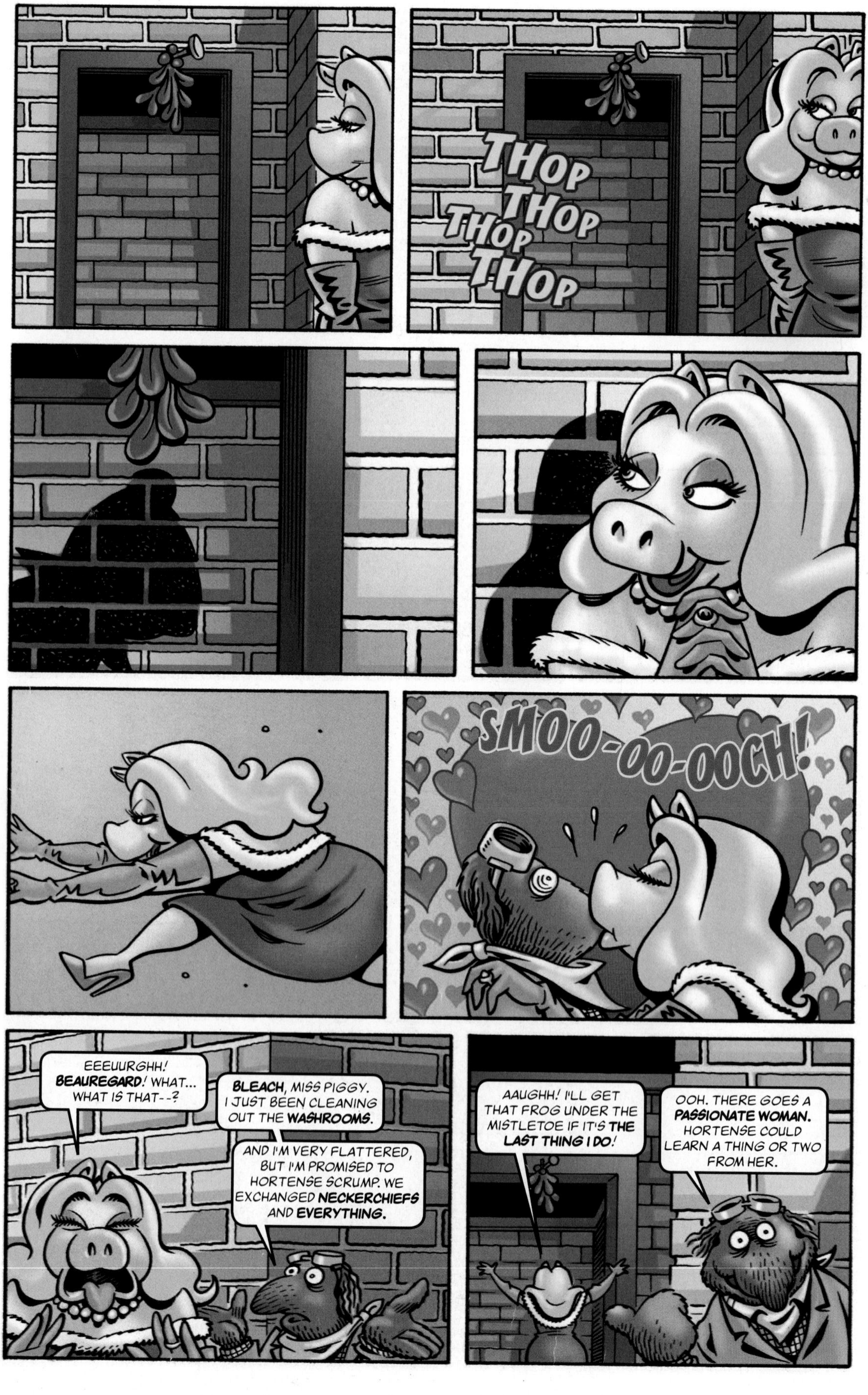
THOP THOP THOP THOP
SMOO-OO-OOCH!
EEEUURGHH! BEAUREGARD! WHAT... WHAT IS THAT--?
BLEACH, MISS PIGGY. I JUST BEEN CLEANING OUT THE WASHROOMS.
AND I'M VERY FLATTERED, BUT I'M PROMISED TO HORTENSE SCRUMP. WE EXCHANGED NECKERCHIEFS AND EVERYTHING.
AAUGHH! I'LL GET THAT FROG UNDER THE MISTLETOE IF IT'S THE LAST THING I DO!
OOH. THERE GOES A PASSIONATE WOMAN. HORTENSE COULD LEARN A THING OR TWO FROM HER.

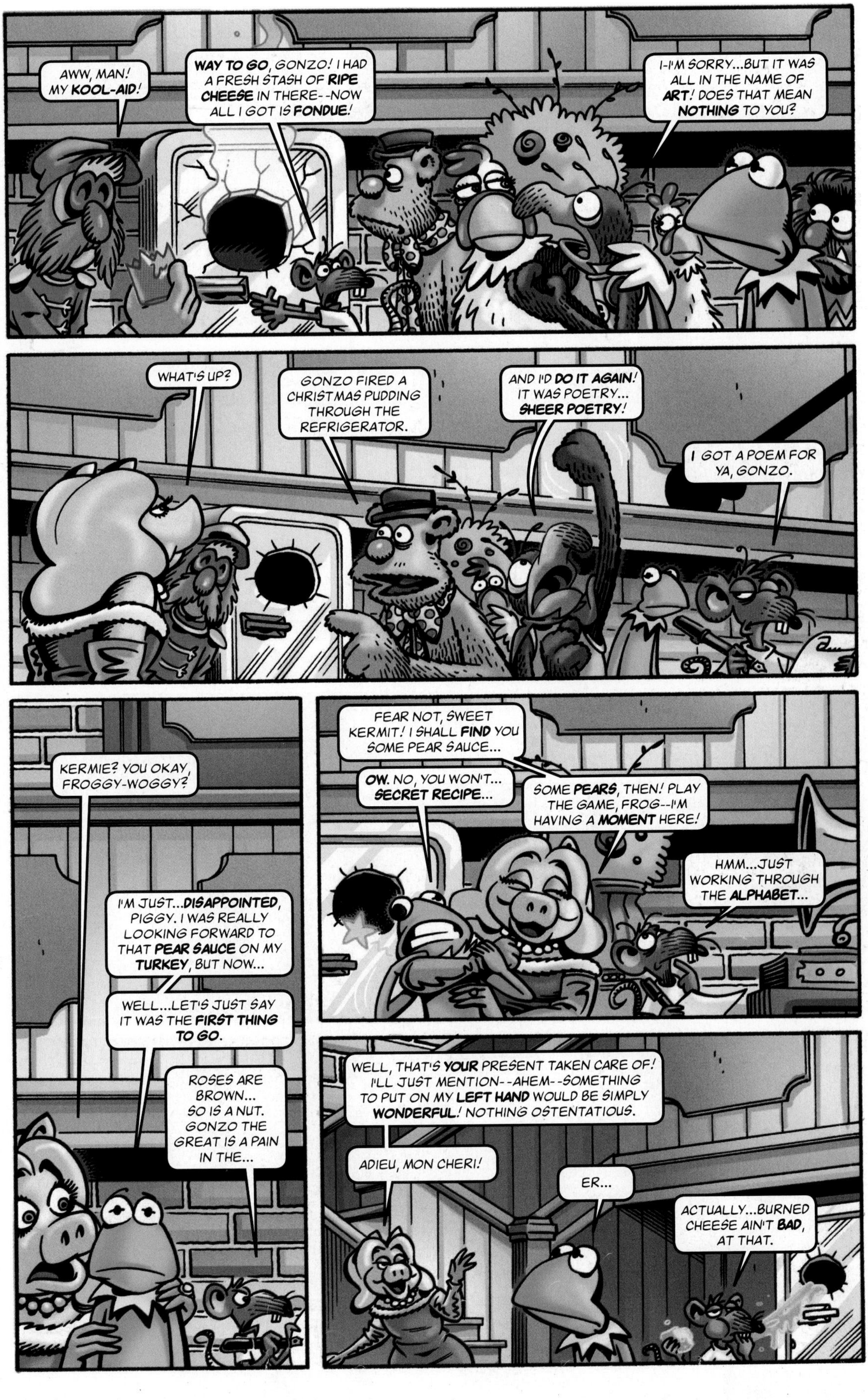
AWW, MAN! MY KOOL-AID!
WAY TO GO, GONZO! I HAD A FRESH STASH OF RIPE CHEESE IN THERE--NOW ALL I GOT IS FONDUE!
I-I'M SORRY...BUT IT WAS ALL IN THE NAME OF ART! DOES THAT MEAN NOTHING TO YOU?
WHAT'S UP?
GONZO FIRED A CHRISTMAS PUDDING THROUGH THE REFRIGERATOR.
AND I'D DO IT AGAIN! IT WAS POETRY... SHEER POETRY!
I GOT A POEM FOR YA, GONZO.
KERMIE? YOU OKAY, FROGGY-WOGGY?
I'M JUST...DISAPPOINTED, PIGGY. I WAS REALLY LOOKING FORWARD TO THAT PEAR SAUCE ON MY TURKEY, BUT NOW...
WELL...LET'S JUST SAY IT WAS THE FIRST THING TO GO.
ROSES ARE BROWN... SO IS A NUT. GONZO THE GREAT IS A PAIN IN THE...
FEAR NOT, SWEET KERMIT! I SHALL FIND YOU SOME PEAR SAUCE...
OW. NO, YOU WON'T... SECRET RECIPE...
SOME PEARS, THEN! PLAY THE GAME, FROG--I'M HAVING A MOMENT HERE!
HMM...JUST WORKING THROUGH THE ALPHABET...
WELL, THAT'S YOUR PRESENT TAKEN CARE OF! I'LL JUST MENTION--AHEM--SOMETHING TO PUT ON MY LEFT HAND WOULD BE SIMPLY WONDERFUL! NOTHING OSTENTATIOUS.
ADIEU, MON CHERI!
ER...
ACTUALLY...BURNED CHEESE AIN'T BAD, AT THAT.

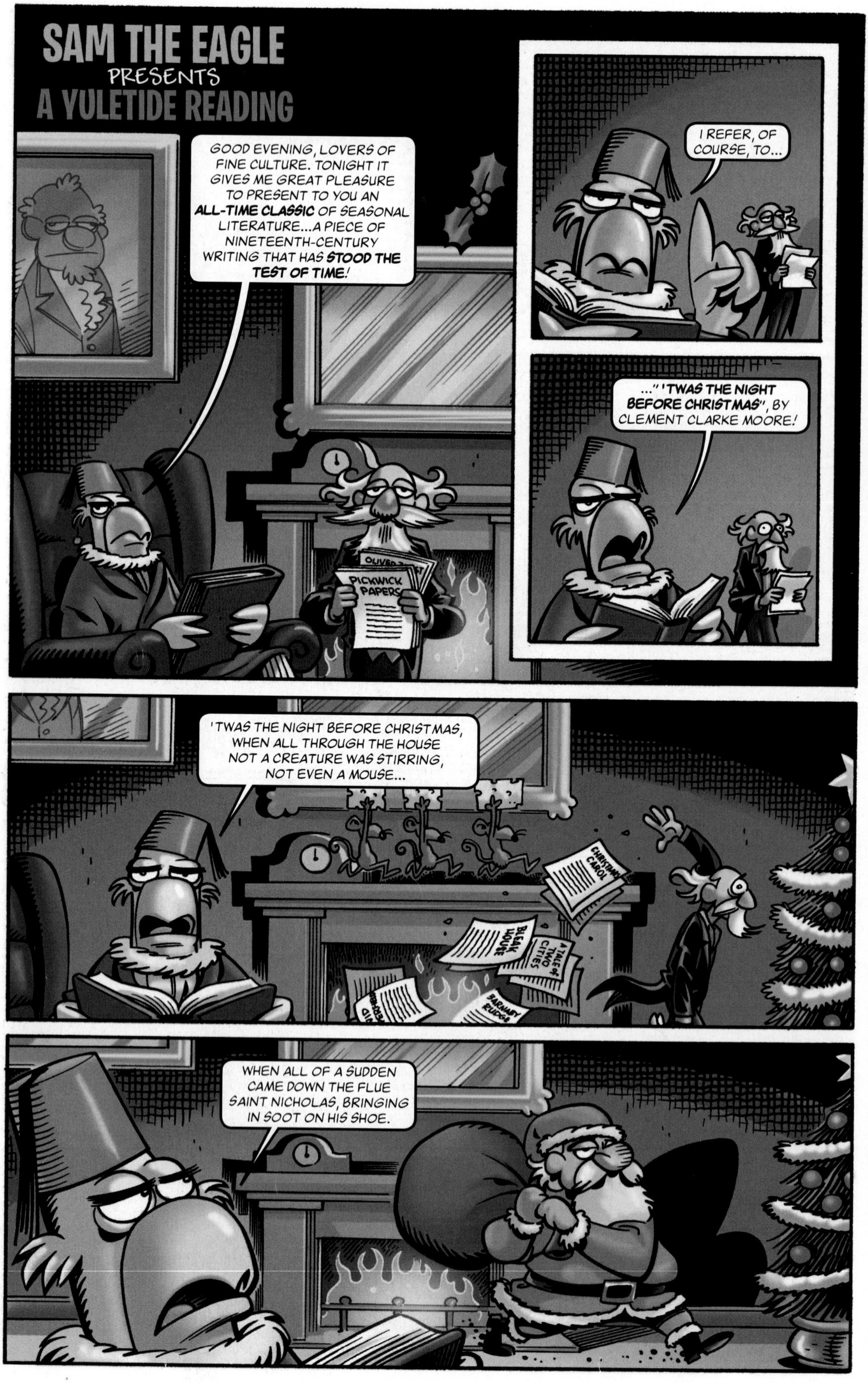
SAM THE EAGLE
PRESENTS
A YULETIDE READING
GOOD EVENING, LOVERS OF FINE CULTURE. TONIGHT IT GIVES ME GREAT PLEASURE TO PRESENT TO YOU AN ALL-TIME CLASSIC OF SEASONAL LITERATURE...A PIECE OF NINETEENTH-CENTURY WRITING THAT HAS STOOD THE TEST OF TIME!
PICKWICK PAPERS
I REFER, OF COURSE, TO...
..."'TWAS THE NIGHT BEFORE CHRISTMAS", BY CLEMENT CLARKE MOORE!
'TWAS THE NIGHT BEFORE CHRISTMAS, WHEN ALL THROUGH THE HOUSE NOT A CREATURE WAS STIRRING, NOT EVEN A MOUSE...
CHRISTMAS CAROL
BLEAK HOUSE
A TALE OF TWO CITIES
BARNABY RUDGE
WHEN ALL OF A SUDDEN CAME DOWN THE FLUE SAINT NICHOLAS, BRINGING IN SOOT ON HIS SHOE.

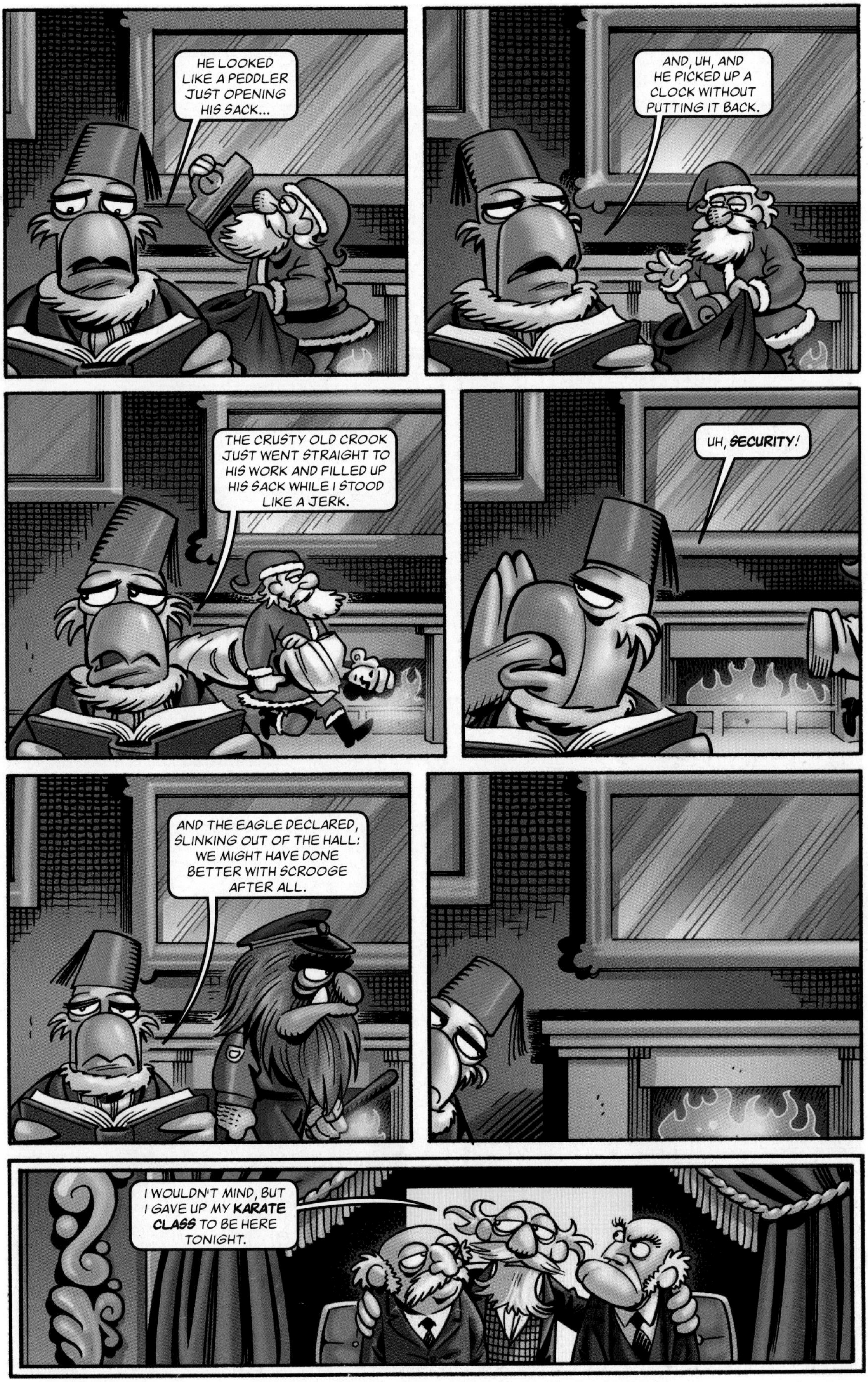
HE LOOKED LIKE A PEDDLER JUST OPENING HIS SACK...
AND, UH, AND HE PICKED UP A CLOCK WITHOUT PUTTING IT BACK.
THE CRUSTY OLD CROOK JUST WENT STRAIGHT TO HIS WORK AND FILLED UP HIS SACK WHILE I STOOD LIKE A JERK.
UH, SECURITY!
AND THE EAGLE DECLARED, SLINKING OUT OF THE HALL: WE MIGHT HAVE DONE BETTER WITH SCROOGE AFTER ALL.
I WOULDN'T MIND, BUT I GAVE UP MY KARATE CLASS TO BE HERE TONIGHT.

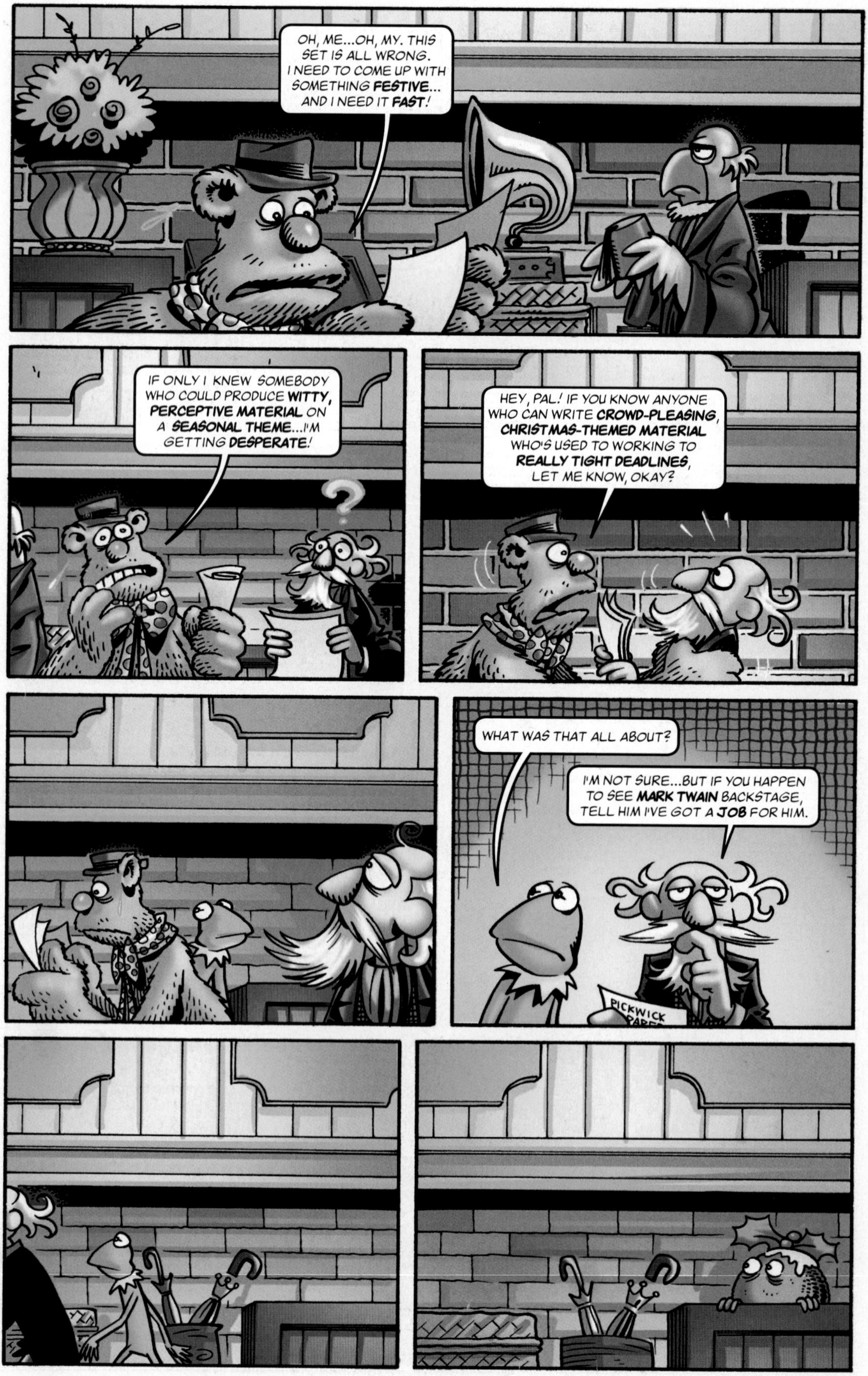
OH, ME...OH, MY. THIS SET IS ALL WRONG. I NEED TO COME UP WITH SOMETHING FESTIVE... AND I NEED IT FAST!
IF ONLY I KNEW SOMEBODY WHO COULD PRODUCE WITTY, PERCEPTIVE MATERIAL ON A SEASONAL THEME...I'M GETTING DESPERATE!
HEY, PAL! IF YOU KNOW ANYONE WHO CAN WRITE CROWD-PLEASING, CHRISTMAS-THEMED MATERIAL WHO'S USED TO WORKING TO REALLY TIGHT DEADLINES, LET ME KNOW, OKAY?
WHAT WAS THAT ALL ABOUT?
I'M NOT SURE...BUT IF YOU HAPPEN TO SEE MARK TWAIN BACKSTAGE, TELL HIM I'VE GOT A JOB FOR HIM.
PICKWICK

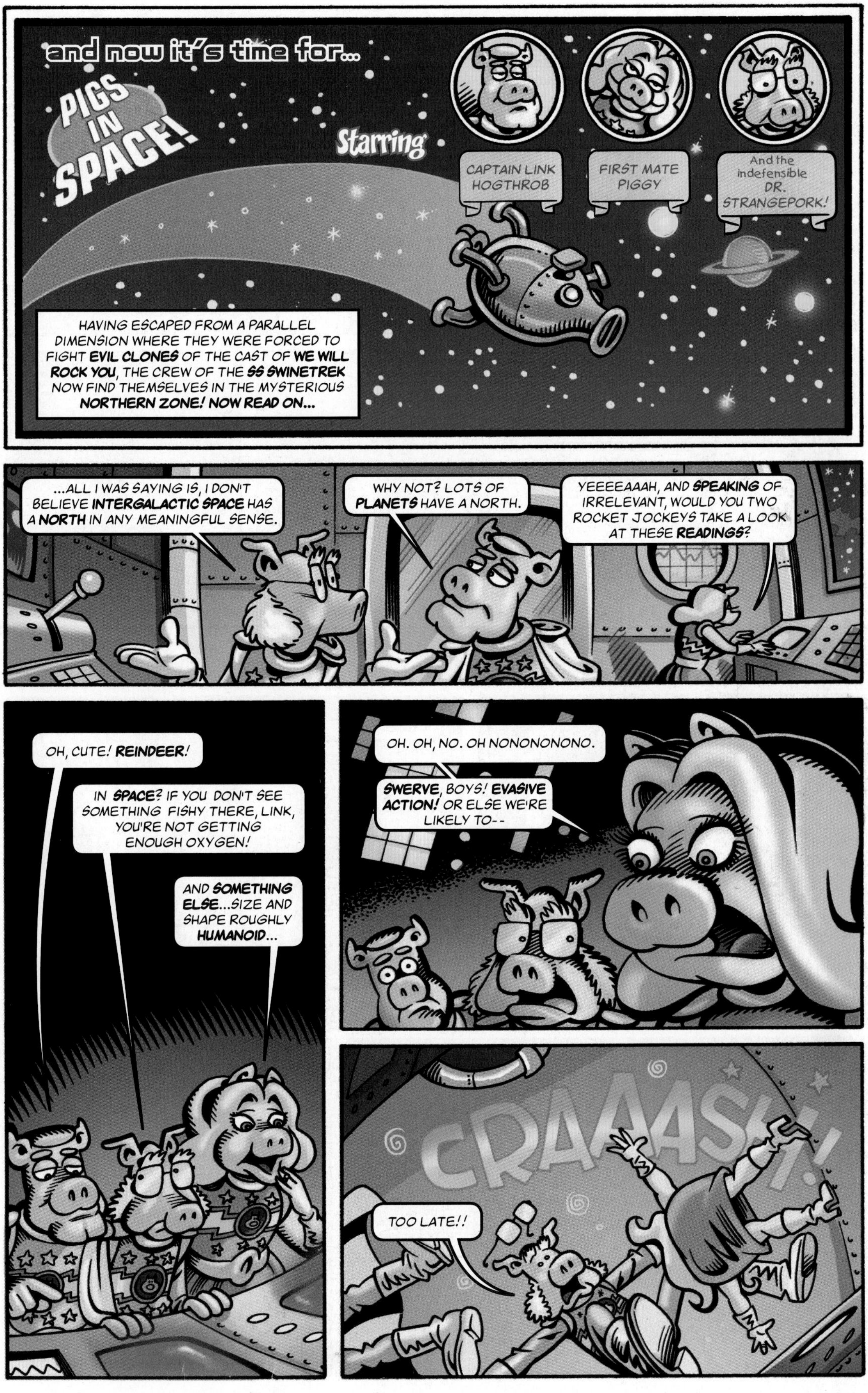

and now it's time for...
PIGS IN SPACE!
Starring
CAPTAIN LINK HOGTHROB
FIRST MATE PIGGY
And the indefensible DR. STRANGEPORK!
HAVING ESCAPED FROM A PARALLEL DIMENSION WHERE THEY WERE FORCED TO FIGHT EVIL CLONES OF THE CAST OF WE WILL ROCK YOU, THE CREW OF THE SS SWINETREK NOW FIND THEMSELVES IN THE MYSTERIOUS NORTHERN ZONE! NOW READ ON...
...ALL I WAS SAYING IS, I DON'T BELIEVE INTERGALACTIC SPACE HAS A NORTH IN ANY MEANINGFUL SENSE.
WHY NOT? LOTS OF PLANETS HAVE A NORTH.
YEEEEAAAH, AND SPEAKING OF IRRELEVANT, WOULD YOU TWO ROCKET JOCKEYS TAKE A LOOK AT THESE READINGS?
OH, CUTE! REINDEER!
IN SPACE? IF YOU DON'T SEE SOMETHING FISHY THERE, LINK, YOU'RE NOT GETTING ENOUGH OXYGEN!
AND SOMETHING ELSE...SIZE AND SHAPE ROUGHLY HUMANOID...
OH. OH, NO. OH NONONONONO.
SWERVE, BOYS! EVASIVE ACTION! OR ELSE WE'RE LIKELY TO--
CRAAASH!
TOO LATE!!

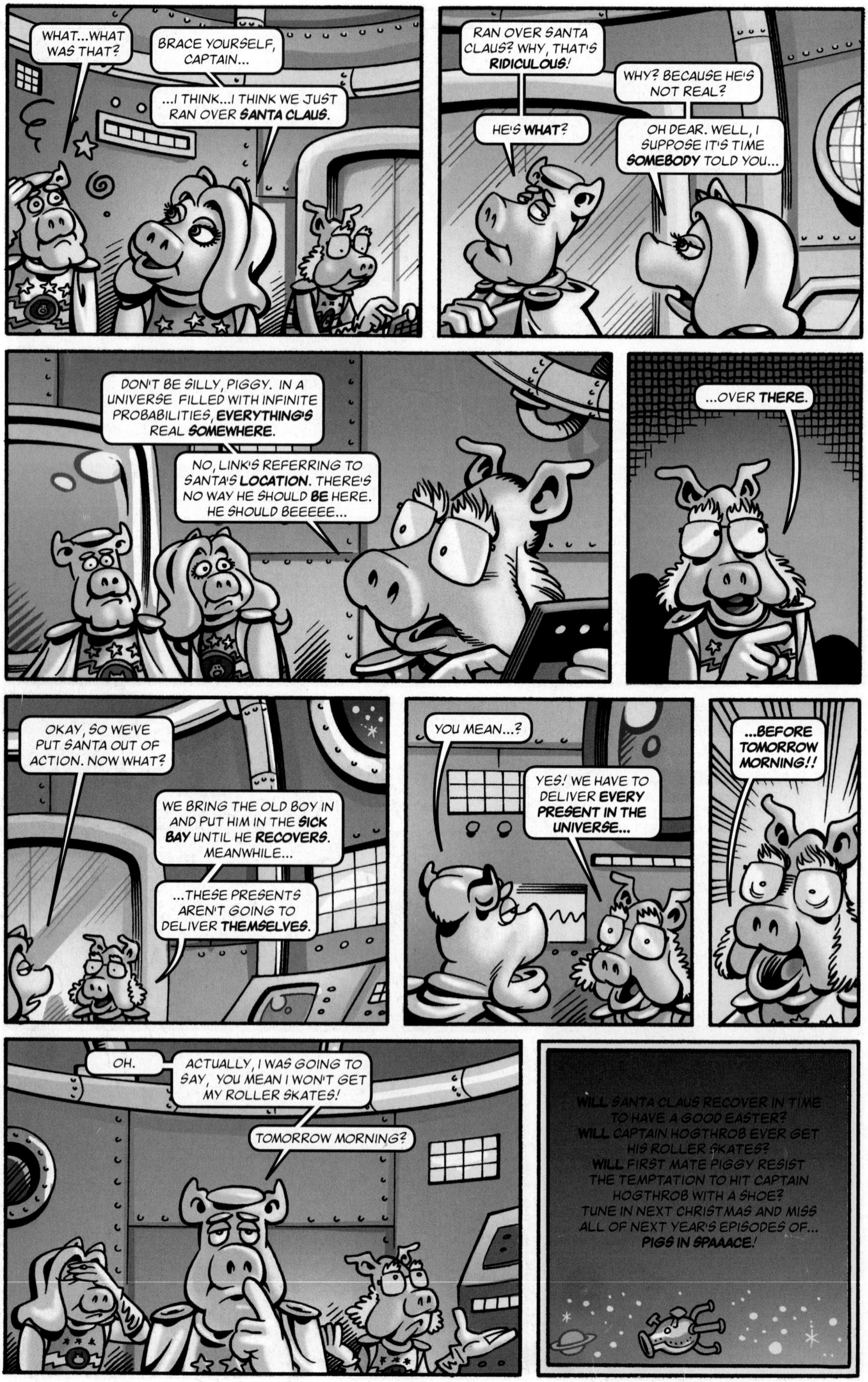
WHAT...WHAT WAS THAT?
BRACE YOURSELF, CAPTAIN...
...I THINK...I THINK WE JUST RAN OVER **SANTA CLAUS**.
HE'S **WHAT**?
RAN OVER SANTA CLAUS? WHY, THAT'S **RIDICULOUS**!
WHY? BECAUSE HE'S NOT REAL?
OH DEAR. WELL, I SUPPOSE IT'S TIME **SOMEBODY** TOLD YOU...
DON'T BE SILLY, PIGGY. IN A UNIVERSE FILLED WITH INFINITE PROBABILITIES, **EVERYTHING'S** REAL **SOMEWHERE**.
NO, LINK'S REFERRING TO SANTA'S **LOCATION**. THERE'S NO WAY HE SHOULD **BE** HERE. HE SHOULD BEEEEE...
...OVER **THERE**.
OKAY, SO WE'VE PUT SANTA OUT OF ACTION. NOW WHAT?
WE BRING THE OLD BOY IN AND PUT HIM IN THE **SICK BAY** UNTIL HE **RECOVERS**. MEANWHILE...
...THESE PRESENTS AREN'T GOING TO DELIVER **THEMSELVES**.
YOU MEAN...?
YES! WE HAVE TO DELIVER **EVERY PRESENT IN THE UNIVERSE...**
...BEFORE TOMORROW MORNING!!
OH.
ACTUALLY, I WAS GOING TO SAY, YOU MEAN I WON'T GET MY ROLLER SKATES!
TOMORROW MORNING?
WILL SANTA CLAUS RECOVER IN TIME TO HAVE A GOOD EASTER? **WILL** CAPTAIN HOGTHROB EVER GET HIS ROLLER SKATES? **WILL** FIRST MATE PIGGY RESIST THE TEMPTATION TO HIT CAPTAIN HOGTHROB WITH A SHOE? TUNE IN NEXT CHRISTMAS AND MISS ALL OF NEXT YEAR'S EPISODES OF... **PIGS IN SPAAACE!**

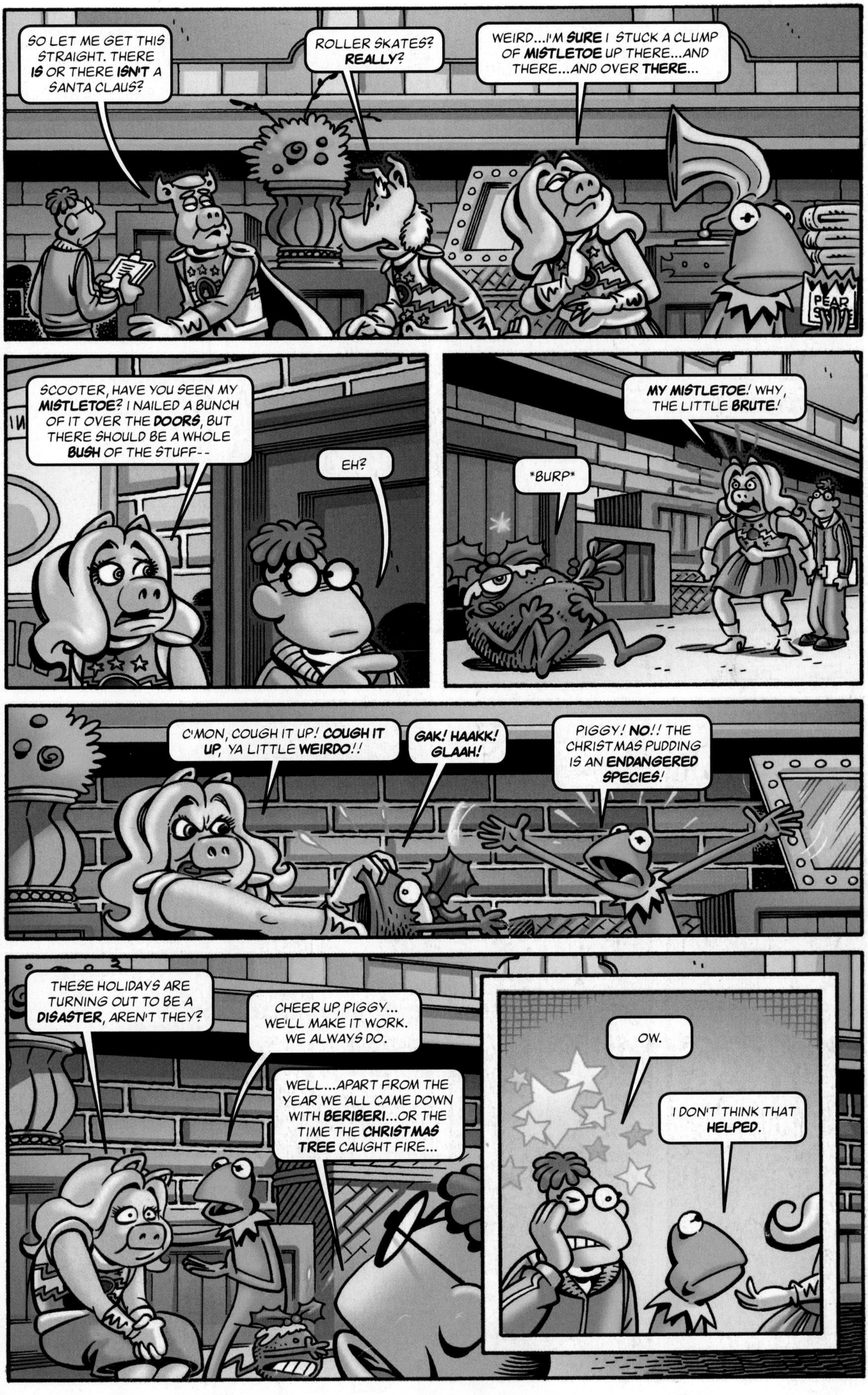
SO LET ME GET THIS STRAIGHT. THERE IS OR THERE ISN'T A SANTA CLAUS?
ROLLER SKATES? REALLY?
WEIRD...I'M SURE I STUCK A CLUMP OF MISTLETOE UP THERE...AND THERE...AND OVER THERE...
PEAR
SCOOTER, HAVE YOU SEEN MY MISTLETOE? I NAILED A BUNCH OF IT OVER THE DOORS, BUT THERE SHOULD BE A WHOLE BUSH OF THE STUFF--
EH?
MY MISTLETOE! WHY, THE LITTLE BRUTE!
BURP
C'MON, COUGH IT UP! COUGH IT UP, YA LITTLE WEIRDO!!
GAK! HAAKK! GLAAH!
PIGGY! NO!! THE CHRISTMAS PUDDING IS AN ENDANGERED SPECIES!
THESE HOLIDAYS ARE TURNING OUT TO BE A DISASTER, AREN'T THEY?
CHEER UP, PIGGY... WE'LL MAKE IT WORK. WE ALWAYS DO.
WELL...APART FROM THE YEAR WE ALL CAME DOWN WITH BERIBERI...OR THE TIME THE CHRISTMAS TREE CAUGHT FIRE...
OW.
I DON'T THINK THAT HELPED.

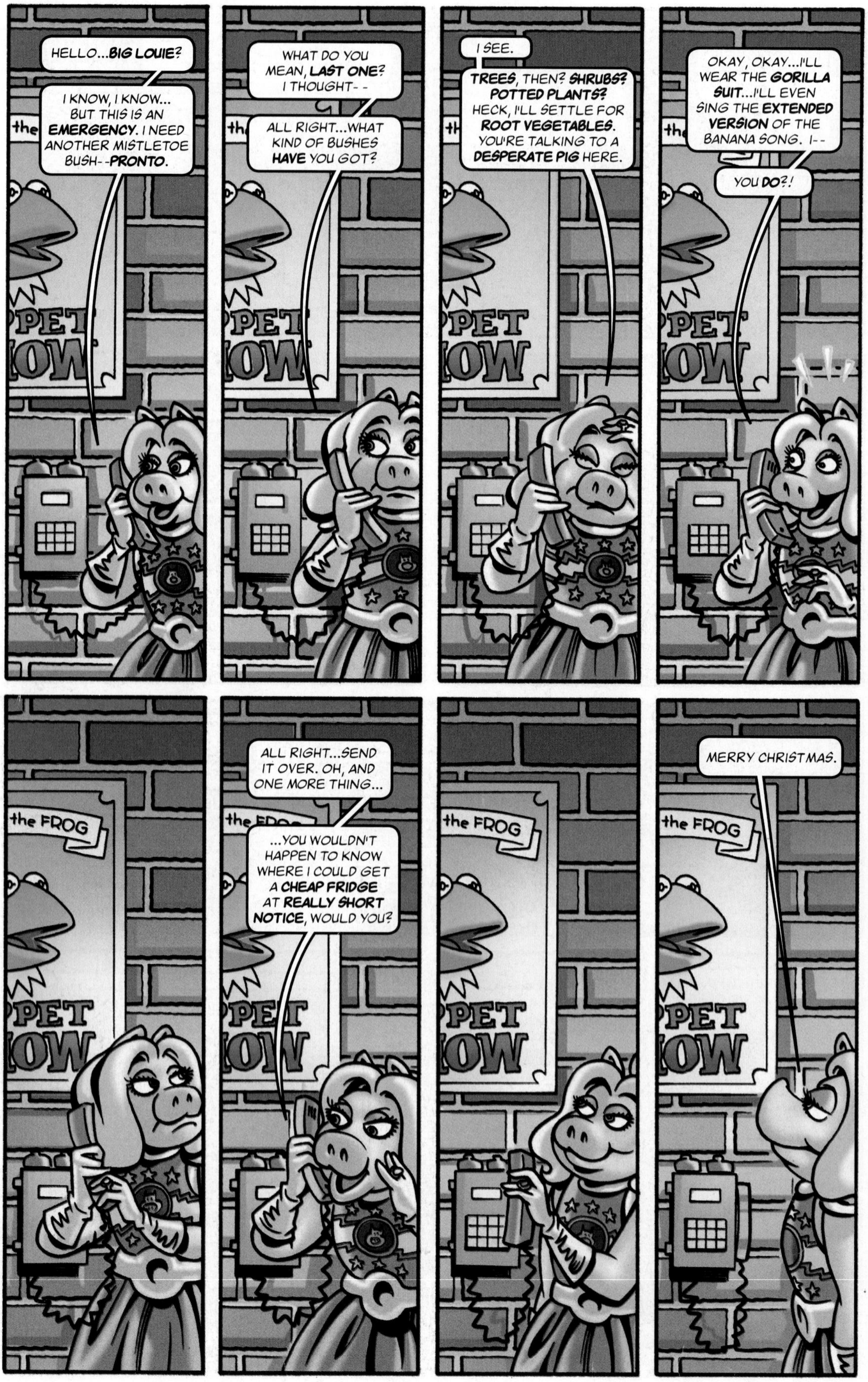

HELLO...BIG LOUIE?
I KNOW, I KNOW... BUT THIS IS AN EMERGENCY. I NEED ANOTHER MISTLETOE BUSH--PRONTO.
WHAT DO YOU MEAN, LAST ONE? I THOUGHT- -
ALL RIGHT...WHAT KIND OF BUSHES HAVE YOU GOT?
I SEE.
TREES, THEN? SHRUBS? POTTED PLANTS? HECK, I'LL SETTLE FOR ROOT VEGETABLES. YOU'RE TALKING TO A DESPERATE PIG HERE.
OKAY, OKAY...I'LL WEAR THE GORILLA SUIT...I'LL EVEN SING THE EXTENDED VERSION OF THE BANANA SONG. I--
YOU DO?!
ALL RIGHT...SEND IT OVER. OH, AND ONE MORE THING...
...YOU WOULDN'T HAPPEN TO KNOW WHERE I COULD GET A CHEAP FRIDGE AT REALLY SHORT NOTICE, WOULD YOU?
MERRY CHRISTMAS.

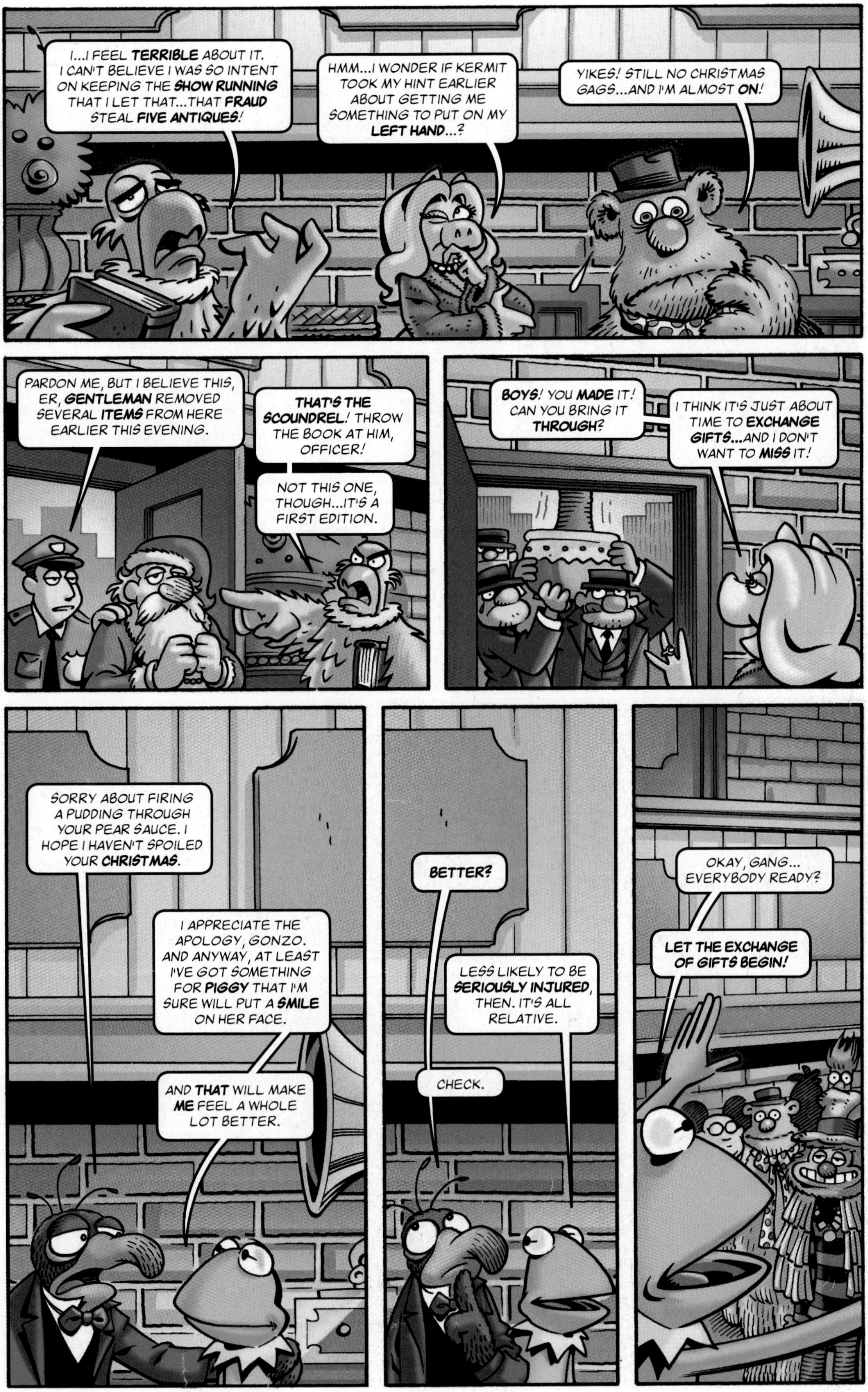
I...I FEEL TERRIBLE ABOUT IT. I CAN'T BELIEVE I WAS SO INTENT ON KEEPING THE SHOW RUNNING THAT I LET THAT...THAT FRAUD STEAL FIVE ANTIQUES!
HMM...I WONDER IF KERMIT TOOK MY HINT EARLIER ABOUT GETTING ME SOMETHING TO PUT ON MY LEFT HAND...?
YIKES! STILL NO CHRISTMAS GAGS...AND I'M ALMOST ON!
PARDON ME, BUT I BELIEVE THIS, ER, GENTLEMAN REMOVED SEVERAL ITEMS FROM HERE EARLIER THIS EVENING.
THAT'S THE SCOUNDREL! THROW THE BOOK AT HIM, OFFICER!
NOT THIS ONE, THOUGH...IT'S A FIRST EDITION.
BOYS! YOU MADE IT! CAN YOU BRING IT THROUGH?
I THINK IT'S JUST ABOUT TIME TO EXCHANGE GIFTS...AND I DON'T WANT TO MISS IT!
SORRY ABOUT FIRING A PUDDING THROUGH YOUR PEAR SAUCE. I HOPE I HAVEN'T SPOILED YOUR CHRISTMAS.
I APPRECIATE THE APOLOGY, GONZO. AND ANYWAY, AT LEAST I'VE GOT SOMETHING FOR PIGGY THAT I'M SURE WILL PUT A SMILE ON HER FACE.
AND THAT WILL MAKE ME FEEL A WHOLE LOT BETTER.
BETTER?
LESS LIKELY TO BE SERIOUSLY INJURED, THEN. IT'S ALL RELATIVE.
CHECK.
OKAY, GANG... EVERYBODY READY?
LET THE EXCHANGE OF GIFTS BEGIN!

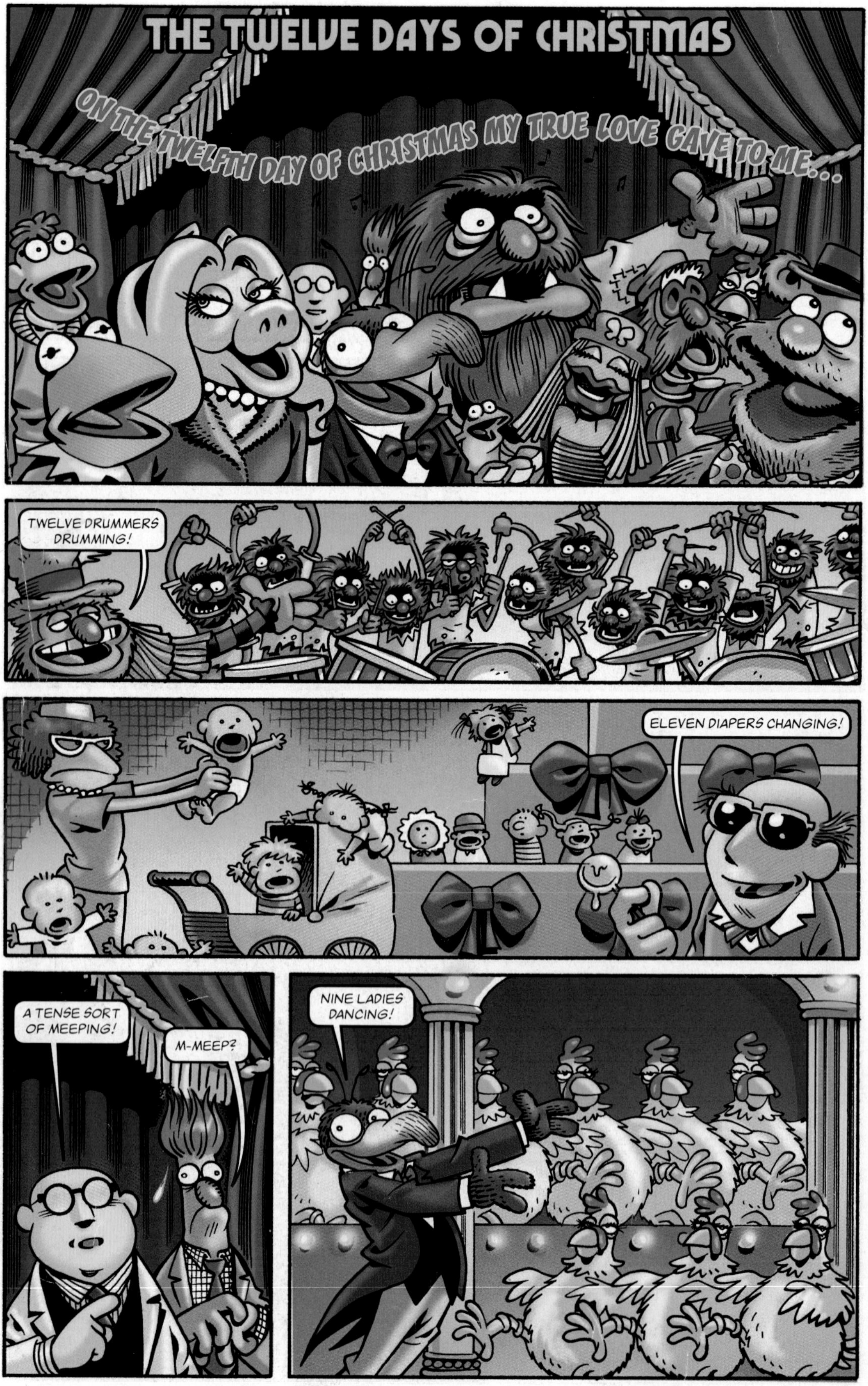
THE TWELVE DAYS OF CHRISTMAS
ON THE TWELFTH DAY OF CHRISTMAS MY TRUE LOVE GAVE TO ME...
TWELVE DRUMMERS DRUMMING!
ELEVEN DIAPERS CHANGING!
A TENSE SORT OF MEEPING!
M-MEEP?
NINE LADIES DANCING!

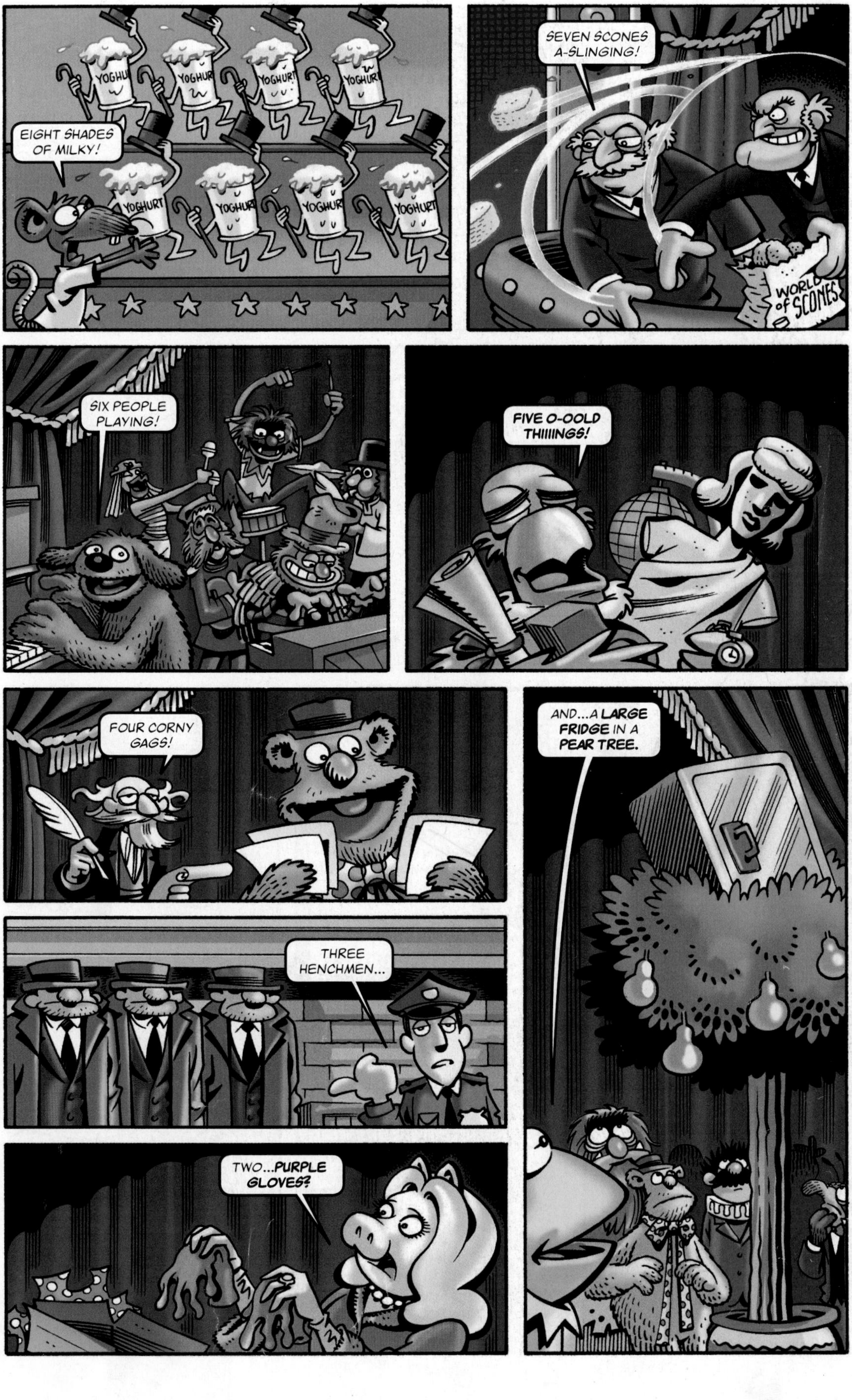
YOGHURT
EIGHT SHADES OF MILKY!
SEVEN SCONES A-SLINGING!
WORLD of SCONES
SIX PEOPLE PLAYING!
FIVE O-OOLD THIIIINGS!
FOUR CORNY GAGS!
AND...A LARGE FRIDGE IN A PEAR TREE.
THREE HENCHMEN...
TWO...PURPLE GLOVES?

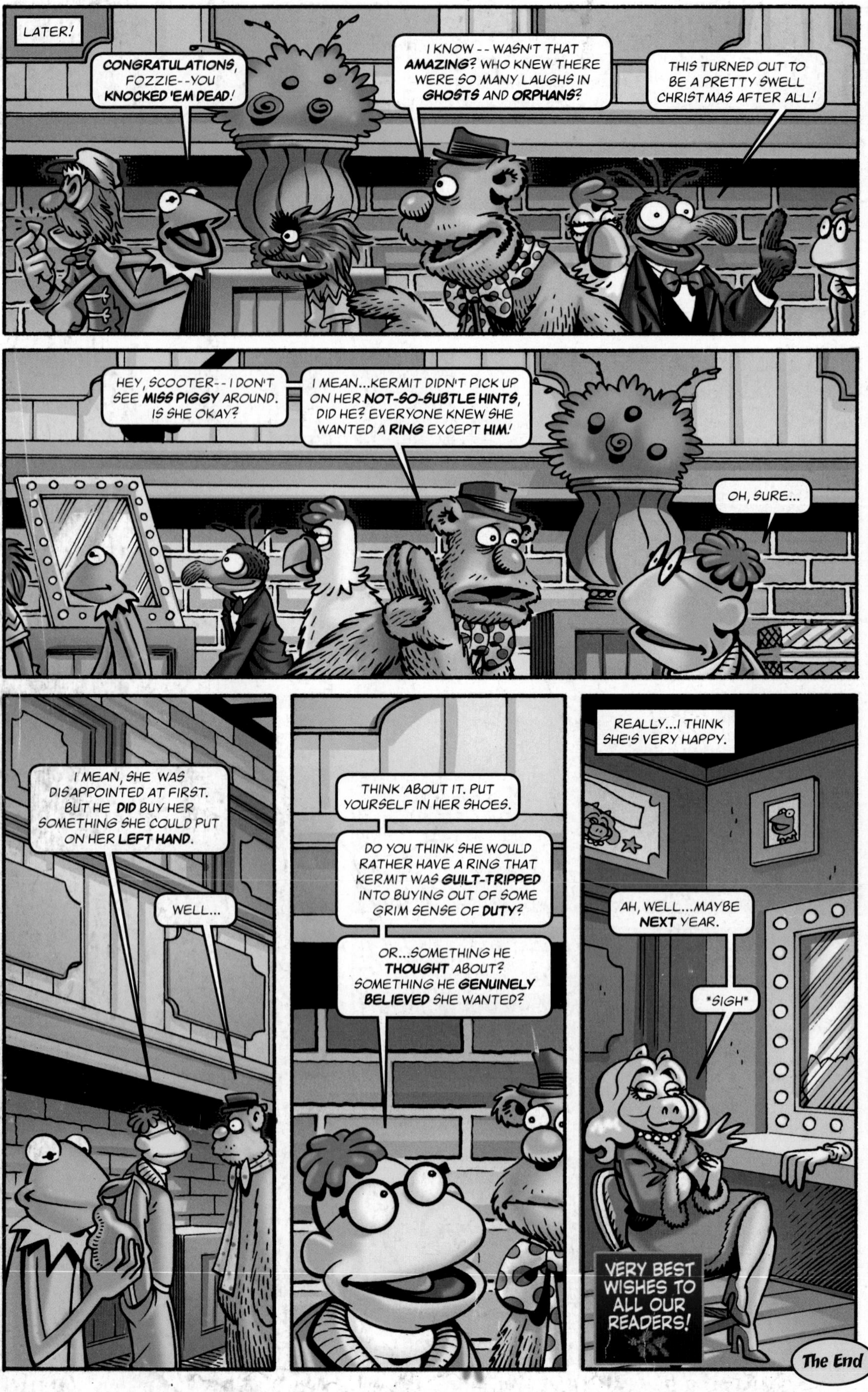
LATER!
CONGRATULATIONS, FOZZIE--YOU KNOCKED 'EM DEAD!
I KNOW -- WASN'T THAT AMAZING? WHO KNEW THERE WERE SO MANY LAUGHS IN GHOSTS AND ORPHANS?
THIS TURNED OUT TO BE A PRETTY SWELL CHRISTMAS AFTER ALL!
HEY, SCOOTER-- I DON'T SEE MISS PIGGY AROUND. IS SHE OKAY?
I MEAN...KERMIT DIDN'T PICK UP ON HER NOT-SO-SUBTLE HINTS, DID HE? EVERYONE KNEW SHE WANTED A RING EXCEPT HIM!
OH, SURE...
I MEAN, SHE WAS DISAPPOINTED AT FIRST. BUT HE DID BUY HER SOMETHING SHE COULD PUT ON HER LEFT HAND.
WELL...
THINK ABOUT IT. PUT YOURSELF IN HER SHOES.
DO YOU THINK SHE WOULD RATHER HAVE A RING THAT KERMIT WAS GUILT-TRIPPED INTO BUYING OUT OF SOME GRIM SENSE OF DUTY?
OR...SOMETHING HE THOUGHT ABOUT? SOMETHING HE GENUINELY BELIEVED SHE WANTED?
REALLY...I THINK SHE'S VERY HAPPY.
AH, WELL...MAYBE NEXT YEAR.
SIGH
VERY BEST WISHES TO ALL OUR READERS!
The End